GOTHIC IMAGINATION IN
LATIN AMERICAN FICTION AND FILM

Gothic Imagination in Latin American Fiction and Film

CARMEN A. SERRANO

University of New Mexico Press | Albuquerque

© 2019 by the University of New Mexico Press
All rights reserved. Published 2019
Printed in the United States of America

First paperback edition, 2021
Paperback ISBN: 978-0-8263-6277-3

Names: Serrano, Carmen A., 1969– author.
Title: Gothic imagination in Latin American fiction and film / Carmen A. Serrano.
Description: Albuquerque: University of New Mexico Press, [2019] | Includes bibliographical references and index. |
Identifiers: LCCN 2018051836 (print) | LCCN 2019004864 (e-book) | ISBN 9780826360458 (e-book) | ISBN 9780826360441 (printed case: alk. paper)
Subjects: LCSH: Gothic fiction (Literary genre), Latin American—History and criticism. | Latin American fiction—European influences. | Latin American fiction—American influences. | Horror films—Latin America—History and criticism.
Classification: LCC PN3448.G68 (e-book) | LCC PN3448.G68 S47 2019 (print) | DDC 700/.415—dc23
LC record available at https://lccn.loc.gov/2018051836

Cover illustration courtesy of Dover Publications
Designed by Felicia Cedillos
Composed in Sabon Lt Std 10/14.5

Gothic Imagination in Latin American Fiction and Film

CARMEN A. SERRANO

University of New Mexico Press | Albuquerque

© 2019 by the University of New Mexico Press
All rights reserved. Published 2019
Printed in the United States of America

First paperback edition, 2021
Paperback ISBN: 978-0-8263-6277-3

Names: Serrano, Carmen A., 1969– author.
Title: Gothic imagination in Latin American fiction and film / Carmen A. Serrano.
Description: Albuquerque: University of New Mexico Press, [2019] | Includes bibliographical references and index. |
Identifiers: LCCN 2018051836 (print) | LCCN 2019004864 (e-book) | ISBN 9780826360458 (e-book) | ISBN 9780826360441 (printed case: alk. paper)
Subjects: LCSH: Gothic fiction (Literary genre), Latin American—History and criticism. | Latin American fiction—European influences. | Latin American fiction—American influences. | Horror films—Latin America—History and criticism.
Classification: LCC PN3448.G68 (e-book) | LCC PN3448.G68 S47 2019 (print) | DDC 700/.415—dc23
LC record available at https://lccn.loc.gov/2018051836

Cover illustration courtesy of Dover Publications
Designed by Felicia Cedillos
Composed in Sabon Lt Std 10/14.5

Dedicated to Brad Ward, heroic companion in both the waking world and in my dreamscapes

Contents

Preface ix

Introduction. Contextualizing the Gothic Presence in Latin America 1

PART 1. THE CONTEXT

Chapter 1. Vampires
    The First Bat-Men Are from the Americas 27
Chapter 2. Films Love Monsters
    Film's Arrival in Latin America 53

PART 2. CULTURAL ANXIETIES AND AESTHETIC CRITIQUES

Chapter 3. Live Burials and Death-Defying Beauties 81
Chapter 4. Vampires Cloaked in Metaphor 109
Chapter 5. The Doppelgänger
    *Split-Selves, Animal-Doubles, and
    Spectral Couples* 141

Epilogue. Globalized Current Monsters 175

Notes 187

Bibliography 207

Index 233

Preface

> La crítica es una de las formas
> modernas de la autobiografía.
> Uno escribe su vida
> cuando cree escribir sus lecturas.[1]
>
> —Ricardo Piglia

Does our writing reveal something unknown about our lives? I'm not sure if this is the case, but Piglia's words are thought provoking. What moves us to read specific genres and, most important, what inspires us to write about what we read? For me, movies, novels, and stories that embody some element of fear are objects of study I find intriguing. Growing up, I was drawn to a mishmash of scary and uncanny things: vampire films, *The Twilight Zone*, *Wuthering Heights*, Walter Mercado's psychic predictions on Spanish television, and Edgar Allan Poe—especially Poe. I loved the delightfully scary stories that my family told about spooky hooded creatures wandering the countryside. My childhood babysitter and her sister, Eloína, a Santera, would at times take me to a *botánica* where I sat quietly behind the display counter filled with herbs, incense, and special talismans for healing. People came for spiritual guidance or to cast out a *mal de ojo*. Eloína, always dressed in white, also told me about her astral traveling at night. Added to this, I was also brought up in a religious home in which the arrival of the Antichrist, the apocalypse, and rapture were going to happen at any moment; that is, fear reigned. This is my backstory, well part of it, anyway.

    Fast forward, many years later. I started a graduate career studying Latin American literature. I became familiar with the critically acclaimed writers Alejo Carpentier, Julio Cortázar, María Luisa Bombal, Carlos Fuentes, Gabriel García Márquez, Elena Garro, Juan Rulfo, and Horacio Quiroga, among many others. As I read articles about these authors' fiction, their texts were described as belonging to the fantastic literary mode, or celebrated for their marvelous real qualities. Some stories were inspired by indigenous worldviews, while others were heralded for their magical realist features. The texts in Latin American courses might be grouped under such titles as Novels of the Mexican Revolution, Dictatorship Novels, Literature of the Avant-Garde, and the Latin American Boom, for example. These terms on the surface seemingly had nothing to do with the Gothic mode, but there was something that felt simultaneously familiar and unfamiliar to me; these texts were haunted.

While reading *Yo el supremo* (I, the Supreme), a novel about the Paraguayan dictator José Gaspar Rodríguez de Francia (1766–1840), an uncanny figure emerged reminiscent of the Gothic. This text, written by the critically acclaimed author Augusto Roa Bastos, speaks to the dictatorships that plagued Paraguay. As I read this postmodern historical novel, the vampire figure distracted me. How could there be a vampire in this, his most celebrated text? Up to this point all I knew was that Gothic novels, especially those featuring vampires, were usually deemed an inferior type of literature that were mere entertainment and explicitly written to provoke fear or some other extreme reaction. Vampires and the Gothic seemed to have little to do with Latin American literary production. As I continued to read Roa Bastos's novel, the vampiric presence became more prevalent. I told my professor Ana María Amar Sánchez that I wanted to write about the vampire in *Yo el supremo*. My professor listened as I rattled off all the textual evidence. She agreed and asked me to explore its significance. She encouraged me to analyze, write about, and publish it: "El vampiro en el espejo: Elementos góticos en *Yo el supremo*" was the article that pushed me into the realm of the Gothic and its monsters.

When I shared my new research interests with my mentor, Juan Bruce-Novoa, he wholeheartedly supported my book project, which would aim to examine how and why the Gothic presence informed Latin American literature. I told him how this book would trace the ways the European Gothic imagination has manifested in the literature and culture of eighteenth- and nineteenth-century Europe. The book would especially examine the Gothic films of the twentieth century and analyze how the Gothic themes altered Latin American literary and film culture, albeit in quite different ways given the multifaceted and multilayered geographies, cultures, histories, and politics of Latin America. The book would also provide a detailed literary history of the genre, contextualizing the evolution of the European genre and documenting its first appearances in Latin American letters, which was appropriated and transformed, thus illustrating how authors were responding to authoritarianism, colonization, modernization, and patriarchy, among other themes that spoke to the corrosiveness of power.

A few months before he died, I sat with Juan and his wife, Mary Ann, in the hospital, and we watched Mexican vampire movies. He told me that he had always hoped to write a book about the Gothic that specifically focused on Mexican architecture. He said Horace Walpole had looked to the premodern past to create his Strawberry Hill House, a Gothic revival villa, and architects in Mexico, too, in a corresponding manner, looked to their premodern ruins to create new designs of the mid-twentieth century. I wonder what that book would have revealed? God rest his soul. I will be eternally thankful for his unwavering support.

In addition to thanking Juan Bruce-Novoa, I want to thank Dorothea Fischer-Hornung, who organized a conference panel about vampires and zombies for the American Studies Association in Washington, DC, which gave birth to the edited collection *Vampires and Zombies: Transcultural Migrations and Transnational Interpretations*. I appreciate the anonymous reviewers for making thoughtful recommendations to improve the book's argument. The following colleagues read chapters of my book and made meaningful suggestions: Milvet Alonso, Daniel Chávez, James Dryden, Glyne Griffith, Michelle Hamilton, Gayle Morse, Timothy Mark Robinson, Jacobo Sefamí, Patty Tovar, Margarita Vargas, Kate Vega, John Waldron, and Maurice Westmoreland. I am especially indebted to my writing group. Every weekday, in a virtual space, we woke up to write at the crack of dawn: Carolyn Fornoff, Emily Hind, Rebecca Janzen, and John Waldron. Lotfi Sayahi, an inspiring force, consistently pushed me to excel beyond what I thought I was capable of accomplishing. Other friends and colleagues motivated me, recommended books, or bought me a scotch because writing is hard: Gonzalo Aguiar, Alejandra Aguilar, Diana Aldrete, Johanna Batman, Joanna Bigfeather, Selma Cohen, Courtney Colon, Angela Commito, José Cruz,

Luis Cuesta, Emma Dryden, Erin Gallo, Norma Klahn, Ilka Kressner, David Marino, Monika Mueller, John Person, Amanda Petersen, Sara Potter, Timothy Sergay, and Kristina Vassil. I appreciate my colleagues in the Department of Languages, Literatures and Cultures and my students, who share the same fascination for vampires and monsters. Our research librarian, Jesús Alonso-Regalado, travels around the globe and finds exquisite books, which continue to fuel my research interests. Thank you.

This book could not have been possible without the Dr. Nuala McGann Drescher Leave Program, which allowed me to dedicate myself fully to the manuscript. I am also grateful to Elise McHugh, the editor at the University of New Mexico Press, who expressed interest in my project and gave me critical feedback so that this book could be published. The editors, Kristy Johnson and Anne Rogers, have been a godsend. I thank the journal editors and the university presses for allowing me to reuse sections of previously published material: "El vampiro en el espejo: Elementos góticos en *Yo el supremo*," as published in *Revista Iberoamericana* 76, no. 232–33 (July 2010): 899–912, which informs part of the book chapter "Vampires Cloaked in Metaphor." The historical context for the book chapter "The First Bat-Men Are from the Americas" represents an expansion of what I initially explored in "Revamping Dracula on the Mexican Silver Screen in Fernando Méndez's *El vampiro*," in *Vampires and Zombies: Transcultural Migrations and Transnational Interpretations*, edited by Dorothea Fischer-Hornung and Monika Mueller (Jackson: University Press of Mississippi, 2016), 149–67. Chapter 2 of this book analyzes the *modernista* characterization of women as vampires; however, in "Duplicitous Vampires Annihilating Tradition in Froylán Turcios's *El vampiro*," which appears in *Latin American Gothic* (London: Routledge, 2018), focuses on the monstrous changes brought on by modernity.

Being an academic does not allow for a lot of free time, so I thank my family for being supportive and for reminding me to enjoy life: Armando, Evangelina, Linda, and Teresa Serrano; Maggie and Ruben Negrete; and Rocky Lucero, for our tea parties in cotton-candy pink rooms. I am grateful for my dear brother, Jaime Serrano, and his wonderful wife, Mizuho, and my niece and nephew, Hanah and Daniel Serrano, who bring me so much joy and laughter. I also am appreciative of Jeanne Galuski, who prayed for me along the way. I thank Brad Ward, who has created a home environment that is peaceful, loving, and stable. Brad's children, too, Lauren and Patrick Ward, remind me to enjoy youth, pizza, and princesses. I am blessed with an enchanted dog, Matilda, who mysteriously digs out articles from hidden alcoves that are somehow connected to the writing theme of the day. She also knows to wake me up at 6:15 a.m. so that I can write and shuts my laptop at 4 p.m. so I can play. Thank you, Matilda.

INTRODUCTION
CONTEXTUALIZING THE GOTHIC PRESENCE IN LATIN AMERICA

The word *Gothic* conjures eerie images of dark labyrinths, monstrous villains, and female victims in tales that unfold in Old World settings. This word, as well as terms such as *fantastic* and *magical realism*, has been used in criticism to define and distinguish among the various forms of writing that feature some element of fantasy. While the terms *fantastic* and *magical realism* commonly appear in discussion of twentieth-century Latin American fictional works that include supernatural or otherworldly events, the word *Gothic* is seldom mentioned in this connection. Yet elements of the Gothic are found here as well. Gothic literature is usually considered a phenomenon of strictly European origins that later became highly significant in the United States, as seen in the Gothic tales of Edgar Allan Poe and the southern Gothic, and, it is not entirely clear how these texts' features crossed over into literary production in Spanish-speaking America in the nineteenth and twentieth centuries. I argue here that Latin American writers were attentive readers of Gothic literature and were drawn to Gothic-themed films, thus becoming thoroughly familiar with Gothic literary conventions, which they then selectively employed and transgressed in their fiction. Critics, however, have generally ignored Gothic's relevance in Latin American texts.

The supernatural and unreal happenings in Latin American literature have been subsumed under magical realism or the fantastic or ascribed to world visions born of autochthonous cultures. However, rereading Latin American literature through a Gothic lens reveals monsters and vampiric entities that have not been previously analyzed as elements of that genre. The Gothic was absolutely present in the Latin American cultural imagination—especially after the advent of film—and these rhetorical devices were appropriated from Gothic sources and transformed, resulting in innovative artistic creations in which characters in made-up worlds also gave shape to fears and apprehensions that artists were experiencing at particular social and political junctures. The analysis presented in this book emphasizes that Latin American texts did not necessarily follow European models but transported Gothic imagination to articulate the social and political realities of their times.

In his meticulous monograph *Gothic*, Fred Botting posits that negative aesthetics inform the Gothic. He illustrates how these eighteenth- and nineteenth-century texts, captivated by premodern times, elicit emotions that are "extreme and negative."[1] Furthermore, authors create dark settings featuring cruel villains who conjure objectionable situations for their victims, designed to cause "fear, anxiety, terror, horror, disgust and revulsion" in the readers.[2] This book examines the common features and aesthetics that usually characterize Gothic texts, which are then strategically utilized, transformed, subverted, and transgressed in literary works produced in Latin America.[3] The authors discussed in this book at times syncretize, creolize, and/or hybridize the Gothic genre by infusing their narratives with myths drawn from indigenous beliefs and colonial folktales. By interweaving such cultural references with European Gothic ones, Latin American authors produced distinctive versions of vampires, doppelgängers, and live burials that repeat, alter, and/or undermine how these menacing figures and oppressive situations have previously been imagined. The Gothic's imaginative representation of bygone times and monstrous creatures informs Latin America's own literary vampires and doubles while also implicitly expressing trepidation about systems such as authoritarianism, colonization, feudalism, and modernization.

Salient Features of the Gothic

Before analyzing how Latin American authors make use of the Gothic, I will summarize its principal features, as well as describe the evolution of the genre over time. The Gothic is a popular form that, in the most conventional sense, is marked by its predilection for supernatural events and mysterious figures in an ambience designed to instill fear while destabilizing dominant notions about the nature of reality. However, further attempts to precisely define this vast body of literature become complicated because of the many variations in form, discourse, and plot that have appeared since 1764, when Horace Walpole published *The Castle of Otranto*, widely considered the first Gothic novel. Critic Marie Mulvey-Roberts emphasizes this quandary when she asks: "What is Gothic literature? Is it a plot, a trope, a topos, a discourse, a mode of representation, conventions of characterisation, or a composite of all these aspects?"[4] Mulvey-Roberts is not the only one to question the scope of the genre or mode; in fact, many critics adopt differing critical approaches, categorizations, and time frames when describing the Gothic. Some discussions of Gothic's salient themes and characteristics are more temporally contained, focusing solely on eighteenth- and early nineteenth-century English literary productions, while others are broader in scope, including later works and those from other countries. Additionally, some studies go beyond literature to incorporate Gothic films (usually film adaptations of Gothic novels) into their analyses of the Gothic tradition.

The first wave of Gothic literature that deployed the popular rhetorical devices (ca. 1764–1820) often takes as its setting castles or ruins in far-off lands and the distant past. The plot frequently focuses on a helpless heroine pursued by a monstrous villain, a scheme meant to evince terror in the character and to provoke it in readers. In the novels of the eighteenth century, villains often emerge from unexpected places, such as monasteries or convents. Mathew Lewis's *The Monk* (1796) and Ann Radcliffe's *The Italian* (1797) feature immoral Catholic friars, an obvious critique of the Church. In *The Monk*, Ambrosio, a Capuchin monk who goes by the appellation "the Man of Holiness," inspires universal awe through his sermons, but he becomes arrogant and falls in with a devil-like witch, Matilda, who enables and encourages his evilness. Possessed by lust, Ambrosio transforms into an evil being, committing acts of murder and rape. In a final attempt to save himself from the Inquisition, he commits the ultimate transgression by selling his soul to the Devil. Similarly, in *The Italian*, the duplicitous confessor and monk Schedoni plots to secure power and wealth through deceit and fratricide.

Whereas eighteenth-century authors created villains who behaved in monstrous ways, writers of nineteenth-century fiction produced more literal monsters, as seen in Mary Shelley's *Frankenstein* (1818), John William Polidori's "The Vampyre" (1819), Sheridan LeFanu's "Carmilla" (1872), and Bram Stoker's *Dracula* (1897). Judith Halberstam succinctly states that "from the eighteenth century to the nineteenth century, the terrain of Gothic horror shifted from the fear of the corrupted aristocracy or clergy, represented by the haunted castle or abbey, to the fear embodied by monstrous bodies."[5] Not only were the monstrosities of the villains made more material, but also the settings were relocated from rural spaces to modern cityscapes, as seen in Robert Louis Stevenson's *The Strange Case of Dr. Jekyll and Mr. Hyde* (1886) and Oscar Wilde's *The Picture of Dorian Gray* (1890). The villains also arrived from distant lands, characterized as premodern, to invade more modern host countries—Dracula, for example, moved from the antiquated Carpathian mountains to the bustle of London.[6] Like their predecessors, these nineteenth-century literary devices used heightened methods to instill fear in the reader, one of the central features of Gothic literature. In the introduction to *Victorian Gothic: Literary and Cultural Manifestations in the Nineteenth Century*, Julian Wolfreys describes the ways monsters migrated to other locations: "Escaping from the tomb and the castle, the gothic in the Victorian period becomes arguably even more potentially terrifying because of its ability to manifest itself anywhere."[7] Authors could invent a myriad of awe-inspiring and spine-tingling scenes undermining the limitations of the materially possible: figures walking out of picture frames (*Castle of Otranto*), people shape-shifting into animals (*Dracula*), or women conjuring the Devil (*The Monk*), for example. These monstrous imaginings also found their way into texts of other countries and, later, onto movie screens around the world.

In spite of the many challenges that can arise in delimiting the literature, we can identify some of its paradigmatic features. Certain devices and plots established in the eighteenth- and nineteenth-century novels are repeated in later texts and films even to this day. These works usually include a passive and persecuted female, a sensitive and ineffectual hero, and a dynamic and tyrannical villain, along with indiscreet servants.[8] The settings are usually antiquated spaces such as castles, abbeys, vast prisons, subterranean crypts, graveyards, and large old houses; within the chambers' hollows; and often a secret from the past haunts the characters, both psychologically and physically.[9] Another common feature of the Gothic is the doppelgänger, the protagonist's *other*, who persecutes the host subject physically and/or mentally. The double undermines a person's authenticity by making him or her feel no longer whole but rather a split entity, and this other is usually a version that the host deplores and seeks to destroy.

Adding to this literature's disturbing qualities are transgressive sexual relations, which are often at the root of the plot and "the most basic common denominator of gothic writing."[10] Manfred, the villain in Walpole's *The Castle of Otranto*, is in fiery pursuit of his prospective daughter-in-law, Isabela. A taboo sexual relationship is also featured in Poe's "The Fall of the House of Usher" (1839), where Roderick has a singular obsession with his sister/wife, Madeline, leading him to a violent act of live burial. Similarly, in Emily Brontë's *Wuthering Heights* (1847), a novel heralded for its Gothic features, Heathcliff and Catherine, raised as brother and sister, are driven by excess and desire to violate familial boundaries in a transgression that eventually causes their mutual demise.

The Gothic novels that first emerged in the eighteenth century were produced during a time when the dominant neoclassical style and the corresponding ideas associated with the Enlightenment were inspiring artists to produce artworks that were beautiful, balanced, and perfect. Gothic literature represented the opposite, preferring plots marked by excess in which instances of tyranny, imprisonment, and torture evoked dreadfulness instead of beauty. This is also true of the literature produced in the nineteenth century. The ideas associated with progress sublated the magical, the miraculous, and the sublime in the scientific reordering of the world. Gothic artists bemoaned the loss of these elements and brought them back in their literature.[11] In addition to doubles, a host of other malevolent entities such as ghosts, vampires, bats, witches, the undead, and magicians—and horrific descriptions of them—garishly adorn the pages of Gothic works. Likewise, the villains also carry out soul-damning acts such as matricide, live burials, and pacts with the Devil, further emphasizing the authors' delight in creating hideous and awful situations that could in turn provoke strong reactions in characters and readers. Most important, though, is not the haunted landscapes and ghoulish characters that serve as the framework for the genre but the emotion that links all of these texts: fear, the cornerstone emotion of the Gothic.[12]

Gothic Anxieties

As previously mentioned, in order to create a more mysterious and fear-inducing environment, Gothic authors often situate the story in an exotic and far-off place and epoch, a device that would seem to suggest a merely escapist literature for mass consumption that has little to do with the social reality of readers. In his 1938 book, *The Gothic Quest*, Montague Summers sought to redeem the Gothic from its subordinated status: "This, then, is exactly the reason why I think the Gothic novelists, with all their faults and failings, have done us infinite service, and proved themselves true friends to those of us who care to withdraw, be it even for a short time, and at rare intervals, from the relentless oppression and carking cares of a bitter actuality."[13] Although Summers, like others, perceives it as a way to escape from "a bitter actuality," Gothic fear negotiate the changes and conflicts linked to the moment of enunciation in which the fear-inducing past could also speak to the present. There is a rich critical tradition that analyzes how Gothicists employ monsters and fear as vehicles to allegorize human life and that also informs the analysis in this book. By escaping into a made-up world, the texts were also addressing contemporaneity. As Maggie Kilgour argues, "Readers have always noted and complained of the gothic's loose and inaccurate use of history. Recalled to life, the past is brought back to critique the present, so that the feudal tyrant is really the modern egoist in historical dress. The paradox of this is, however, that the revived past cannot be an alternative to the present for it is a nightmare version of it."[14] Jerrold Hogle comments that the "Gothic is inherently connected to an exploitation of the emptied-out past to symbolize and disguise present concerns, including prejudices," while Botting states that "Gothic narratives never escaped the concerns of their own times, despite the heavy historical trappings."[15] The addressing of present concerns by conjuring a previous moment in history, so often attributed to the Gothic, mirrors the expression of anxieties associated with the social and political milieu via the vampires, doubles, and live burials of Latin American texts. The texts analyzed here evoke creatures and punishments associated with an illusory bygone time; however, these authors not only summon European Old World castles, labyrinths, and vampires, but they also mention pre-Columbian gods and myths and age-old temples and ruins to create nightmares that speak to the particularities of the region's history and culture. That is, authors, often double back to both historical settings, adding to the stories' mystery and wonder and paralleling the way the Gothicists approached their historical past. The evocation of an archaic past—a terrifying one that is feudal, dark, and monstrous—was a way for authors in Spanish-speaking America to express contemporary conflicts, both social conflicts associated with encroaching modernity and conflicts with a colonial legacy; it also reflected the authors' hesitation in asserting their literary autonomy.

Modernistas

Two questions remain: when and how Gothic literature was appropriated and transformed in Latin American letters and why it has been understudied in the Latin American context. One reason critics usually ignore the Gothic literature presence in Latin American literary creations may be that the Gothic has been confined to a specific historical period and place. That is to say, the first wave of English Gothic novels reached the peak of popularity in the 1790s, so it seems unlikely that its fame would have any bearing on creative production in a region that was still under Spanish colonial rule. National literature in Latin America was still in its nascent stages and would not develop a rich body of texts until after the Spanish colonies secured their independence in the first half of the nineteenth century. Even after independence, Spanish-speaking authors maintained close bonds with Spain and, for the most part, followed its literary trajectory. Artists would eventually exert their autonomy forcefully when, at the end of the nineteenth century, the *modernistas* (ca. 1880–1920), usually celebrated for their poetry, arrived on the scene, breaking with old traditions and creating new ones.[16] Their short stories, in fact, were some of the first to explicitly feature vampires, reminiscent of Gothic ones.

Just as ideas of reason and progress informed culture in Europe, they also corresponded to social changes in Latin America, which was shifting from an agrarian economy to a more industrialized one. Theories of progress dominated the rhetoric of the time, while that which was deemed premodern was losing its relevance, as Lee Skinner succinctly posits in *Gender and the Rhetoric of Modernity in Spanish America, 1850–1910*: "Many nineteenth-century Latin Americans emphasized the importance of rationality and logic and created a classification system in which all that was not rational, logical, or scientific was deemed negative, anti-modern, and retrograde, while everything categorized as rational and scientific was lauded and embraced."[17] Rejecting the prosaic world being created at the time, in which progress and logic dominated political and social thought, some Latin American artists conjured bygone times, lugubrious landscapes, and flawed protagonists.

The modernista poets analyzed in this book, including Rubén Darío, Leopoldo Lugones, Clemente Palma, and Froylán Turcios, were an influential group responding to the spiritual vacuum brought about by modernity and the positivism that infused the politics and culture of the time. Institutions promoting progress turned away from more spiritual aspects of the world and instead privileged rational and empirical approaches to the pursuit of knowledge. In contrast, the modernistas responded by embracing a former time when people still had faith and could believe in awe-inspiring myths and the supernatural. As Cathy Jrade asserts, the "modernistas' real and immediate ties to premodern modes of perception and belief offered a reservoir of responses to the modern world that they had entered."[18] The modernistas drew from mysterious and occult themes rather than from literary realism, which was emerging as the predominant artistic style.[19] Modernity, with its pervasive application of reason, sought to inter the possibility of the magical and the unknowable; the modernistas responded to this trend by invoking vampires and doppelgängers, which embodied the archaic, the irrational, excess, and mystery.[20] The romantic atavism characteristic of their texts is their response to the overly rational world that was, in the words of Summers, "the relentless oppression" of their time.

The turn toward the Gothic and its monsters highlights the way that authors on both sides of the Atlantic—accosted by so much light, reason, and progress—resisted being seduced by modernity's penchant for a scientific and rational ordering in the world. Stimulated by the premodern era and drawing from it, these authors created unreal creatures, such as vampires and doubles, emanating from dark places shrouded in excess, mystery, contradictions, and the impossible. Yet, despite the relevance of these themes to the analysis of modern literature, modernistas' vampiric short stories are rarely, if ever, mentioned in studies of Latin American literature.

Literature of "Bad Taste"

One of the more salient reasons that the Gothic and its monsters have been under-studied in Latin America is the inferior status of the genre in literary criticism. Gothic works have been marginalized because of the genre's sensationalistic tendencies and predictable form; it has long been described as a literature of bad taste or as lowbrow Romanticism, among many other disdainful criticisms. As Botting says, "Invoking ideas and objects of displeasure, gothic texts were invariably considered to be of little artistic merit, crude, formulaic productions for vulgar, uncultivated tastes."[21] In their chapter "Gothic Criticism," Chris Baldick and Robert Mighall also describe the novel's general subordinated status: "Until the 1930s, most accounts of Gothic fiction were modestly content to admit that the Gothic was an undistinguished curiosity of literary evolution, which nonetheless merited some scholarly treatment of its sources, influences, biographical contexts and generic features."[22]

As an "undistinguished curiosity" it would be even more obscure in a Latin American context, thus further indicating why the Gothic has usually been deemed irrelevant in Spanish-speaking America. Carol Margaret Davidson remarks in *History of the Gothic: Gothic Literature, 1764–1824* that detractors considered the Gothic morally dangerous in its appeal to corrupt tastes.[23] The aforementioned anti-Gothic evaluations demonstrate the ways scholars rejected the literary merits of Gothic novels produced by their own citizens, so it is unsurprising that critics in Spanish-speaking countries might also cast off a genre of literature that was deemed predictable, unpleasant, and obsessed with depraved characters that appealed to substandard tastes. Nevertheless, even though important critics and authors dismissed the Gothic, others utilized Gothic features in their prose, especially those whose works stand out for their surrealist features.

It was only at the start of the twentieth century, with the avant-garde and the invention of film, that this body of literature gained recognition. André Breton, the initiator and iconic figure of Surrealism, who was drawn to automatic writing and Sigmund Freud's theories of the unconscious, explains in his 1924 manifesto that he was inspired by "psychic automatism in its pure state, by which one proposes to express—verbally, by the means of the written word, or in any other manner—the actual functioning of thought."[24] Gothic narratives emphasized characters' irrational and unbridled passions, a theme that resonated with the Surrealists, who were also drawn to dreamscapes that could reveal secret and unspoken desires. Furthermore, the stark departure of Gothicists from neoclassicism's penchant for decorum and balance was parallel to the perception of Surrealist artists that bourgeois moral values were limiting and that classical models were a "force of oppression."[25]

Breton was one of the first to value Gothic literature beyond its gratuitous fear-instilling qualities, as exemplified in *The Castle of Otranto*. He considered Walpole the first Surrealist writer because of his style of automatic writing, fundamentally similar to Breton's technique of seeking to access the unconscious, free from moral and rational constraints, to create art. According to Breton, the Gothic fictional characters created by eighteenth-century writers—as found in Lewis's *The Monk*, Radcliffe's *The Italian*, and Charles Maturin's *Melmoth the Wanderer* (1820)—inspired celebrated writers such as Charles Baudelaire, Lord Byron, Thomas Moore, and Victor Hugo. In other words, the first wave of Gothic literature established many of the characteristics that would later emerge in the Romanticism of the nineteenth century, including the French novels. Exalting the many qualities of this writing, Breton observes: "In this connection it has always appeared to me that nothing could be more opportune than to call attention to that extraordinary efflorescence of English novels at the end of the eighteenth century, known in France as the 'romans noirs.' When we consider, at the present time, this literary style now forgotten or in disrepute, we cannot fail to be struck, not only by its prodigious success, but also by the very singular fascination it exercised for some time upon the most critical minds."[26] In the 1930s the Gothic novels began to fascinate the "most critical minds" all over Europe, a time when Surrealists, among other avant-garde artists, were reevaluating the norms of the art world. Surrealists asserted the Gothic as a legitimate genre with complexities worthy of attention that could inform their vanguard art.

Unlike the modernistas' romantic atavism, which was a means of expressing their loathing of modernity's noisy register, the avant-garde artists adopted Gothic features in their texts for other reasons. The vanguard artists, including Surrealists, were drawn to modernity's bustle and accelerating trajectory. As the word indicates, *avant-garde* is a military term that means a movement forward, encapsulating the vanguards' rebellious and onward-looking approach to art. The vanguard movements of the 1920s and 1930s celebrated speed, machines, progress, cinema, and all things modern that could inform artistic innovation, destroy worn-out modes, and establish new paradigms of what could be deemed "artful." Yet the Surrealists' response to modernity was multifaceted: artists simultaneously looked toward the future and the "new" but also turned inward, toward the unconscious, where unspoken desires, unmediated by social norms, could inspire another type of art. Moreover, they looked to esoteric knowledge from previous epochs and distant lands, finding within them monstrous visions that fed their desire to undermine reality's illusion.

Surrealists of the 1930s, which included Spanish and Latin American artists, were also drawn to modernity's promises that could inspire their art. Furthermore, Freud's groundbreaking psychoanalytic theories motivated Surrealists to draw from dreams, nightmares, and the unconscious mind. They sought new places that evoked another time that was more magical, or as Breton states, "in a violent reaction against the impoverishment and sterility of thought processes that resulted from centuries of rationalism, we turned toward the marvelous and advocated it unconditionally."[27] Their continued search for the marvelous also meant retrieving aspects belonging to a previous era, for instance, finding inspiration in pre-Columbian culture and its artifacts.[28]

Another Unreal Term

Several of the stories and novels examined in this book have already been studied under the overarching umbrella of the fantastic. Unlike the Gothic, the fantastic is a more widely accepted and used term, usually referring to a genre of writing popularized in the nineteenth century by such authors as E. T. A. Hoffman, Henry James, Guy de Maupassant, and Edgar Allan Poe, among the more recognizable figures, and is also often associated with the stories of Jorge Luis Borges, Julio Cortázar, Carlos Fuentes, and Horacio Quiroga, among others. However, the Gothic is not usually at the crux of these analyses.

The fantastic mode of literature was popularized in Latin America during the 1940s with the publication of an anthology edited by some of the most influential writers: Jorge Luis Borges, Adolfo Bioy Casares, and Silvina Ocampo's *Antología de la literatura fantástica* (The Book of Fantasy). As Casares notes in the introduction, the stories depict mysterious moods, ghostly apparitions, the element of surprise, and even time travel (as found in H. G. Wells). Some of the stories present realistic depictions of the material world that are then transgressed by seemingly supernatural or strange occurrences.

Casares's broad understanding of the fantastic, which encroaches on characteristics often used to describe those found in fantasy literature and science fiction, is less restrictive than that of Tzvetan Todorov. Todorov's groundbreaking text, *The Fantastic: A Structural Approach to a Literary Genre* (1973), thoroughly examines the most salient feature of fantastic literature as illustrated in *Arabian Nights*, Franz Kafka's *Metamorphosis* (1915), and Edgar Allan Poe's "The Fall of the House of Usher" (1839); however, his book focuses on mostly European and US texts while ignoring Latin America's rich tradition of fantastic literature. Newer studies such as Cynthia Duncan's insightful *Unraveling the Real: The Fantastic in Spanish-American Ficciones* (2010) and Omar Nieto's discerning *Teoría general de lo fantástico: Del fantástico clásico al posmoderno* (General Theory of the Fantastic: From the Classic to the Postmodern Fantastic) (2015) analyze the ways fantastic literature has evolved and has been imagined over time, thus contributing meaningfully to the understanding of Latin American literary production under this rubric.[29]

While the fantastic, as recent criticism emphasizes, is a more accepted term for texts produced in Latin America, the Gothic has often been relegated to an inferior class. In the prologue to *Antología de la literatura fantástica,* Casares explains that he, along with the other editors, brought together ghostly and otherworldly stories from literatures around the world. Their collection includes such literary giants as Borges, as well as Julio Cortázar, James Joyce, Franz Kafka, Guy de Maupassant, and Edgar Allan Poe. Given the anthology's subject matter, one might assume that the Gothic and the modernistas' vampire stories would figure prominently, but none appear. The editors of this anthology explicitly exclude the Gothic and its vampires, underscoring the subordinated status of the genre. Casares mentions the Gothic works of Sheridan LeFanu, Bram Stoker, and Horace Walpole, but only to denigrate their artistic value. He derisively comments that vampires and castles have had an unhappy journey through literature and thus do not figure in the collection. He notes how *la literatura fantástica* emerged in the nineteenth century primarily in English and also acknowledges the Gothic tradition as one of its predecessors. Yet for him, Gothic literature is tasteless, as he makes clear in discussing Walpole's *The Castle of Otranto*. Of this work, Casares states, "*The Castle of Otranto* debe ser considerado antecesor de la pérfida raza de castillos teutónicos, abandonados a una decrepitud en telarañas, en tormentas, en cadenas, en mal gusto" (*The Castle of Otranto* should be considered an antecessor to the fake lineage of Germanic castles, abandoned to the decrepitude of cobwebs, in torments, in chains, in bad taste).[30] In no uncertain terms, Casares, like many other authors, assigns the Gothic and its vampires to the nonliterary category of phoniness and poor taste. Nevertheless, the fact that he diminishes the Gothic suggests that Casares, along with Borges and Ocampo, has read enough of these works to develop definite opinions about them. Since the anthology's publication, the fantastic, not altogether surprisingly, has become a more widely accepted term. Yet the Gothic, by comparison, has either been dismissed or relegated to the periphery of critical literary analysis in Latin America. In response, the present study illustrates how the fear and negative aesthetics that characterize the Gothic offer another way to analyze canonical texts.

While theories of the fantastic contribute to innovative readings of classic Latin American texts, this book examines narratives that could have fantastic as well as Gothic qualities. Depending on the definition employed, Gothic literature can have characteristics similar to those usually bestowed on the fantastic, but not all fantastic narratives necessarily illustrate Gothic tropes and aesthetics. The fantastic, usually in the form of short stories, often depicts hesitation in the characters and perhaps evokes it in the reader, especially in its use of ambiguous endings.[31] In the Gothic, dreadful monsters or monsterlike creatures rule. The characters in the Gothic tale experience unreal and threatening environments as material ones in which they are being persecuted by monsters or monstrous people: Ambrosio buries Antonia alive, Dracula drains Lucy of her blood, and Dr. Jekyll shape-shifts into a beastly creature. That is to say, the ominous figures almost always are "real" or cross over into the characters' material world in very palpable ways; they are not typically represented as flickering specters that merely haunt their characters' imaginations.

The reframing of the Gothic disassociates Latin American novels from the seductive and overarching magical realist mode under which texts that embody any unreal quality are so commonly subsumed. In large part because of Angel Flores's 1955 seminal essay, "Magical Realism in Spanish American Fiction," magical realism is often associated with literature coming out of Spanish-speaking America. Flores situates Borges, María Luisa Bombal, and Adolfo Bioy Casares, among other writers, within the magical realist tradition and acknowledges that, through their art, Latin America finally finds an authentic form of expression. Flores and others were critically forging space for writers in the worldwide canon by grouping them under the heading of magical realism to exalt their innovative writing, thus contributing to a new literary typology. The magical realist mode has since transcended Spanish-speaking America to become a more global and "preeminent form of fiction in the contemporary world," attracting writers from Europe, Africa, the Middle and Far East.[32] Additionally, several thought-provoking studies consider magical realism to be a decolonizing literature.

For reasons noted earlier, readers outside Latin America often perceive magical realism as the primary style of literary production coming out of Latin America that includes supernatural elements. Indeed, much of the fiction written by Latin Americans is automatically categorized as magical realism, especially whenever unexplainable or strange events occur, as in works by authors such as Julio Cortázar, Carlos Fuentes, and Juan Rulfo. Critics and authors have questioned the legitimacy of this all-encompassing term because it has no fixed definition: it can be broad, referring to any texts that mix realism with fantasy, or it can be limited in various ways. However, critics usually suggest that in these texts the supernatural events do not cause fear but form part of the everyday or, as Maggie Bowers states in Magic(al) Realism, "One of the unique features of magical realism is its reliance upon the reader to follow the example of the narrator in accepting both realistic and magical perspectives of reality on the same level."[33] The magical realist application to several renowned texts undermines other possibilities of interpretation derived from various literary forms such as, for example, modernism or the Gothic, which are also antimimetic artistic approaches that undermine the material world, displace linear time, and reimagine dreams or nightmares.

Despite the continuing debate over the validity of using magical realism as a critical term, many novels and stories described herein have consistently been framed by notions of magical realism. In truth, certain passages—or, in fact, entire novels and short stories—would benefit from being unhinged from such notions, allowing for other modes of analysis. I ask readers to view some of Latin America's most esteemed writers and literary texts through another paradigm, the Gothic. When reread through a Gothic frame, the texts reveal aspects that have been overshadowed by the previous focus on elements of magical realism or the fantastic.

Why So Much Context?

Because of the unfavorable fame of the Gothic texts, mentioning it as influential in Latin American literature often creates unease among literary critics who might view the connection as an attempt to debase the esteemed status of critically acclaimed Latin American works. Detractors suggest that the coalescing of these two literary traditions—one esteemed, the other perceived as artless—somehow diminishes the texts' status and originality. Yet, esteemed authors have created innovative works based on the Gothic. Edgar Allan Poe, for example, used, parodied, and theorized the genre and created his own Gothic-inspired short stories. Poe, whose works are often analyzed for both their fantastic qualities and their Gothic aesthetics, is the one author whom almost all Latin American writers discussed here admired and cited in their texts, explicitly or implicitly. George Haggerty considers Poe to be the first American to produce remarkable Gothic fiction: "Poe was not only the first American to excel in the Gothic mode, he was the first writer in either England or America to formulate a thorough and convincing theory of the Gothic and to create a complementary collection of tales both to support and develop his critical theory."[34]

Haggerty convincingly argues that Poe was fascinated by the mechanics behind the Gothic and claims that Poe's "self-conscious Gothicism" allowed him to transcend the genre. He appropriates sensational excess among other traits found in this type of literature and transforms it for his own aims, creating focused and highly macabre and tormenting scenarios in his short stories. Like Poe, Latin American artists associated with *el modernismo*, the fantastic mode, and the vanguards also appropriated and transcended the Gothic. As will become evident in the following chapters, these writers used and transformed Gothic texts, both from the eighteenth and nineteenth centuries, as did film adaptations based on such literature.

The vanguard and neo-avant-garde texts discussed in this book also implicitly question the parameters used to distinguish the artful from the artless. As already mentioned, words such as *unique*, *balanced*, and *original* were often used to celebrate classic and neoclassic art, for example, while the opposite is true for those works considered artless. The language used to describe the Gothic (*formulaic, predictable, tasteless, unbalanced, excessive*, etc.) illustrates this point. Such condemnatory words also might extend to other cultural artifacts emerging from mass culture, such as films and comic books, produced for a consumer industry in which the need for profit drives content. These commercial products, deemed mere entertainment, have usually been excluded from a place such as the consecrated art world.[35] Yet artists raised prosaic objects to the level of art, as best illustrated by visual arts: Marcel Duchamp's 1917 *Fountain* transforms a urinal into an art piece, Roy Lichtenstein's comic strip art parodies crude newspaper print productions, while Andy Warhol repurposes a Campbell's soup ad, creating a new art sensation and thus illustrating how the concept of art was being undermined and reimagined by the vanguards and neo-vanguards.

This reevaluation of art objects also had a lasting impact on literary production in the Americas throughout the twentieth century.[36] Latin

American authors created pioneering texts by borrowing from many sources, including those associated with ill-famed texts and mass culture, such as Gothic novels and Gothic-inspired films. By doing so, they were implicitly undermining more traditional views of aesthetics and the corresponding value of originality often bestowed upon aesthetic objects. That writers should use and transform popular forms, which include the Gothic, in the creation of their own innovative texts is not unusual. Literary critic Ana María Amar Sánchez, in her groundbreaking *Juegos de seducción y traición: Literatura y cultura de masas* (Games of Seduction and Betrayal: Mass Literature and Culture) asserts that the use and elaboration of popular forms has been prevalent among esteemed writers in Latin America in her discussion of "the manner in which a whole body of literature belonging to the 'cultured' utilizes, appropriates and transforms codes belonging to mass culture."[37] By incorporating and reworking popular genres—usually held in low esteem by criticism due to their perceived literary inferiority—writers expanded boundaries, creating revolutionary texts that addressed their own time period and context. Borges's rearticulation of the police novel, as well as Manuel Puig's play on popular radio programs and reimagination of B movies in his prose, are examples of these reappropriations. In particular, Borges, an admirer of Poe, used detective fiction as a means to turn "narrative action into philosophical speculation."[38] By incorporating media associated with mass culture, the authors were subverting consecrated cultural and social constructs bestowed upon aesthetic objects. Amar Sánchez's discussion of the amalgamation of antithetical forms that have resulted in innovative texts provides the frame for the inclusion of the Gothic in Latin American literary studies. Authors drew on the Gothic tradition—a literature that aimed to please and entice its mass culture readership—and transformed it in a new context, deploying its rhetorical devices for their own purposes.

Transatlantic Interactions

The texts analyzed here also illustrate the ongoing global and cross-cultural interactions that have constantly altered cultures and their respective cultural creations. The development of concepts such as intertextuality (Julia Kristeva), palimpsests (Roland Barthes), parody (Linda

Hutcheon), and hybridity (Nestor García Canclini), in which origins are no longer at the root of critical evaluation, has led to fruitful discussions. García Canclini, in his pioneering study *Culturas híbridas: Estrategias para entrar y salir de la modernidad* (Hybrid Cultures: Strategies for Entering and Leaving Modernity), acknowledges that the process of hybridization is in perpetual flux in Latin America culture. The process of negotiation between cultures, a result of modernization and the mass media, has engendered relationships that are in constant flux. I argue that this dynamic relation also expresses itself through the intertextual interplay between Gothic (novels, stories, films) and Latin American literary production.

Latin American writers, who often traveled, studied, and/or resided in Europe, especially in Paris, actively participated in vanguards. The Cuban author Alejo Carpentier joined Surrealists in Paris but later broke away from them because he found their art was too contrived; he instead found inspiration in the magical and mystical aspects he found in Latin American and Caribbean culture, whose social reality he described as *lo real maravilloso*. The Chilean poet Vicente Huidobro also joined the Surrealists and interacted with their most iconic figures, including Breton, Salvador Dalí, and Luis Buñuel. Buñuel lauded Huidobro's poetry, while Huidobro admired Buñuel's films, but Huidobro rejected Surrealists' penchant for automatic writing and created his own avant-garde movement known as *el Creacionismo*, addressed in chapter 2. María Luisa Bombal, whose texts feature surrealist qualities, lived in Paris from 1922 to 1931, when the vanguard was in its heyday. Octavio Paz, one of Mexico's most renowned poets of the twentieth century, lived in Paris in the 1940s, when he wrote his famous *El laberinto de la soledad* (The Labyrinth of Solitude). While there, he joined the Surrealists and developed a close friendship with Breton, as corroborated in Breton's interviews. Although Latin American artists were initially drawn to the Surrealists, they later left the movement and went on to create poetry and prose that spoke to a Latin American identity.

The vanguards were an international, transatlantic, symbiotic movement, in which artists from both sides of the Atlantic drew from many sources. Breton was fascinated with Mexico and the Day of the Dead, and suggested that Mexico was already a surreal place. In 1939 he organized a Mexican art exhibit in Paris, and in 1940, along with Wolfgang Paalen and César Moro, he planned the "Exposición internacional del surrealismo: Aparición de la gran esfinge nocturna" (International Exhibition of Surrealism: Apparition of the Great Sphinx of the Night) at the Galería de Arte Mexicano in Mexico City, further illustrating their mutual influence.[39] Through enduring conversations with artists across the Atlantic, especially those associated with the vanguards, the writers analyzed in this book became thoroughly familiar with and contributed to international movements, through which they would also have become familiar with European Gothic texts.

In our global world, all arts can be seen as influenced by previous works; even if the author does not consciously intend to imprint her or his work with previous works, knowledge of it imbues the new text. As T. S. Eliot writes in his 1919 essay, "Tradition and the Individual Talent," "[It is] our tendency to insist, when we praise a poet, upon those aspects of his work in which he least resembles anyone else. . . . No poet, no artist of any art, has his complete meaning alone. His significance, his appreciation is the appreciation of this relation to the dead poets and artists. You cannot value him alone; you must set him, for contrast and comparison, among the dead."[40]

Eliot's words underscore that individual originality is often the principal factor in evaluation of newly produced cultural objects, as exemplified in his description of the long-standing maxim "novelty is better than repetition."[41] Yet Eliot argues that thoughtful writers are historically aware of tradition, thus acknowledging the whole of literature, produced over the centuries, in their own literary creations. Similarly, when critics asked acclaimed Mexican author Alfonso Reyes about his literary predecessors, he responded, "Three thousand years of universal literature."[42] Eliot and Reyes, among others, appreciated that art is not created in a vacuum but rather represents a continuation and altering of what was already present. However, evaluations based on originality have not been altogether overcome.

Acknowledging the Gothic and embedding it in a Latin American frame recognizes the process of the constant adoption, repudiation, and/or transformation of a backgrounded text. All cultures transmit influences of previous exchanges with other cultures and vice versa.[43] Wendy

Doniger, in the introduction to *Splitting the Difference*, a comparative study of ancient Greece and India exploring representations of doubles, twoness, and split-selves, reminds readers that acknowledging contact should not automatically suggest a hierarchical relationship of originator and receiver but rather a more complex relationship. The consistent transatlantic interchange between cultures and media, from west to east, east to west, north to south, south to north, film to novel, novel to film, and all other possible permutations imaginable—further facilitated after the turn of the twentieth century with accelerating modernity and globalization—manifests itself clearly in the literatures and films analyzed in this book. The authors featured herein appropriate, transform, and renew previous works of art, thus forging groundbreaking texts that merit more careful analyses under the rubric of the Gothic.

The negative aesthetics and unreal events found in the Gothic have a pivotal place in the Latin American novels and stories examined in this book, wherein unreal characters enter into the character's material world (animal doubles, ghosts, revenants, walking corpses, and witches), reflecting the oppressive social circumstances in which their writers found themselves. Some of the characters feel fear, terror, and revulsion when they find themselves in desperate situations wherein they are at the mercy of malevolent entities. Thus, negative aesthetics, inspired by the Gothic, spoke to political and social subjections that authors found overwhelming. Through their villains, they emphasized the corrosive effects of power of their time.

Part One: The Context

Chapter 1, "Vampires: The First Bat-Men Are from the Americas," begins by posing the question "What do vampires have to do with Latin America, anyway?" and then traces the history of vampire characters, beginning with a description of the most salient characteristics of the pre-Columbian American hematophagous bat, a creature often portrayed as a sacred entity associated with the mystery of the cosmos and the underworld. Yet the anthropomorphic bat and bat deity, as represented in the codices and in the *Popul vuh* (the creation story of the Quiche Maya), respectively, never really found their way onto the pages of modern Latin American literature as sacrosanct beings. Although the vampire figure had no obvious influence in the region's literary culture during the eighteenth and early nineteenth centuries, the American bat, after the Spanish Conquest, did transform vampiric imaginings in Europe. Chroniclers, travelers, and scientists who ventured to the Americas wrote about their grisly encounters with blood-sucking bats (a species unknown in Europe), prompting the creature's incorporation into European vampire folklore and literature. Also, by renaming this flying mammal the vampire bat, they not only bestowed more monstrous qualities on the American bat but also made it synonymous with the vampire monster. The vampire's association with the bat inspired Stoker's Dracula, who in the novel is described as having the ability to shape-shift into a bat, a device which would later appear in popular vampire films and other media, further cementing the association. The American vampire bat thus made a transatlantic journey wherein it was repackaged and returned to the Americas, burdened with a new monstrous identity that had little to do with its pre-Columbian divine nature.

Latin American modernistas, who were drawn to Romanticism and the Gothic tales of Poe, feature vampiric entities in their prose, as illustrated in Rubén Darío's "Thanatopia" (1893), Leopoldo Lugones's "La vampira" (1897), and Clemente Palma's "Vampiras" (Female Vampires) (1906).[44] Froylán Turcios, a writer from Honduras and also a modernista, published his novel El vampiro in 1910. The novel represents one of the first Gothic novels of the Spanish-speaking continent. It coalesces traditional vampire lore with regional notions of shape-shifting, as found in the nagual, or animal double. The modernistas' deployment of the vampire figure implicitly characterized modernity's impact in the region as monstrous. Although vampires are not central to Latin American literary production, they continued to inspire texts beyond el modernismo, as illustrated by master storytellers Horacio Quiroga (in "El vampiro" [1927]) and Julio Cortázar (in "El hijo del vampiro" [1937]) (The Son of the Vampire), who are better known for their *literatura fantástica*.[45]

Chapter 2, "Films Love Monsters: Film's Arrival in Latin America," further contextualizes the Gothic's presence in Latin America, examining how Gothic images entered the national imagination with film's arrival. The first part of this chapter presents a history of early film to firmly establish the ways in which classic movies such as *The Cabinet of*

Dr. Caligari (1920), *Dracula* (1931) and its Spanish counterpart, *Drácula* (1931), were screened in Latin American cities mere months after their original release in Europe and the United States. Both foreign and domestic films attracted significant public attention in Spanish-speaking America, becoming culturally significant and influential in artistic production. Poets and prose writers, fascinated by cinema, were moved to become film critics and/or screenwriters as well. The interplay between the Gothic and film become especially evident in three examples: Vicente Huidobro's *Cagliostro* (1934) and Quiroga's short stories such as "El espectro" (1921) and "El vampiro." As demonstrated in the first two chapters of this book, when these works are seen within their historical context, the salience and plausibility of a Gothic transatlantic connection are evident. The authors themselves, at times, explicitly mention Gothic texts, but the works demonstrate how authors of the time were parodying and transcending features associated with Gothic literature and film.[46]

Part Two: Cultural Anxieties and Aesthetic Critiques

Chapter 3, "Live Burials and Death-Defying Beauties," considers a device for which Gothic writers are especially known: evoking terror through detailed descriptions of live burials, particularly those of female heroines. After summarizing instances of live burials in Gothic novels and Gothic-inspired short stories, the chapter explores how authors reimagine these oppressive situations in *La amortajada* (The Shrouded Woman) (1938) by María Luisa Bombal, and *Pedro Páramo* (1955) by Juan Rulfo, which are often analyzed for their surrealist qualities. Latin American authors sometimes deploy the image of live burial and the female corpse in a manner similar to that used by Gothic writers; however, Latin American authors also complicate and rewrite these literary tropes through the use of surprising endings that would not be found in traditional Gothic plots. Whereas in English-language texts characters who are buried alive desperately want to return to the world of the living, where life was good, the characters in the Latin American novels discussed here do not wish to return. The female heroines speak from beyond the grave, from an afterlife imagined as a safe haven, far from tyranny. They express how in life they felt fear and suffered from injustice and oppression, whereas in the afterlife they are free to dream and imagine.

Chapter 4, "Vampires Cloaked in Metaphor," analyzes the use of the vampire as a metaphor for oppressive regimes and violent atmospheres. *Yo el supremo* (1974) by Augusto Roa Bastos and *Vlad* (2010) by Carlos Fuentes feature villains who are ubiquitous, violent, and powerful, and, most importantly, do not die. These authors use the vampire figure and Gothic themes in fascinating ways that speak to many forms of persecution in a Latin American context. Framed within the notions of metaphor, the novels evoke vampiric figures that articulate fears about contemporary culture while simultaneously demonstrating the ways the mythic entities and controversial figures of the historical past continue to haunt the present. In these texts, a redressed Dracula, as imagined by Stoker, emerges from the pages of a novel that illustrates the persistence of oppressive and infectious totalitarian regimes in Latin America, as elsewhere in the world and throughout history. These despots are similar to vampiric entities, which return in different times, in different continents, in different bodies to terrorize and feed off their citizens.

The final chapter, "The Doppelgänger: Split-Selves, Animal-Doubles, and Spectral Couples," revisits the many manifestations of doubles in the texts discussed in this book and then focuses on the particular use of animal doubles—mainly, the lycanthrope—in Alejo Carpentier's novel *El reino de esto mundo* (The Kingdom of This World) (1949), underscoring the emancipation of the animal-double from its usual monstrous imaginings. Conversely, Carlos Fuentes coalesces indigenous worldviews with Gothic aesthetics, evoking pre-Columbian rituals of human sacrifice. In Fuentes's literary works, many of the characters are spectral duplications and reembodiments of previous historical, literary, and mythical figures. These characters, virtual doppelgängers, demand sacrificial victims to secure immortality—an obvious reference to pre-Columbian rituals—thus altering the usual literary representations that feature split entities. In Fuentes's "Chac Mool" (1954) and *Aura* (1965), the doubles ask for small offerings and, eventually, for a human life in order to continue their existence, thus restaging Mesoamerican sacrificial ceremonies to the gods.

Whereas chapters 3 and 4 offer a social and political critique, chapter 5 examines how literary texts behave like virtual doppelgängers. More than any other author examined in this book, Carlos Fuentes has been studied for his pervasive use of the double and appropriation of Gothic features, which he cites openly. Fuentes's purposeful use of the double and the Gothic also implicitly critiques notions of authenticity, demonstrating how authors are often bound to their literary predecessors. Doubles often destabilize the subject's fantasy of being whole, authentic, and autonomous, leading the protagonist to realize that he or she is no longer the original and has been, in a sense, plagiarized. Similarly, ancestors, acting as virtual doubles, become interlopers asserting their presence vigorously with each new literary creation, thus undermining notions of complete originality. Just as the authentic self cannot kill the "other" without causing his or her mutual destruction, authors cannot erase former literary entities—they are haunted by more than three thousand years of literature.

The chapters in this book illustrate that writers reacted to hegemonic movements and philosophies bearing down on them, whether rigid rationalism or realism. They looked elsewhere to invigorate their prose and, at times, turned to antimimetic art and, more specifically, to the Gothic.[47] The texts discussed here undermine realistic fiction's predilection for verisimilitude and documenting of social life, which many times becomes a means of social or political comment. Writers who wrote fantastic literature after the modernistas, as well as those authors associated with the vanguards, transcended the scientific and overly rational world and reincorporated myths, dreams, and nightmares into their literature, which could also speak, albeit more obliquely, to confining social circumstances. Through their Gothic interplay, the authors discussed in this book allegorize in their literature the political, cultural, aesthetic, and/or existential angst that they and their contemporaries grappled with in their own lives.

PART 1
THE CONTEXT

CHAPTER 1

VAMPIRES

The First Bat-Men Are from the Americas

What do vampires have to do with Latin America, anyway? It would seem to many that vampire monsters originally formed part of eastern European folklore and were later made infamous in literature by John William Polidori, Sheridan LeFanu, and Bram Stoker in "The Vampyre" (1819), "Carmilla" (1872), and *Dracula* (1897), respectively. In these works, both male and female vampires are portrayed as cunning aristocratic beings that were engendered in the distant past but exist in the present to feed off the living. They have many supernatural abilities, including seduction, hypnotism, mind reading, shape-shifting, and magically disappearing. They can live forever. Their most frightful trait is their insatiable thirst for human blood, which provokes them to seek out victims, whom they attack and kill, sometimes converting them into the undead.

Even though the vampire figure did not have an extensive manifestation in Latin American literature in the nineteenth and early twentieth century, as it did in Europe, it was an evocative monster that was appealing to the most canonical authors from this region, appearing in Latin American literature in the nineteenth century as best illustrated by modernista poets such as Rubén Darío, Leopoldo Lugones, Clemente Palma, and Froylán Turcios, all of whom feature vampiric entities in their prose.[1] Later in the twentieth century, writers associated with literatura fantástica also deployed the vampire figure in their stories; Horacio Quiroga and Julio Cortázar are two singular examples. Yet, before analyzing the vampire figure found in the literature in the nineteenth and twentieth century, it is necessary to give a brief synopsis of the American bat's journey through the archives of history in order to understand how the pre-Columbian anthropomorphic bat, usually a venerated and sacred being, never figured prominently in the modern Latin American literary landscape.

Transatlantic Context

Although initially the relationship is not obvious, the blood-sucking bats of the Americas shaped some of the notions of the vampire monster as we understand it today. The innocuous European bats were very different from American blood-consuming ones. There are more than 1,000 species of bats found worldwide, and approximately 250 inhabit the American continent. Of all the species found around the world, only three species—*Desmodus rotundus*, *Diphylla ecaudata*, and *Diaemus youngi*—consume blood; they are found exclusively in tropical areas of the American continent, mainly southern Mexico, Central America, and parts of South America.[2] Yet the blood-sucking bat species, or hematophagous bats, have received the most fervent attention in popular culture, eclipsing the harmless bats that feast merely on fruits and insects.

The chronicles relating to the conquest of America introduced the hematophagous bat species to the European imagination. The hematophagous bat was mentioned in early conquest literature as found in the second volume of *The Memoirs of the Conquistador Bernal Díaz del Castillo*, in which the author describes the bats that he encountered when traveling with Hernán Cortés during the invasion and conquest of Mexico (1519–1521).[3] Similarly, according to his memoirs, Álvar Núñez Cabeza de Vaca had an unfortunate encounter with bats while he was traveling through Paraguay: one morning he awoke to a gruesome and bloody scene after a bat attached itself to his toe and pruned off a piece of it.[4] Before the identification of the Latin American blood-sucking bat species by explorers and travelers, the vampire monster, as conceived in eastern European folklore, had no metaphoric association with the bat. Until then, the European vampire monster was usually described as a zombie-like dunce, a revenant, and associated with other animals—it was thought to be able to shape-shift into a cat, dog, wolf, rat, or other creature—but it was not narrowly associated with the bat.[5]

The American vampire bat was known by other names before it was rechristened and made monstrous. In Nahuatl the bats are known as *quimichpatlan* (bat) and *tzinacan* (bat that bites); in Mayan, the bat is known as *zotz*. That is to say there was nothing explicitly monstrous in their names. French biologist Georges-Louis Leclerc, Comte de Buffon, first used the term *vampire* in the mid-eighteenth century to describe the blood-sucking bat species of the Americas and bestowed upon them a more sinister status. Charles Darwin further advanced the existence of this creature when he refers to them as "Vampire bats" and by their taxonomic binomial name, *Desmodus d'orbignyi*. He had encountered this bat species in Chile and described it in the following way in his *Voyage of the Beagle* (1839):

> The Vampire bat is often the cause of much trouble, by biting the horses on their withers. The injury is generally not so much owing to the loss of blood as to the inflammation, which the pressure of the saddle afterwards produces. The whole circumstance has lately been doubted in England; I was therefore fortunate in being present when one (*Desmodus d'orbignyi* [sic], Bat) was actually caught on a horse's back. We were bivouacking late one evening near Coquimbo, in Chile, when my servant, noticing that one of the horses was very restive, went to see what was the matter, and fancying he could distinguish something, suddenly put his hand on the beast's withers, and secured the vampire. In the morning the spot where the bite had been inflicted was easily distinguished from being slightly swollen and bloody. The third day afterward we rode the horse, without any ill effect.[6]

According to Darwin, in 1839 the Latin American hematophagous bat was still thought to be part of folklore; however, he brought the bat creature into the realm of the "real" not only by creating a sketch depicting it but also by sharing the personal anecdote of his vampire bat encounter. Over time, the American bat almost always came to be considered a monstrous figure thanks to those who ventured through the American continent beginning in colonial times and wrote travel letters about blood-sucking bats, fueling the imagination of those who read the letters.

Given Díaz del Castillo's chronicles of the Mexican conquest, Cabeza de Vaca's memoirs, Darwin's scientific naming, and travel letters, the subsequent amalgamation of the blood-sucking American bat with the European vampire monster seemed inevitable. Consequently, the vampire bat species of the Americas was important in altering the vampire folklore and literature in Europe.[7]

In creating his quintessential vampire, Stoker was not only informed by European and eastern European folklore, but he also drew from American legends as well. More specifically, Stoker's Dracula creation is also partly based on the American bat species, as described in the following, in which he mentions the fatal power of the bat's bite: "I have not seen anything pulled down so quick since I was on the Pampas and had a mare that I was fond of go to grass all in a night. One of those big bats that they call vampires had got at her in the night, and what with his gorge and the vein left open, there wasn't enough blood in her to let her stand up, and I had to put a bullet through her as she lay."[8] In mentioning these bats from South America in his novel, Stoker further crystallizes the association of the vampire with the Latin American bat and establishes many of the defining features associated with the vampire figure that still continue in popular culture.

Pre-Columbian Vampires

The anthropomorphic bat, or the bat-man, was not solely a European creation. The bat-man was part of pre-Columbian culture long before the modernized vampire monster took hold of the Latin American literary landscape. Bats in Latin American autochthonous cultures were not usually associated with evil. Instead, they were perceived as powerful creatures, mediums, and occasionally gods. In El Tajín, the site of pre-Columbian stone sculptures of Veracruz, vampire bats are depicted as important gods in postsacrificial ceremonies.[9] The powerful bats appear in the *Popul vuh*, the book of creation and epic myths of the Quiche Maya.[10] In the *Popul vuh*, a "death bat" (*camazotz*) takes the head of one of the twin heroes and carries it to the ritual ball game. According to J. Eric S. Thompson, in several of the codices (for example, those of Borgia, Porfirio Díaz, or Fejérváry-Mayer), anthropomorphized bats are depicted as being involved in human sacrifice.[11] The Zotzil

Maya, of the Chiapas plateau, used to call themselves *Zotzil uinic* (bat-men), claiming that their ancestors found a stone bat that they took as their god.[12] Furthermore, Elizabeth Wilson cites the bats' presence in Colombia and Mexico. She also documents a bat-man deity, or hero, as found in the Toba people's creation story. In other words, the first bat-men or bat-people could be found in the Americas.[13]

In his 2013 book, *Zotz: El murciélago en la cultura maya* (Zotz: The Bat in Mayan Culture), Roberto Romero Sandoval explores the vampire bat's presence in Mayan tradition. He reports that the bat image is found on ceramic pots, urns, lintels, and sculptures.[14] Like Thompson, he explains how the vampire bat is often a manifestation of the sacred. As the bat is a nocturnal creature, Romero Sandoval argues, in Mayan culture the bat is associated with the underworld and the more somber aspects of the shadowy cosmos. The vampire bat is also depicted on various thresholds that are supposed to lead to interior spaces of the subterranean universe. Romero Sandoval also notes that the vampire bat was not only significant in Mayan culture but also important among the Zapotec indigenous cultures in Oaxaca, Mexico; although not necessarily considered a deity, in Zapotec culture the vampire bat was similarly associated with the supernatural.[15] Today in Oaxaca, farmers consider all bats to be important for controlling the pests that could ruin their crops, emphasizing how the bat has been a venerated and helpful creature that is not specifically diabolical but rather one that has contributed to their livelihood. Kampen, Thompson, Romero Sandoval, and Wilson emphasize how the bat of the Americas was a powerful being associated with the sacred, the mythic underworld, and the supernatural long before the bat was solely allied with the profane in contemporary culture.

Other than in the *Popul vuh*, the mythic bats as documented in pre-Columbian culture have largely vanished from the Latin American literary scene, thus illustrating how colonial projects often erased and replaced pre-Columbian knowledge with new European representations. The anthropomorphic bat emerges in the Americas in the nineteenth century refashioned in European attire, having had its indigenous past covered up. That is to say, the expression of the vampire figure in Latin America has usually been deemed a foreign creature; however, this book illustrates how authors reappropriated and rearticulated the vampire in a new context.

The Modernistas' Vampires

As mentioned in the introduction, el modernismo was an important literary current that attracted writers from across the Spanish-speaking American continent beginning in the late nineteenth century and including such poets as Delmira Agustini (Uruguay), Rubén Darío (Nicaragua), Leopoldo Lugones (Argentina), Clemente Palma (Peru), and Froylán Turcios (Honduras). These authors feature vampire figures in their writings, making them some of the first to collectively usher in the vampire monster shaped by Romantic European renditions of vampiric entities to the region.

Before the modernistas became an influential literary force, works produced in Spanish-speaking America mostly followed Spain's literary tradition. However, Latin American modernista poets expanded their literary scope in terms of time and space by looking to the past and turning their focus away from Spain. They included places perceived as more exotic, such as Asia, and at times incorporated Orientalist aesthetics. They looked toward more cosmopolitan regions, such as Paris, and emulated the Parisian Symbolist poets. The modernistas were drawn to these Parisian poets' forms and themes and dedicated some of their essays and poems to artists such as Charles Baudelaire, Stéphane Mallarmé, and Paul Verlaine. The modernistas were attracted to the idea of "art for art's sake," and they sought refuge in a more idealized or mythic world, recoiling from the scientific and materialistic tendencies bearing down on them as a result of modernity. The modernistas were drawn to foreign authors and forms, and their poems were at times criticized for being overly global, escapist, and lacking a recognizable national identity. Yet their work pivoted from solely evoking foreign imagery to finding inspiration in the local folklore and pre-Columbian cultures, as illustrated by Darío's "Caupolicán," "Chinampa," and "El sueño del Inca," sonnets that celebrate indigenous heroes and the Latin American landscape.[16]

Rubén Darío was one of the movement's leading poets and his work is representative of many of the modernista aims and styles. In Darío's poems, he mentions mythic figures and gods from ancient Greek, Roman, and Norse traditions as well as from pre-Columbian American civilizations: characters such as centaurs, Venus, and Thor, along with the native mythic heroes Caupolicán and Cuauhtémoc, appear in his poems. At times Darío includes opulent themes and imagery, which on occasion feature melancholic heroes, sad princesses, and his emblematic majestic swans. In addition to his luxurious figures, he often mentions rubies, gold, and other precious stones and minerals in his works to draw attention to and emphasize their beauty. "Sonatina," "El Cisne," and "Caupolicán" are three examples of Darío's poems that have some of the features most associated with his works and el modernismo in general.

The modernistas, like Darío, also explored occult and esoteric themes in their works, which Cathy Jrade explores in detail in her book *Rubén Darío and the Romantic Search for Unity: The Modernist Recourse to Esoteric Tradition*. The modernistas, the successors of Romanticism, were also inspired by darker themes of death and the grotesque, especially those found in Edgar Allan Poe's writings. Poe, Baudelaire, and Darío were kindred spirits drawn to many of the same themes of death, beauty, and even the beauty of death, especially when it came to female figures. Darío's admiration for Poe is evidenced by his many allusions and explicit references to Poe's work, exemplified by his essay "Edgar Poe y los sueños" (Edgar Poe and Dreams). Darío read many of Poe's original works in English as well as the French translations of Poe published by Baudelaire, Mallarmé, and Camille Mauclair.[17] Darío's essay "Los raros" indicates that he held Poe in high esteem, and his admiration for Poe is especially evident in the anthology *Verónica y otros cuentos fantásticos* (1995), which includes Dario's short stories about a female vampire, the Devil, and other hauntings. This collection features Darío's prose published in newspapers and journals beginning in 1893 and is unlike most anthologies of his work, which usually include only his poems. This principal if not singular interest in modernistas' poetry is true for most of these poets since literary criticism has privileged their verse, while their prose has been, by comparison, understudied. The collection of Darío's stories in *Verónica y otros cuentos fantásticos* is also significant because it represents an early example of the literatura fantástica produced in the region, which would later become important to writers associated with this mode of literature, as illustrated by Jorge Luis Borges, Adolfo Bioy Casares, Julio Cortázar, and Horacio Quiroga.[18] That is to say, modernista themes were precursors to a type of literature that would become popular later in the twentieth century in Latin America.[19]

Darío was not the only modernista who was drawn to vampires.

Other writers associated with el modernismo also delved into vampire lore: in his early years, Leopoldo Lugones wrote about a female vampire in "La vampira" (1897), as did Clemente Palma in "Las vampiras" (1906). In 1910 Froylán Turcios published his novel *El vampiro*, which is one of the first Gothic novels of the Spanish-speaking continent. The vampire figure emerges in modernista poems as well. For example, Delmira Agustini wrote the poem "El vampiro," which appeared in her 1910 book *Cantos de la mañana*.[20] Latin American authors such as Darío and Lugones, among other modernistas, were admirers of Baudelaire, so it is not surprising that they were drawn to the female vampire figure, which reflected in the way vampires had been represented in French letters and in Baudelaire's poems "Le vampire" (The Vampire) and "Les métamorphoses du vampire" (The Metamorphoses of the Vampire), both of which appeared in Baudelaire's *Les fleurs du mal* (1857)[21]—a fundamental work for many Latin American poets of this era. In Baudelaire's poem "The Vampire," he likens women to a herd of demons that shackle their male lovers, and in "The Metamorphoses of the Vampire," the vixen seductress turns into a monstrous and grotesque figure whose lover reacts in horror when he sees that the beautiful woman is transformed into a putrescent thing and a skeleton. Similarly, in Darío's story "Thanatopia," he speaks of a female vampire who has been invited to cross the familial threshold because the protagonist's father has married her.

In *Verónica y otros cuentos fantásticos*, we find Darío's "Thanatopia" (1893), one of the first vampire short stories written by a Latin American modernista. The title of the story is a reference to the Greek god Thanatos, associated with death, and *topia* references topos or place. As the title indicates, this story concerns a place of death where the main character encounters a vampire and barely escapes with his life, but perhaps at the expense of his sanity. In the story, a young man, James Leen, is at a bar drinking a beer and telling friends about his lonely, difficult childhood. An unnamed narrator occasionally interrupts James's monologue to describe James's delicate physical and unstable mental state, which calls into question the truthfulness of James's testimony. The narrator describes James as thin, quiet, and strange, but also as an esteemed teacher well liked by friends and colleagues. In spite of his general amiability, he sometimes has melancholic bouts like the one he is experiencing as he speaks of his traumatic past. After describing James's moodiness, the narrator explains that those at the bar consider this particular brooding *fumisterie*, or an unpleasant prank, which creates more ambiguity for the reader and further thwarts interpretation since James's story could be simply a way for him to amuse himself and/or his friends. The ambiguity that might create hesitation in the reader situates the story within the fantastic mode; however, the story also evokes the aesthetics associated with the Gothic.

James recounts that when he was a young boy his mother died prematurely and his cold and austere father, John Leen, a celebrated scientist, sent him to an Oxford boarding school. He spent many lonely and miserable years there, rarely seeing his father. At age twenty, James's father visits and asks that he return to their home so that he can meet his new stepmother. James returns to his London mansion only to find that his dreadful father has married an equally dreadful woman. He later describes how she carries the putrid scent of death; she is, in fact, a cold female corpse and a vampire. The final sentences are especially horrifying when James describes how the cold corpse wants to give him a kiss on his forehead, eyes, and mouth. The narrator suggests that the father, a man of science, has delved into the occult and has managed to resurrect a dead female body. On the night that he is asked to meet his stepmother, James describes his father's retinas as being as red as those of a rabbit and details how his father's intense gaze made him tremble with fear. According to James, his father eventually had him institutionalized so that no one would discover his father's macabre life. Nevertheless, James eventually escapes from the asylum and finds refuge in Buenos Aires, the place from which he is narrating the story.

Similar to writers associated with literatura fantástica, the story is narrated in an ambiguous way so that the reader can opt for either a rational or supernatural interpretation of the events. James could be mentally ill and has imagined this episode, or he could, in fact, be suffering a breakdown because he has a vampiric stepmother. Or perhaps James's account could be a hoax, as the narrator suggests. However, what is important here is that this is one of the first times that the vampire figure appears in a Latin American short story, and other authors associated with this movement followed suit. "Thanatopia" exemplifies how Darío, as well as other modernistas, was drawn to occult and esoteric themes that had little to do with the rational and positivistic ideas that dominated intellectual thought at that time. Darío's story features a female vampire that John Leen has resurrected through his experiments with occult practices, though her origins remain unclear; however, in Lugones and Palma's stories, female characters are the principal actors that bring about death and destruction, thus also revealing how modernistas were imagining women at that time.

Female Vampires

Beginning with Darío, the modernistas illustrate how they were drawn to female vampires; unless confined, these monstrous and passionate women could threaten the sanctity of the home. Their evocation of the vampire figure also recalls the way this monster condenses many threats into a single body, which Judith Halberstam describes in her book *Skin Shows*. Halberstam states that "Dracula is the deviant or the criminal, the other against whom the normal and the lawful, the marriageable and the heterosexual can be known and quantified."[22] William Hughes observes that "there appears to be a critical imperative that dissociates the vampire from conventional humanity, polarizing the un-dead in a cultural Other whose practices constitute an intervention into the integrity of race and nation or an invasion to the sanctity of home and family."[23] Halberstam and Hughes underscore the ways the vampire monster embodies a threat to what is usually accepted as the norm in terms of family, gender, and sexuality; and the modernista female characters analyzed here were corrupting well-established gender norms. That is, these featured female vampires are independent and impassioned, behaving in monstrous ways that cause the death of the males in their wake.

In particular, the vampire stories featuring females illustrate how modernista poets might also be apprehensive about the shifts in gender roles brought on by modernity. As if reacting to the changing social structure, their prose intimates that women should remain confined to domestic spaces and not venture into spheres considered masculine. This corroborates what Margarita Vargas states about modernistas, "whose representations of women consist primarily of monolithic figures marked by beauty, confinement, and servitude."[24] Their literary production also corresponds to a time when industrialization and nascent globalization were having a profound impact on the Latin American economy, during which regions were being transformed from the rural and agrarian model to a money-based market economy, allowing more women to enter the workforce. Women in Latin America, as in other places around the globe, were expected to behave according to certain social norms; however, the changing economy was altering family dynamics. Lee Skinner succinctly outlines the pervasive modes of behavior ascribed to women in *Gender and the Rhetoric of Modernity in Spanish America, 1850–1910*, stating, "Women should be malleable, gentle, and submissive; the writers specifically rejected the notion that a woman could or should outshine her male counterpart."[25] Furthermore, as Skinner illustrates, women at that time were to operate as "angels of the home" whose main purpose was to protect the family's honor. Additionally, women should demonstrate virtuous qualities and sacrifice personal desires. The modernistas evoked women as beautiful goddesses, sublime angels, sad princesses, but when they included female characters who demonstrated sexual desires, outperformed men, and/or behaved contrary to established social norms, they were transmogrified into dark angels and monsters.

Their texts also suggest changes brought on by modernization altered traditional gender roles and contributed to monstrous transformations and even death, and implicitly addressed how the nation was being ruined by the modern. In particular, the portrayal of vampiric females emphasized the way women's sexuality was perceived to undermine society's moral order, which, as Bram Dijkstra argues in his book *Evil Sisters: The Threat of Female Sexuality and the Cult of Manhood*, was reaffirmed by scientific discourse emerging in the nineteenth century and more clearly methodized in the early twentieth century. According to Dijkstra, "The 'discoveries' of early-twentieth-century biology saddled Western culture with a vicious eroticism centered on images of the sexual woman as vampire." He describes how female sexuality was represented as a degenerative disease. Women were described as predators, destroyers, witches, and vampires that brought about male death. These independent women could also very well destroy manhood, resulting in an "effeminate" race of men.[26] These pseudoscientific notions formed part of literature as well, which might partially explain why the modernistas' stories feature mostly female vampires intent on destroying men. These writers also represent women as ominous figures who cause madness and death. They are frequently described as predatory monsters that threaten the sanctity of family and home, which reinforced how scientists, according to Dijkstra, were constructing female sexuality as primitive, menacing, and deadly. Sometimes women were not willingly causing harm, but their alluring presence was enough to bring about death and madness.

Leopoldo Lugones, like Darío, published a short story about a female vampire, "La vampira" (1897). In this story, the nameless female character does not bite or suck the blood from her victims but draws out the life and intellect from her lovers. She belongs to an aristocratic class and was once married to an esteemed and wealthy colonel, who died mysteriously. When they first met, they were madly and passionately in love, but one day he begins to feel melancholic and soon loses his health and, apparently, his good judgment. As he begins to weaken, his intellect and speech are also affected. Paradoxically, while he is fading away, she begins to exude life. Before his illness, she was described as plain, timid, short, and dull, but as his health and mental state deteriorate, she begins to usurp his knowledge and health, becoming more expressive, voluptuous, beautiful, independent, and even taller. She outshines him. She relates to Adolfo, her new young suitor and the protagonist of the story, how she has absorbed all of the colonel's energy; in fact, the colonel now inhabits her body and she has, in a sense, "consumed" his masculine traits.[27] She found the passionate love that led to a complete unification delightful at first; however, this union with the colonel is anything but ideal because now his specter haunts her, not allowing her to love anyone else. Seemingly, she has an interior doppelgänger of sorts—both a female and male presence within her body.

This coalescing of male and female identities in a single body also brings into play various myths associated with androgyny. According to creation myths, the androgynous figure was a primal and idealized body that became fragmented after the fall of humanity. This fall results in a yearning for a return to that utopian androgynous state.[28] This unification of the bodies, according to myth, would signify a return to some imagined paradise. A body that has both male and female features could mean perfection and a return to a primal and innocent place before humankind's fall from grace. However, in "La vampira" the female character's experience with this union does not bring her closer to heavenly existence as imagined in the world of myth. Rather, her life becomes a living nightmare. She is a haunted being that kills those who love her, as Adolfo will soon discover. The debasing of the notions of androgyny, in which unification brings about damnation rather than a paradise, is not surprising given the cultural context. The discourse at the time, recalling Dijkstra's and Skinner's words, was reaffirming the cult of manhood by excluding women from domains that were deemed masculine. There were borders that women should not cross, and when venturing into spaces associated with masculinity they were branded as monsters.

Men had codes of behavior to follow as well, and not obeying them could lead to terrible endings. In some of the stories analyzed here, men who demonstrate excessive emotions or behave irrationally become mad or die. In the case of Adolfo, he falls madly in love with his beloved and, like the colonel, slowly begins to lose his senses and good health because of his passionate feelings for her. Sensing danger, Adolfo tries to leave and forget her. Yet, unable to control his feelings, he returns for a final meeting and while Adolfo kisses her, she strangles him to death. She is seemingly possessed by the colonel's spirit who, driven by jealousy, kills Adolfo. Arguably, at the moment of the murder, she is a two-sexed being—a female body with a masculine presence at her core. This doubling of the protagonist also evokes the figure of the doppelgänger, but instead of being a divided self, in which the double is scurrying around town causing havoc, the monster is embodied within the female heroine. What is suggested here is that independent women who dare to appropriate male qualities—as she has done by absorbing the colonel's intelligence, eloquence, and independence—become monsters and present an implicit threat. The text suggests that men were not to assume behavior deemed feminine and women were to behave in ways considered womanlike and avoid spaces associated with masculinity. Transgressing these norms brings about death, which is what Adolfo finds in the end. Unlike typical vampire stories, there are no fangs or drawing of blood, but the female character is taking the lives and intelligence of her unsuspecting lovers. Unbridled, passionate love leads to unfortunate consequences, like death and mental instability, especially for male characters. The way

Lugones characterizes this heroine exemplifies what Dijkstra also argues in his book. Men were to remain free of independent women and avoid emotional excess, thereby maintaining behavior deemed appropriate to their gender and class.

Whereas Lugones uses the vampire as metaphor, Palma presents the vampire figure in a more classic and literal way. His female vampires do have fangs and come out at night to draw blood from their male victims. Palma, a Peruvian writer associated with the modernistas, was similarly attracted to themes of the monstrous; his story "Vampiras" (Female Vampires) highlights how emotional excess leads to unfortunate ends. The story first appeared in 1906 and was later republished in the second edition of *Cuentos malévolos* (Malevolent Stories) in 1913.[29] In it the narrator describes how a coven of female vampires stalk and kill young men at night. The protagonist, Stanislas, also the narrator of the story, is concerned about his sickly and fragile state and does not know why or how he has become ill.

Stanislas's fiancée, Natalia, is often at his bedside caring for him, yet as his symptoms worsen he seeks additional attention. He visits the family doctor, Max Bing, who warns of impending death if Stanislas does not place himself completely under Bing's care. The doctor shares that he has seen the same symptoms in a previous patient, Hansen, who was devoured by female vampires while he slept. The doctor says that in spite of our living in an enlightened era, which offers no reasonable explanations for these monsters, there still exists malignant shadows, occult powers, and strange forces that have not yet formed part of scientific discourse. This comment illustrates the ways modernistas were drawn to the more mysterious aspects of existence and underscores the ways life's marvels could not be solely approached through scientific inquiry.

Doctor Bing explains that Hansen was engaged to Alicia but courted many young women prior to Alicia who were madly in love with him. These female figures, described very much like a coven of witches, apparently returned every night as vampires to drain Hansen of his blood and life. In Stanislas's case, he does not have a coven of vampire witches attacking him at night; rather, his beloved, Natalia, is visiting him at night in the form of a vampire. Paradoxically, instead of suggesting that he leave or kill her, the doctor urges that in order to save himself,

Stanislas must marry Natalia immediately so as to impede her further monstrous transformation.

Palma's eerie story utilizes the usual tropes found in vampire stories; however, his short story concludes with a more concrete, albeit unreal, explanation of vampirism associated with frustrated female sexual desire. The story suggests that passionate women turn into vampires, threatening the lives of their unsuspecting partners, and the only way to prevent their monstrous transformation is through women's domestication—that is, marriage. In other words, through domesticity she can assume her "angel of the house" position. Palma's story also speaks to bourgeois sensibility of the time because his story prescribes, very much like Doctor Bing did with Stanislas, a traditional, well-established marriage while discouraging destructive, passionate desire, which could have detrimental effects such as female vampirism and male death.

In the works of the modernistas discussed earlier, vampire women bring about the demise of men. However, the way these writers ascribe vampiric qualities to women is different from how Delmira Agustini, also associated with el modernismo, approaches the vampire figure in her poem "El vampiro." Cathy Jrade's book *Delmira Agustini, Sexual Seduction, and Vampiric Conquest* explores the deployment of the vampire metaphor and problematizes the way male poets of Agustini's time were objectifying and vilifying women when they described them as vampires. In Agustini's work, the poetic voice assumes the role of the vampire and is one of power, not victimization. Although a woman wrote the poem and it would seem that the poetic voice would come from a female subject, it is unclear who is declaiming the words in "El vampiro." Why does she not title the poem "La vampira" instead of using the masculine article and noun? Has Agustini assumed the role of a male vampire, as the title "El vampiro" suggests? If she were supposed to be a woman speaking as if she were a male vampire, this would make the poem doubly subversive because she not only assumes a male voice but is also the vampire that speaks to a subjective presence. This is unlike the way in which the other modernistas related to the vampire figure. We usually are presented with a perspective from the vampire's victims—typically a young male under a vampiric woman's spell. Agustini's transgression is not unusual if we consider how critics have already underscored the way she rearticulated and contested modernista strategies.[30] Although sharing the thematic interests of the modernistas, she undermined and criticized their aesthetic representations. Jrade shows how Agustini's work was a way for her to reaffirm female autonomy and subvert the way women were being imagined at the time. Delmira Agustini's social reality was one of asserting herself as a poet in a male-dominated field, and "El vampiro," by appropriating a vampiric male subjectivity, is a clear example of how she was altering the way women could speak about themselves.

Although Jrade explores the vampire metaphor in Agustini's poetry, a similar study has not been done on modernista prose. Darío, Lugones, and Palma are widely read authors, yet their stories (much less the ones about vampires) are rarely mentioned in criticism, and most modernista anthologies focus on their verse. However, the fact that their short vampire stories exist underscores how writers on both sides of the Atlantic had a common affinity for vampires in the late nineteenth and early twentieth centuries. Moreover, by evoking these vampiric entities modernistas could also express anxieties brought on by modernity and the accompanying social changes that were impacting the family and nation. While the stories mentioned thus far feature vampiric women, there were writers who also included other types of vampires in their literature.

A Latin American Gothic Novel: *El Vampiro*

Similar to Poe, Darío, and Lugones, Turcios explores the inexplicable and monstrous in his fiction, as depicted in *El vampiro*. This is a noteworthy short novel because Turcios uses the lyrical language celebrated by the modernista poets as well as conventions associated with Romanticism. He also incorporates many Gothic literary features, making it one of the first Gothic novels from Latin America. His vampire monster coalesces the demonic monk as conceived by Matthew Lewis in his Gothic novel *The Monk* (1796) and the vampire figure articulated by Stoker in *Dracula*. Turcios's villain is a corrupt cleric who can shape-shift into the form of a vampire bat to stalk and kill his victims at night. Turcios not only appropriates features found in well-known Gothic novels, but also includes the Gothic setting and a female vampiric character as imagined in Poe's "Ligeia" (1838).

Before analyzing Turcios's vampire figure, a summary of the author's context is necessary. Although Turcios was an emblematic figure of Central American letters, he is less well known than his contemporaries, which include Darío, José Martí, and Agustini. Turcios was born into a moneyed family in Honduras, but due to his family's financial difficulties, he had to abandon his university studies. When his financial situation changed, Turcios secured a livelihood by becoming a journalist and by holding various positions in public offices that allowed him to travel throughout Latin America and Europe. During his travels he met with the most esteemed writers, including Darío, Lugones, and Alfonso Reyes, among other renowned poets of his time. In *Froylán Turcios: Su vida y sus obras* (Froylán Turcios: His Life and Works), Moisés Vincenzi chronicles the author's life and describes the admiration many of the modernistas had for Turcios's poetry and prose. Vincenzi's book also emphasizes that Turcios was drawn to features that defined certain aspects of el modernismo: "los marmoles, las sedas, los perfumes, las piedras preciosas, y sobre todo la perfección del espíritu, la belleza de la formas helénicas . . . en general todas las formas de la elegancia y del lujo" (marble, silks, perfumes, precious stones, and above all spiritual perfection, the beauty of Hellenic forms . . . in general, all forms of elegance and luxury).[31] Turcios was drawn to the luxurious and elegant, exalting the beauty of people, places, and objects using *preciosista*, or affected language; yet, like his contemporaries, he was also seduced by the lugubrious, as illustrated in *El vampiro*.

However, unlike the other modernista vampire tales, his novel's plot unfolds in a Latin American setting, which emphasizes the narrator's as well as the author's deep admiration for the region's colonial past, its cultural traditions, and its former claim to glory. La Antigua, which also means former, old, ancient, was once the influential capital and is famous for its colonial architecture, its impressive volcanic topography, and its Mayan ruins, all of which the narrator in *El vampiro* lyrically describes in detail. This romanticized atavism, coupled with disdain for the modern, characterizes the modernista movement, revealing the writers' loathing of modernity's noisy register. Yet they escaped and found refuge in Gothic language as another means by which to express these feelings.

Turcios includes such common Gothic characters and tropes as an orphaned heroine, an ineffectual hero, a double, a family secret, a superstitious and loquacious servant, a vampire, a revenant, and a malignant cleric. Most of the events unfold in a familial mansion located in La Antigua, Guatemala, the country's former capital, which he describes as lugubrious and ghostly. The novel's most Gothic quality is that it is a story of hauntings and of a family troubled by an ominous past that will bring about an ill-fated future. An underlying tension present throughout is the existence of a menacing, vampiric priest who appears early on and remains lurking in the shadows, materializing at the novel's end to ruin the blissful aspirations of the young protagonist, Rogerio.

Unlike the modernista stories discussed previously, Turcios's principal vampire villain is not a woman but rather a corrupt priest, Fray Félix Aguilar, who is admired by all in the town; however, this seemingly benevolent man is diabolical in his pursuit of Rogerio's beloved orphaned cousin, Luz. Turcios's malevolent priest is similar to Matthew Lewis's character Ambrosio from *The Monk*. Ambrosio is also a much-adored cleric, but this supposedly godly man is evil and lustful and relentlessly pursues Antonia, the female heroine. When Antonia rejects him as a lover, he drugs her, tortures her with live entombment, rapes her, and later murders her. In Turcios's novel, the lust-driven Fray Félix is similarly stalking Luz and will stop at nothing to possess her. He also seems to be driving her into darker depths with his bewitching words during confession. Luz tells Rogerio that the priest is damning her: "Me voy a condenar . . . desde la primera confesión está hundiéndome en el infierno"[32] (I am being condemned . . . since the very first confession he is submerging me into the depths of hell). This passage describes the way Fray Félix is placing her under his spell and how she too is being driven to the underworld.

When Rogerio discovers that the priest tried to rape Luz, he does everything possible to save her, confronting the monstrous priest with a crucifix in one hand and whip in the other, shouting sacred words to cast out Fray Félix from their home and lives. After one of these confrontations, the priest rushes out of the de Mendoza home, appearing to float, and his ominous cape splits into two, resembling batlike wings, thus establishing the connection between the priest and the vampire bat figure, as found in *Dracula*. At the novel's end a terrible fight ensues between Rogerio and a vampire bat. Although it is not made entirely clear, it is suggested that the priest can shape-shift into a bat, and that the bat is Fray Felix's familiar and/or his nagual, his animal double, which explains why when Rogerio strangles the vampire bat the priest also dies by strangulation, even though he is presumably in another town.

Rogerio kills the bat and, by extension, the priest. Still, Rogerio is ultimately unable to save Luz. Before dying, the priest had already slain Luz and perhaps even turned her into a vampire as well. In the final words of the novel, Rogerio describes her corpse and bloodstained neck: "Un bucle negro caíle sobre el rostro palídisimo. En la nieve del cuello desnudo brillaba una ligera mancha de sangre"[33] (A black curl fell on her pale face. On her snowy naked neck, a bloodstain glistened). The author foreshadows a vampiric transformation for the reader because she has been bitten on the neck by a vampire and also because the narrator explicitly and repeatedly references Poe's "Ligeia" when describing Luz's exceptional intelligence and beauty. Like Lugones and Palma, Turcios characterizes women as alluring, vampiric, and destructive.

The reference to "Ligeia" suggests that we should understand Luz within the specific context of Poe's story, in which Ligeia is resurrected from the dead by usurping the body of Lady Rowena. In Poe's story, Ligeia's ghost poisons Lady Rowena, and as she dies her physical features change. Lady Rowena's corpse assumes Ligeia's features. Her blonde tresses transform into raven-black curls, her blue eyes turn dark colored, and her corpse even grows taller. In Turcios's novel, the narrator's description of Luz is similar to the way Poe describes Ligeia. Both are women of fifteen with remarkable intelligence and beauty, and both have pale, transparent skin and dark, bewitching eyes. Of Luz, Rogerio says that her eyes are full of life as well as shadows that evoke dreams of an unknown supernatural Eden, which is comparable to Poe's description of Ligeia's eyes. Similar to Ligeia's raven-black tresses, Luz's curls are described as black with blue highlights that resemble the feathers of certain remarkable birds found in the mountains.[34]

Turcios's admiration for and referencing of Poe is illustrated in the story when Rogerio and Luz describe how they both are enchanted by the texts of one of the greatest poets of the Americas, Poe.[35] Luz herself recites Poe's "Ulalume," and "Annabel Lee" in a way the author describes as mesmerizing and lugubrious. In addition to reciting Poe's poems, Luz also knows the words to "Berenice" and "Ligeia" by heart and utters the words of the texts for Rogerio and others in a way that causes them all to shudder—according to the narrator, she had read a version of "Ligeia" that was translated into Spanish from Baudelaire's French translation of Poe's original English version. Turcios replicates the final words of "Ligeia" word for word, and in this way, the reader is hearing "Ligeia" in Spanish as performed by Luz:

> Pero . . . ¿Había crecido mi esposa durante su enfermedad? ¿Qué indefinible delirio se apoderó de mí al concebir esta idea? De un salto caí a sus pies; pero ella se retiró a mi contacto: desprendió su cabeza del horrible sudario que la rodeaba, y entonces se desbordó en la atmósfera de la habitación una masa de largos cabellos desordenados: ¡eran más negros que las alas de la noche, más que el plumaje del cuervo! Y vi que los ojos de aquel rostro lívido se abrían lentamente. "—¡Al fin! exclamé con voz sonora.—¿Podría engañarme yo jamás? ¡He ahí los ojos admirablemente rasgados, los ojos negros, los extraños ojos de mi amor perdido, de los mi adorada Ligeia!"[36]

> [But had she then grown taller since her malady? What inexpressible madness seized me with that thought? One bound, and I had reached her feet! Shrinking from my touch, she let fall from her head, unloosened, the ghastly cerements which had confined it, and there streamed forth, into the rushing atmosphere of the chamber, huge masses of long and dishevelled hair; it was blacker than the raven wings of the midnight! And now slowly opened the eyes of the figure which stood before me. "Here then, at least," I shrieked aloud, "can I never—can I never be mistaken—these are the full, and the black, and the wild eyes—of my lost love—of the Lady—of the Lady Ligeia."][37]

As Luz declaims the words, it is as if Rogerio is witnessing the transformation of Luz into Ligeia, suggesting that during the declamation Luz momentarily becomes Ligeia's double. This merging of characters is achieved by Turcios's strategic use of Poe's exact words from "Ligeia" and by conflating his own narration with that of Poe's. Thus, Poe's Ligeia seemingly usurps Luz's position in Turcio's text.

As in "La vampira" and "Vampiras" mentioned previously, men fall under a woman's vampiric spell; similarly Luz's enchanting words seem to have a damning effect on Rogerio. Luz, whom the author describes as beautiful, intelligent, and otherworldly, outperforms Rogerio in every respect, thus transgressing women's prescribed roles as described by Skinner, in which women were not to outshine men. As illustrated in Palma's and Lugones's stories, demonstrating such intense passion could portend a fatal end. After the night in which Luz passionately recites Poe's works, when everyone, especially Rogerio, is affected by her words, things take a turn for the worse. One day Rogerio and Luz go hunting, and even though he is an experienced hunter, Rogerio is accidently shot when Luz mishandles a revolver. He then spends many days hallucinating and almost dies. His doctor says that because of the gunshot and subsequent tuberculosis, any other mishap or frightful event will certainly kill him.

Luz is a metaphoric vampire who is beautiful but dangerous and brings about Rogerio's demise by causing madness, sickness, and, perhaps, death. As Rogerio becomes increasingly devoted to Luz, he loses his good judgment and good health. He foolishly enters a cursed and forbidden room that once belonged to his grandfather, another ominous and mysterious figure. In it he finds the vampire's hidden lair, and this is where he has his final encounter with the monster. During their fight, Rogerio kills the vampire bat, but not before being bitten on the neck, which later causes him, yet again, to suffer delirious hell-bound dreams and hallucinations. Even though he barely survives, the vampire bite might damn him to another form of existence; of course, in accordance with folklore, such an injury could also destine him to the realm of the undead. This final violent encounter with the vampire bat could have been the one to possibly provoke his premature demise. However, the novel ends without us knowing for certain whether Rogerio dies or whether he and Luz have become vampires.

Luz and the other female characters discussed in this chapter are similar in that they are described as vampires—either literally or metaphorically. These extraordinary women, by seeming to cast maleficent spells, often cause male suffering and death. The modernista stories underscore the dangers of emotional excess and demarcate appropriate spheres of action for both men and women. They describe sexual, intelligent, and independent women as being bestowed with vampiric and witchlike qualities that somehow drain men of their vitality. The stories also demonstrate the way these authors reaffirmed the gender roles of their time period. Later in the twentieth century, however, the vampire figure begins to be imagined differently.

Other Vampiric Short Stories

The vampire did not entirely disappear from the literary scene when interest in modernista literature waned. Vampires were occasional characters in Latin American short stories later in the twentieth century, as seen in the works of Horacio Quiroga and Julio Cortázar. Vampirism is an important theme in two short stories in Quiroga's "El almohadón de pluma" (The Feather Pillow) and "El vampiro." "El almohadón de pluma" was first published in 1907 and later republished—reaching a broader readership—in Quiroga's famous short story collection, *Cuentos de amor, de locura y de muerte* (1917) (Stories of Love, Madness, and Death). In "El almohadón de pluma," Quiroga narrates the story of newlyweds Alicia and Jordán. The bride, Alicia, is mysteriously dying of an unknown illness. Her husband, Jordán, cares for her as she becomes weaker and mentally unstable. She has visions of an "anthropoid" or humanlike creature stalking her. In spite of being under her doctor's care, she still continues to suffer hallucinations and soon dies. Afterward, her husband discovers a small, blood-filled, and hairy animal hidden in her pillow, which has apparently drained her of blood and life. The tick-like insect had not bitten her on the neck; rather, it had been sucking blood from her temples, suggesting that the monster was first draining her of her intellect. This story is unlike the previously discussed modernista works; here the female figure is an entirely passive victim, rather than being the source of evil that brings about the demise of a lover.

Quiroga's "El vampiro" first appeared in 1927 and was later reprinted in his short story collection *Más allá* (1934) (Beyond). In this story, two men, Don Guillen Orzúa y Rosales and Guillermo Grant, are obsessed with a famous and beautiful Hollywood actress. These characters specifically mention Poe's "The Oval Portrait," in which the life of a woman is sucked out of her and transfigured onto a picture frame, which they believe to be a scientific possibility. Apparently, these two men wish to replicate this phenomenon through some mysterious use of gamma rays. They somehow succeed in drawing her body out of the screen, materializing her filmic specter. However, this scientific experiment goes awry because she emerges from the screen not as a beautiful woman but as a frightful skeleton. She also becomes a vampire-type figure that begins to suck the life and sanity out of the two men. Don Guillen Orzúa y Rosales dies, and Guillermo Grant finds himself in an asylum awaiting a similar fate. As analyzed in more detail in chapter 2, this short story has more to do with cinema and its inherent spectral qualities. That is to say, Quiroga, familiar with vampire lore and its literary tradition, employs the vampire to comment on film as an art form, which is awe-inspiring but unsettling too.

In 1937 another master of the short story, Julio Cortázar, speaks of vampires in "El hijo del vampiro" (The Son of the Vampire), which was published in *La otra orilla* (a compilation of stories written by Cortázar between 1937 and 1945). "El hijo del vampiro" is perhaps the most subversive text in the short stories mentioned in this chapter because the author challenges many notions associated with bourgeois sensibilities, in which the idea of family is completely shattered. In Cortázar's work, Duggu Van is a vampire who falls in love with Lady Vanda, which is unusual because, in the world of vampires, the monster does not usually fall in love but instead only feels hunger, lust, and desire, but not necessarily love. Since Duggu Van is enamored, he feeds on animals or other creatures to satisfy his urges. He not only falls in love with Lady Vanda, he also impregnates her, which again represents a new twist on the traditional vampire tale. What is most unusual is the way Lady Vanda carries the pregnancy. Her unborn child begins to devour her from the inside and gains a monstrous life by feeding off her. He also begins to change Lady Vanda's body from that of a female body to a male one. Thus, Lady Vanda's body is not destroyed but rather becomes transgendered. The story describes how her female organs transform into those of a male when the narrators says, "Su piel se había puesto repentinamente oscura, sus piernas se llenaban de relieves musculares, el vientre se aplanaba suavemente y, con una naturalidad que parecía casi familiar, su sexo se transformaba en el contrario"[38] (Her skin had turned darker suddenly, her legs developed muscles, her stomach was flattening slowly and, with a spontaneity that seemed almost familiar, her sexual organs transformed into the opposite). In the end, the vampire Duggu Van comes into the building where she has been transformed into a young boy. That is to say, Lady Vanda is now reborn in the form of Duggu Van's son. The final line of the story describes Duggu Van walking out of the hospital holding hands with his "neonatal" son.

Lady Vanda has died, but she takes on the form of a man, and not just any man; she has been transmogrified as her own son. This new body transgresses all notions of what constitutes humanness because she/it is simultaneously a human, a monster, a mother, and a son. Does the vampire father then have an amorous relationship with his son, which would imply incest? In this case, the vampire figure corrupts the clear delineation of family relationships. In either case, Cortázar has skillfully managed to create a vampire that transgresses many boundaries having to do with notions of death, gender, sexuality, and family. Unlike the modernistas, who often domesticate the female vampire through marriage, there is no such recuperation of a preestablished order in Cortázar's story.

The Importance of Poe

As discussed earlier, the works of Poe were important not only for the modernistas, but also for subsequent writers. Quiroga and Cortázar sought to create tension and surprise endings in ways similar to Poe, and all three usually created more ambiguity than clear explanations for readers. Poe's work and theories about short story writing were widely read by Latin American writers even after the modernistas. Critics have discussed Quiroga's, Cortázar's, and even Borges's texts in relation to Poe's literary creation.[39] In Quiroga's 1927 *Decálogo del perfecto cuentista* (Decalogue of the Perfect Short Story Writer), he cites Poe, Guy de Maupassant, Rudyard Kipling, and Anton Chekhov as models for his story writing. Cortázar also wrote about Poe, and he translated many, if not all, of Poe's short stories and other critical works.[40] The fact that

Quiroga and Cortázar experimented with vampire monsters in their literature is not all that surprising given that Poe, a formidable figure in both authors' literary development, also featured women who have vampiric qualities, as found in "Ligeia," "Berenice," and "Morella." Arguably, "The Oval Portrait," as well as some of Poe's other stories, can also be interpreted as implicit instances of vampirism.

However, with the exception of Turcios, whose short novel emphasizes the local traditions and landscapes, all the vampire short stories referenced in this chapter have a universal quality and could take place anywhere. Other than being written in Spanish by Latin American authors, there are no specific markers that make them particularly Latin American. This is not unusual, as Poe himself often opted for more European rather than American settings.[41] This approach to milieu in Latin American vampire stories might explain why critics have overlooked these works. On the surface there is nothing particularly autochthonous about them, especially if we look at the names of the characters. In Darío's story, the characters are John and James Leen, residents of London. In Clemente Palma's work, the characters' names are Stanislas, Doctor Max Bing, and Hansen. In Cortázar's short story, the vampire's name is Duggu Van and the female victim is named Lady Vanda. Most of these vampires do not usually evoke the regional folklore of the American continent.

These vampire tales are unlike most of these authors' well-known works in which the American landscape and history are central to the text. For example, the South American jungle is integral to and palpable in Quiroga's work in his short story collection *Anaconda* (1921). The marvelous and menacing jungle is especially powerful in his stories "El hombre muerto" (The Dead Man) and "A la deriva" (Adrift). Similarly, Aztec myths are more relevant in Cortázar's renowned stories "La noche boca arriba" (The Night Face Up) and "Axolotl." Even though the vampire is not a prevalent figure in Latin American prose, these vampire stories are thought-provoking and demonstrate the vampire's presence in the literary imagination among some of the region's most esteemed writers.

Poe, as a quintessential figure of the English-speaking North American Gothic, informed the southern Gothic of the United States, which was especially popular from the 1940s to the 1960s. This time period is also when the literatura fantástica was widely read in Latin America, suggesting that this turn toward the fantastic and "self conscious Gothicism" was a literary phenomenon that reverberated throughout the continent. It is difficult to argue that the Gothic tradition, as articulated by English and American Gothic, was not part of the literary tapestry in Latin America, given that Gothic setting and the vampiric were appealing to the most erudite authors from the Spanish-speaking region since at least the nineteenth century.

CHAPTER 2

FILMS LOVE MONSTERS

Film's Arrival in Latin America

Moving pictures have projected fantasy films brimming with specters since their inception, and Latin American filmgoers started attending them soon after the Lumière apparatus arrived at the urban centers of this region in 1896. The films appearing on the silver screen in Latin America were not only popular among general audiences, but many eminent Spanish-speaking authors such as María Luisa Bombal, Martín Luis Guzmán, and Horacio Quiroga also became keen admirers of the "seventh art" and took notice of the cinematic innovations that premiered in thriving metropolitan movie houses, as illustrated in their movie reviews and their fiction of the 1920s and 1930s. Quiroga's film-inspired stories feature starstruck filmgoers as well as Hollywood movie stars from the silent-film era; Guzmán's historical novel, *El águila y la serpiente* (1928) (The Eagle and the Serpent), describes revolutionary soldiers in 1914 watching the latest newsreels in theaters in Mexico City. Whereas some authors touched on film culture in their literature, others changed their writing at a compositional level; for example, events were narrated in a fragmentary way or in rapid succession in a manner similar to cinematic montage, as in the case of Mariano Azuela's *Los de abajo* (1925) (The Underdogs). At times, authors' cinematic-themed works were inspired by the Gothic, particularly when the stories introduced ominous characters imbued with occult powers, as illustrated in Quiroga's short stories "El espectro" (1921) (The Specter) and "El vampiro" (1927), as well as Vicente Huidobro's German Expressionist-like filmic novel *Cagliostro* (1934).

Because scholars often have considered the Gothic presence in Latin

America irrelevant or merely tangential, it is imperative to first explore early film history in order to firmly establish the ways classic movies—including Gothic and German Expressionist films—were screened and became the focus of public attention in Spanish-speaking America, thus developing cultural significance and influencing artistic production.[1]

Motion Pictures Reach Latin America

In Latin America, as in Europe, the new film apparatus astounded audiences. When the Lumière brothers screened their first films in 1895 at Le Salon Indien du Grand Café in Paris, the spectators were amazed by the moving images projected on the screen. Little did anyone realize that the presentation of this new invention, at the time deemed merely a passing fancy, was the debut of a prolific art form and lucrative commercial product that would influence many aspects of cultural production around the world. According to anecdotal accounts, several spectators in Paris were so startled when they saw the oncoming train in the film *L'arrivée d'un train en gare de La Ciotat* (The Arrival of a Train at La Ciotat Station) (1896) that they screamed and fled the tent to avoid being crushed.[2] This unsubstantiated story nevertheless highlights the fear and surprise that film provoked when audiences saw the latest spectral novelty for the first time. Georges Méliès, a magician and master of optical illusions who was thoroughly accustomed to seeing the newest marvels, still responded with wonder at his first Lumière film premiere: "[A] still photograph showing the place Bellecour in Lyon was projected. A little surprised, I just had time to say to my neighbor: 'They got us all stirred up for projections like this? I've been doing them for over ten years.' I had hardly finished speaking when a horse pulling a wagon began to walk towards us followed by other vehicles and the pedestrians, in short all the animation of the street. Before this spectacle we sat with gaping mouths, struck with amazement, astonished beyond all expression."[3] This statement not only emphasizes the way in which Méliès was astonished by the new film phenomenon but also foreshadows how others would react when seeing these moving images for the first time.

The Lumières' movie projector and its accompanying films caused a public sensation and soon began to appear in other countries outside France. Beginning in the summer of 1896, the Lumière films appeared in the urban centers of Argentina, Brazil, Chile, and Mexico. Mirroring Méliès's reaction, Latin America's most notable artists also were amazed by this new invention, which is best illustrated by the celebrated Mexican poet José Juan Tablada who, in 1896, penned his reaction to the films:

> El cinematógrafo Lumière continúa exhibiéndose con un éxito grande y merecido. Aquellos metros de blanco lienzo se animan al golpe de la proyección luminosa con una vida intensa, sorprendente y prodigiosa. El primer sentimiento que ese espectáculo sugiere es la superstición y el fanatismo: se busca vivamente al Nostradamus de negra túnica constelada de signos zodiacales que, abierta el libro de la cábala y tendida la diestra en imperioso conjuro, ordena y suscita aquellas fantásticas visiones que aunque la reflexión sorprende las leyes físicas que rigen ese aparato, la ilusión supersticiosa persiste y se siente uno perdido en una atmósfera de ensueño y de misterio.[4]

> [The Lumière films continue to be exhibited with much deserved success. Those meters of white canvas become alive when they are struck by a luminous projection with an intense life that is surprising and prodigious. The first feeling of this spectacle suggests superstition and fanaticism. One seeks Nostradamus dressed in his black tunic covered in zodiac signs. When he opens to the book of the Kabala to his left, with imperious convocation, he orders those fantastic visions, that upon reflection one understands the amazing physical laws that govern the machine, yet the superstitious illusion persists and one feels lost in the atmosphere of mystery and illusion.][5]

Tablada was clearly mesmerized, and his words express the magical and mysterious features inherent in film, emphasizing the impact this new visual medium was having on both sides of the Atlantic.

The attraction to cinema's fantasy and mystery never dissipated, and it continued to intrigue more patrons eager to watch the latest specters created by film. With advanced technology, short films developed into longer features, which drew crowds and resulted in the construction of more theaters. The number of venues that were created to screen these films in fewer than forty years is significant; for example, by 1934, according to the newspaper *Variety*, of the many Latin American countries with theaters, Argentina had the most with 1,985 cinema houses, and Mexico had 701.[6] These figures indicate that Argentina and Mexico were major consumers of film, and subsequently they produced a stimulating and vibrant film culture. These two countries soon began developing their own national film industry and eventually became influential producers of critically acclaimed works both nationally and internationally.

Early in the twentieth century, cinema culture was robust in the city centers of Spanish-speaking America, and many movie houses screened the first films coming out of Europe and the United States. Luis Reyes de la Maza, in his book *Salón rojo*, gives detailed program descriptions of the silent films that were screened between 1895 and 1920 in the most important cinema houses in Mexico City, including Salón Rojo.[7] The screenings at Salón Rojo and the surrounding theaters at the turn of the twentieth century were representative of the types of movies projected at other metropolitan centers. According to Reyes de la Maza, by 1900 motion pictures had become such an integral part of the everyday metropolitan experience in Mexico City that spectators often attended movie theaters eager to watch the latest releases.[8] He notes the thousands of films that premiered at Salón Rojo, including historical dramas, newsreels, serialized films, and nascent Mexican productions. In addition, the films screened were some of the most popular ones coming out of France, including the Lumières' *L'arrivée d'un train en gare de La Ciotat* and Méliès's film *Le voyage dans la lune* (1902) (A Trip to the Moon). Similarly, the films of Max Linder, a French silent-film pioneer and comedian, found their way onto Mexican screens. These venues premiered comedies as well as more mysterious films, such as the 1911 version of *Notre-Dame de Paris* (The Hunchback of Notre Dame) and the Italian film based on Milton's *Paradise Lost*, *Satanás* (1912). Although Reyes de la Maza focuses primarily on Italian, French, and US productions, he does occasionally mention German film screenings. Furthermore, Reyes de la Maza illustrates that, during the silent-film era, the international moving pictures being projected in Mexico City had not yet become a

US-controlled industry; this situation would, of course, change after 1914 when Europe became embroiled in the First World War.

After World War I, the US film industry displaced Europe's dominance over film distributions and screenings in Latin America, as John King points out in his book *Magical Reels: A History of Cinema in Latin America*. In his study, King explains that, by 1926, Argentina was second only to Europe in the film market, in which US films could represent as much as 95 percent of screen time. King points out that a major Argentinean film distributor, Max Glücksmann,[9] had offices in New York, Paris, and other European capitals. In addition to these film-distribution enterprises, Glücksmann owned as many as fifty movie houses in Argentina, Uruguay, Paraguay, and Chile, and they regularly featured foreign films.[10] King particularly underscores that the national film industry struggled to develop in Argentina and Mexico because it competed with the foreign interests controlling the industry; his research also emphasizes that Latin American metropolitan centers were transnational in terms of film distribution. Mexico and Argentina screened the German Expressionist films *The Cabinet of Dr. Caligari* (1920) and *Metropolis* (1927), as well as Gothic films such as *Dracula* (1931), soon after their initial European or American premiere.[11]

Gothic Film

When filmmakers wanted to provoke intense feelings in spectators through the images projected on the screen, they often did so by utilizing the descriptions written by the work's author. One of the sources that filmmakers looked to for inspiration was the Gothic narrative, especially works of fiction written during the nineteenth century. It is likely that filmmakers looked to these Gothic tales because this tradition of literature exploited mysterious events and the "monstrous" to achieve one of its primary goals: the provocation of fear. Moreover, authors were able to do this with florid descriptions of horrific acts such as hauntings, live burials, abductions, and persecutions, among other disturbing passages. Most important, the Gothic established a popular literary genre that created especially memorable madmen, revenants, and doppelgängers, which filmmakers were clearly drawn to early on. By exploiting this rich source material, moving pictures could now provide their audiences with a more concrete form of the nightmares and terrors that Gothic writers had already imagined and established in the public imagination.

Critic Heidi Kaye, among others, emphasizes that "some of the earliest motion pictures were based on Gothic fiction."[12] There are many examples of nineteenth-century Gothic literary works that inspired films early in the century: *Frankenstein* (Shelley, 1818; films, 1910, 1931), "The Fall of the House of Usher" (Poe, 1839; film, 1928), "Carmilla" (LeFanu, 1872; film titled *Vampyr*, 1932), *The Strange Case of Dr. Jekyll and Mr. Hyde* (Stevenson, 1886; film titled *Dr. Jekyll and Mr. Hyde*, 1931), *The Picture of Dorian Gray* (Wilde, 1890; film, 1913), and *Dracula* (Stoker, 1897; films titled *Nosferatu*, 1922, and *Dracula*, 1931), to cite only a few. Frankenstein's monster first appeared in film in 1910, and since then more than seventy movies have been made and continue to be made based on the monster created by Mary Shelley. However, even more popular than film versions of Shelley's monster, then and today, are those featuring vampires. *Nosferatu* (1922), directed by F. W. Murnau and Max Schreck, was the first film adaptation (albeit unauthorized) of Stoker's *Dracula*, and it has since become a German Expressionist classic. Ten years later, acclaimed Danish director Carl Theodor Dreyer released *Vampyr* (1932), a story based on LeFanu's vampire tale "Carmilla," in which the master vampire is played by a woman. As with many filmmakers, Dreyer was inspired by German Expressionist films; most notably he replicates several scenes found in Murnau's *Nosferatu*. Perhaps the most well known of these early film adaptations was the Hollywood 1931 horror classic *Dracula*, directed by Tod Browning, which became a remarkable international sensation and also borrowed traits from Expressionist films.

The Popularity of German Expressionist Films

Famous for featuring shadowy themes and ominous villains, German Expressionist films were successful commercially and critically in Germany and transnationally. Remarkably, in spite of the near destruction of the European film industry after World War I, German films had moved to the forefront of film production and distribution by the 1920s.[13] Some of these films include *The Cabinet of Dr. Caligari* (1920) by Robert Wiene; *Nosferatu* (1922) and *Faust* (1926) by F. W. Murnau; *The Student* of Prague (1926) by Henrik Galeen; and *Metropolis* (1927) by Fritz Lang, Alfred Abel, and Friedrich W. Murnau. In spite of the great resistance to German films by the allied countries (France and the United States in particular), the German film *The Cabinet of Dr. Caligari*, as well as other films, still reached these countries. Wiene's *Caligari* continuously screened in Paris throughout the decade, which emphasizes the film's appeal.[14] Furthermore, the French director Henry Roussel, during a visit to the United States, claimed that the US screening was so popular a spectacle that it "caused the flood of printers' ink to flow, discussing it all over America."[15] The moving pictures being screened in Europe and the United States also were making their way to Latin America; *The Cabinet of Dr. Caligari* premiered in Argentina in June 1921 and in Mexico in December of that same year. This is also true for *Metropolis*, which debuted in Buenos Aires and Mexico City the same year, 1927, it had in Germany.[16]

In his book German Expressionist Film, John Barlow highlights the general features found in these films and shows their "persistence in Hollywood and elsewhere in later years."[17] He illustrates some of the most salient qualities of German Expressionist films and especially notes those found in *The Cabinet of Dr. Caligari*. For example, Wiene, among others, opted for highly stylized and abstract sets, preferring fantastic settings instead of natural ones. The distorted landscapes metaphorically conveyed the mental instability of the characters; as Siegfried Kracauer asserts, "The settings amounted to a perfect transformation from material objects into emotional ornaments."[18] In addition, these filmmakers heightened visual communication through the actors' dramatic gestures, as found in their pantomimic acting, and also in their fanciful costumes. This emphasis on visual elements even appears in the elaborate and striking typesetting and typefaces used in the intertitles, in which the words appear slanted, underlined, wedge-shaped, or otherwise embellished.[19] In order to dramatize unreal backgrounds, directors often used unusual camera angles and stark lighting to accentuate warped perspectives. Disfavoring tonality, at times the sets were painted with black paint, creating acute angles and dark, unnatural contours in order to stress the contrast between light and shadow. These stark contrasts were found not only in the sets but also in the vivid makeup used on the actors, such as for the characters Cesare in *Caligari* and Count Orlok in *Nosferatu*. For example, as the camera closes in on their faces, their eyes, heavily outlined with black makeup, appear phosphorescent, making their gaze seem all the more dramatic and strange. Lastly and most importantly, in addition to the many visual elements shared by these films, at the thematic level these films deal with unreal and supernatural situations in which monstrous villains and madmen persecute innocent victims.

Filmmakers outside of Germany appreciated these Expressionist innovations and subsequently imported some of their techniques into their own filmic creations. For example, in 1928 two films were released, both based on Poe's stories and displaying Expressionist qualities: *La chute du la maison Usher* by French Surrealist movie director Jean Epstein, and *The Fall of the House of Usher* by US film director J. S. Watson Jr. Although Epstein's film—which is based on Poe's "The Oval Portrait" as well as "The Fall of the House of Usher"—is considered a Surrealist classic, many critics—among them John Barlow, Roger Ebert, and Fernando González de León—describe qualities that are associated with Expressionist films, such as the use of chiaroscuro illumination to fill in a sparsely decorated set to make the ambience more eerie and the use of close-ups and dramatic gestures to reveal the character's unstable emotional state. The film also takes place almost entirely in an interior space that seems purposely artificial, a trait common to Expressionist film staging.

To give this film a Latin American context, it is important to note that Luis Buñuel—a leading force in the Surrealist movement who worked in Europe as well as in Mexico—was the assistant director and also wrote the screenplay for *La chute du la maison Usher* and, in collaboration with Salvador Dalí, he also directed one of the most influential Surrealist films, *Un chien Andalou* (1929). Buñuel resided in Mexico from 1946 until his death in 1983, and contributed to national film development in a meaningful way with his critically acclaimed films *Los olvidados* (1950) (The Young and the Damned), *Viridiana* (1961), and *El ángel exterminador* (1962) (The Exterminating Angel). According to Fernando González de León's article "Buñuel, Poe and Gothic Cinema," some of the Gothic conventions Buñuel adopted in his early career would surface in some of his later films produced in Mexico, which is especially true in the case of *Viridiana*, in which the male character bears a tacit resemblance to the Gothic villain found in Matthew Lewis's *The Monk* (1796). This apparent appropriation is not that surprising given that, in an interview, Buñuel explicitly describes how he was drawn to Gothic novels since his childhood, and he also wrote a screenplay based on the Gothic novel *The Monk*.[20]

German Expressionist films were innovative compared with those produced by France or Hollywood up until then, and these commercially successful German Expressionist films not only resonated with filmmakers in the 1920s but also influenced Hollywood horror films of the 1930s and film noirs produced in the 1940s and 1950s.[21] In fact, many of the directors and film crews who had worked on Expressionist films in Germany fled the Nazi regime and came to the United States, finding work in Hollywood studios, where they revisited some of the aesthetics and themes associated with the once commercially successful German films; for example, these are seen in the US-produced works of directors Fritz Lang, Paul Leni, and Billy Wilder, to name just a few. Heidi Kaye substantiates German Expressionism's legacy as well by pointing out how German films inspired later films: "Perhaps the film most influential on later Gothic movies is one not based on a Gothic novel. But its sticking imagery and evocative themes inspirited the genre. As such, the German Expressionism of Robert Wiene's *The Cabinet of Dr. Caligari* (1920) transformed the American approach to the Gothic cinema."[22] Thus, the Hollywood studios, affected by the earlier silent era, continued with what Expressionist films had already created, leading to their own versions of terror on screen.

As previously mentioned, *Dracula*, starring Bela Lugosi, was such a sensation that at the film's US premiere in 1931 it sold more than fifty thousand tickets in just two days and ultimately grossed over twenty-five million dollars[23]—all the more remarkable given that the country was suffering through the Great Depression. This year also represented the start of Hollywood's horror-film boom, which included some of the most famous films of the era: *Dracula*, *Dr. Jekyll and Mr. Hyde*, and *Frankenstein*, all of which were released in 1931 and were film adaptions based on Gothic literature. Not surprisingly, the numerous productions of horror films led to the coining of the term *Hollywood Gothic* by David Skal "because of the genre's debt to Gothic literature and the visual style of German expressionism."[24] Most important to this discussion, these films subsequently made their way to Latin America.

The specific case of Hollywood's Spanish version of *Dracula*, or *Drácula*, is particularly elucidating because the Spanish versions illustrate how both European and US studios went to great lengths to protect their interests.[25] More specifically, Hollywood horror films promised large revenues, but studios faced a real challenge in terms of reaching and maintaining their international audiences as a result of improved audio technology. The addition of sound—in English—in 1927, as first incorporated in *The Jazz Singer*, forever changed the landscape, and US studio executives feared they would lose their financial footing because of the language differences. According to Alfonso Pinto, Hollywood studios produced more than a hundred Spanish-language films between 1930 and 1935.[26] The most famous of these Spanish-language film versions was *Drácula* (1931), directed by George Melford. The Spanish crew filmed at night using the same film sets that were used to produce the English-language version, as well as the identical script and shot list—but with Spanish-speaking actors. In April of that same year, the Spanish-language version of the film showed in Mexico City, where it played for a month.[27] According to John Flynn, the Spanish *Drácula* continued to play for many years in various Spanish-speaking countries, underscoring the popularity of these films in the region.[28]

However, the rush to create multiple iterations of the same film in a different language proved to be a miscalculation; foreign audiences preferred seeing the original, subtitled versions instead.[29] Consequently, Spanish-language film production ceased; in the end, the English-language "talkies" did not undermine Hollywood's presence in foreign markets as the studios had originally surmised. This short-lived Hollywood language experiment, however, emphasizes the financial significance of the Spanish-speaking audiences, which was important enough for the studios to invest valuable resources into holding on to foreign moviegoers and maintain their dominance over Latin American film industries.[30]

With the advent of sound and other technological innovations such as improved color and advanced special effects, many Gothic works that had first been made into silent moving pictures were regularly re-created in newer and more up-to-date versions later in the twentieth century, especially movies that had once been financially lucrative. When a more modernized version of an earlier moneymaking Gothic film classic was reborn, these prolific movies became all the more ubiquitous. This brief film history provides a background and context to better appreciate how Latin American authors may have viewed early films and, at times, adopted cinematic features and themes into their own literary creations.

Artistic Reaction to Foreign Films

The arrival of film and its sustained popularity in Latin America at the beginning of the twentieth century attracted many enthusiasts, including certain authors who manipulated their prose in order to narrate their works more cinematically. Patrick Duffey convincingly argues that cinema influenced Mexican literature in a profound way in his book *De la pantalla al texto: La influencia del cine en la narrativa mexicana del siglo veinte* (From Screen to Text: The Influence of Cinema in Mexican Narratives of the Twentieth Century) and his article "Pancho Villa at the Movies: Cinematic Techniques in the Works of Guzmán and Muñoz." Mexican authors such as Mariano Azuela, Nellie Campobello, and Martín Luis Guzmán, in *Los de abajo* (The Underdogs) (1925), *Cartucho* (1931), and *El águila y la serpiente* (The Eagle and the Serpent) (1928), respectively, incorporated cinematic references, themes, and techniques into their prose. These three texts, published in the 1920s and early 1930s, focus more on Mexico's social reality, especially with events having to do with the Mexican Revolution (ca. 1910–1920). Thus, one might expect a more realist literary style in which authors represented historical events without employing an overly experimental style of writing; however, this is not entirely the case because some of these authors remodeled their prose to be more cinematic. Their filmic-inspired wordplay was comparable, in certain respects, to avant-garde writers' more notorious and purposeful utilization of innovative cinematic techniques as exemplified by Vicente Huidobro, a vanguard author, who deliberately altered his fiction to be more cinematic.

Cinematic references and literary strategies are also found in works not associated with the avant-garde. As Duffey and others have already noted, Azuela's fragmented narrative style in *Los de abajo* functions like that of cinematic montage, as does Campobello's *Cartucho*, in which scholars, such as Castro Leal, have described the short vignettes as picture frames in rapid movement.[31] Guzmán's *El águila y la serpiente* is significant because, according to Duffey, this was one of the first times that film was referenced in a Mexican novel.[32] As previously mentioned, Guzmán describes revolutionary soldiers attending one of the popular cinema houses in 1914 to see the latest newsreels on the revolution, which affirms that many people still went to these theaters despite being in the midst of a civil war. Guzmán not only mentions films explicitly, but his descriptions also seem to replicate certain filmic qualities found in German Expressionist films, as noted by film critic Aurelio de los Reyes.[33] Artists across different literary movements were using film's pervasive influences in their literary creations.

Another artistic outgrowth of this new art form was the transformation of well-known authors into film critics and screenwriters. Jason Borge, in his book *Avances de Hollywood: Crítica cinematográfica en Latinoamérica, 1915–1945*, emphasizes that many writers were so fascinated by Hollywood cinema that they felt compelled to express themselves through film reviews. The movie reviews he features in his book include renowned authors from Chile, Argentina, Mexico, and Uruguay such as María Luisa Bombal, Jorge Luis Borges, Martín Luis Guzmán, and Horacio Quiroga, among others. Manuel González Casanova, in his *El cine que vió fósforo: Alfonso Reyes y Martín Luis Guzmán*, compiles film reviews written by Mexican authors Gúzman and Alfonso Reyes under the pseudonym fósforo while they were exiled in Spain. Some of the films they reviewed were Paul Wegener's *Der Golem*, Louis Feuillade's serial films *Fantomas*, and Cecil B. DeMille's *Carmen*, among many other films shown in Spain between 1915 and 1918.[34] Similarly, in the Horacio Quiroga anthology *Cine y literatura* there is a notable collection of his film reviews that appeared in newspapers and magazines from 1919 through 1931. Quiroga wrote reviews for Argentinean magazines such as *Caras y Caretas*, *El Hogar*, *Atlántida*, and others in which he primarily evaluated US and Argentinean films.[35] He preferred Hollywood films and was quite critical of the German Expressionist films generally—and of *The Cabinet of Dr. Caligari* specifically—because he found the aesthetics too decorative and in no way representative of the "realism" he appreciated in US-produced films.[36] In the reviews found in the above-mentioned books one can see how Latin American authors were reacting to the moving pictures coming out of Europe and the United States—some critics appreciated the artistic innovations of European films, whereas others preferred those from Hollywood.

Another artist who took notice of filmic possibilities, and whose work I explore more fully in terms of its Gothic qualities in chapter 3, was the Chilean author María Luisa Bombal (1910–1980), who was a novelist, film critic, and screenwriter. Critic Lucía Guerra-Cunningham, an expert on and friend of Bombal, asserts that Bombal was both a film lover and a great admirer of the Gothic.[37] It is widely known that she and Jorge Luis Borges spent many hours at the cinema in Buenos Aires watching the latest releases. Prior to that, she spent much of her youth in Paris (1922–1931), where she most likely saw the newest movies and where, as critics have noted, she had the opportunity to interview Carl Theodor Dreyer. In fact, she was present at the filming of one of his most famous films, *Le passion de Jeanne d'Arc* (1928), further chronicling the connection between the author and the director's work. Bombal most certainly would have been familiar with Dreyer's *Vampyr* (1932), a partial film adaptation of LeFanu's Gothic tale "Carmilla." In her Surrealist-inspired novel *La amortajada* (1938), Bombal's words seem to reproduce some of the scenes found in Dreyer's *Vampyr*. Maribel Acosta-Lugo and Emma Susana Speratti-Piñero have already analyzed Bombal's novel in relation to Dreyer's work and go into great detail, noting parallel themes and techniques born out of film.[38]

Recalling Dreyer's close-up techniques in *Joan of Arc*, Acosta-Lugo describes the careful attention Bombal dedicates to describing the landscape and characters. The most important cinematic scene shared between Bombal's novel and Dreyer's film is when they carry the bodies to the cemetery. In the film, the hero, Allan Gray, has a dream in which he finds himself trapped in a coffin, which has a small glass window through which he can see the vampire and his sinister assistants seal the lid of the casket. The camera angle tilts up so that for several minutes spectators share Gray's field of vision. As the henchmen move his body from the interior of the house toward his the gravesite, spectators can see the landscape via the entrapped victim's perspective, thus showing the ceiling, the foliage, the cloudy sky, and the church buildings. Gray can see his surroundings, but he can neither speak nor move, which is similar to Bombal's character, Ana María, who according to the narrator can see and feel in spite of being dead. Bombal uses a comparable camera technique in her writing: as they carry Ana María to her final resting place, the narrator describes how the character can see the interior of the house, the trees, and the sky, thereby readers, in a certain sense, share her visual perspective as was done in Dreyer's film. Even without knowing Bombal's connection to Dreyer and his work, it becomes apparent in reading her novels that Gothic and filmic images of the time period are embodied in Bombal's texts.

While Bombal's texts feature certain allusions to film, Horacio Quiroga (1878–1937) speaks of film culture explicitly. Born in Uruguay, he resided for most of his life in Buenos Aires, where he thrived as a writer and most likely viewed the films that inspired some of his fiction. Quiroga's short stories "Miss Dorothy Phillips, mi esposa" (1919) (Miss Dorothy Phillips, My Wife) and "El puritano" (1926) (The Puritan) emphasize that he was so fascinated with film that he wanted to include cinematic themes in his prose. In "Miss Dorothy Phillips, mi esposa," Guillermo Grant, the main character, indicates that he is fascinated by cinema and states that film represents the beginning of a truly new era. According to him, because of film, spectators can now longingly stare at a remarkably beautiful woman for a prolonged period on the moving screen. Of his new opportunity to admire Hollywood starlets, Grant says, "Pero no sé si ellos comprenderán la vibración que sacude a un pobre mortal, de la cabeza a los pies, cuando una hermosísima muchacha nos tiende por una hora su propia vibración personal al alcance de la boca"[39] (But I am not sure that they will understand the vibration that shakes a mere mortal from head to toe when a most beautiful girl, who is almost within reach, for an hour extends her own personal vibration). Grant's obsession with Hollywood's beautiful actresses—whose eyes he finds especially alluring—inspires him to travel to Los Angeles so that he can meet, charm, and eventually marry the famous Dorothy Phillips, who was an actual Hollywood actress of the time. The narrator's fascination with Hollywood films and their rising young stars, in a sense, also corresponds to the way Quiroga was himself admiring these moving images, which then inspired new types of stories based on film.

Similarly, Vicente Huidobro (1893–1949) was first and foremost an avant-garde poet, yet he tried his luck as screenwriter and filmmaker, although his scripts were never realized on the big screen as he had originally imagined. At one point he met with Douglas Fairbanks and even attempted to write a screenplay in which Fairbanks would star.[40] Like many authors, Vicente Huidobro was intrigued by how cinema could change literature, and he created poetry and prose that, at times, were visual and cinematic. His most cinematic work, however, was *Cagliostro*, which was initially conceived as a film but later transformed into a cinematic novel. Huidobro emphasized this overt homage to cinema: "Character drawing today has to be more synthetic, more compact, than it was before. Action cannot be slow. Events have to move more rapidly. Otherwise the public is bored."[41] Huidobro, like the Futurists and other vanguard artists, was excited by this new technology and the bustle of cosmopolitan culture in which cinematic fervor was at its center.

Huidobro first wrote this text in script form with the goal of having it produced into a silent film in the same vein as German Expressionist films; however, his dreams were dashed when, in 1927, *The Jazz Singer*, the first film with synchronized sound, premiered. Because he originally envisioned the film as a silent one, he abandoned the script and converted it into an experimental film-text. The script was first serialized in various magazines between 1921 and 1922. In 1931 it was finally published as a book but, oddly enough, in English. It was not published in Spanish until 1934.[42]

Gothic Filmic Appropriations

The cinematic apparatus became a central theme and even a protagonist in some Gothic-inspired prose. Horacio Quiroga, as noted earlier, incorporated specters and vampires in his stories "El espectro" and "El vampiro," for which early Hollywood films were clearly his muse, and Vicente Huidobro, contemptuous of realism, drew from German Expressionist films *The Cabinet of Dr. Caligari*, *Nosferatu*, and *The Student of Prague* (1913) in his *Cagliostro*.[43] The reasons authors employed Gothic features and filmic themes, and the manner in which they did so, vary. On the one hand, it was an aesthetic experiment in which authors could break away from worn-out traditions to create something entirely new, as the avant-garde artists, like Huidobro, consistently strived to do. Quiroga, on the other hand, was intently preoccupied with themes of death and madness; and films provided Quiroga another means by which to explore how modern technology could simultaneously be awe-inspiring and portentous; characters either become unhinged or find an early grave.

Quiroga's interests in film, vampires, doubles, and specters especially coalesce in the short story "El vampiro." In it, a moribund man, Grant, residing in what appears to be a mental hospital, narrates the tale of how he came to his state of shattered nerves due to an experiment that went awry. Grant describes how an enigmatic and wealthy man of seemingly aristocratic lineage, Don Guillen Orzúa y Rosales, initially contacted him because they shared common interests in filmic images, specters, and the transference of energy. Don Rosales talks about Poe's "The Oval Portrait" as an example of an obsessive desire that can give as well as take away life through the energy that can be transmuted through an intense gaze—an experiment that he seems to want to replicate.

This ominous man invites him to his luxurious home for an equally sumptuous dinner that is described eerily—possibly reminding readers of Jonathan Harker's dinner at Count Dracula's castle, and thus suggesting that Don Rosales is, perhaps, a vampire. At this unusual dinner Grant discovers that his host is attempting to conjure the body of a famous Hollywood actress through the use of gamma rays (referred to as N-1 rays). Inexplicably, he is able to draw the starlet's specter from the screen, somehow placing her at the dinner table where she interacts with both men, who are obviously infatuated with the beautiful Hollywood star. However, the obsessed Don Rosales wants to possess the cinematic specter in bodily form; this reveals the fact that Don Rosales has become fixated with the Hollywood star's filmic specter that is also, in a certain sense, the movie star's doppelgänger.

He is not interested in going to Hollywood to seduce the actual actress, as the narrator did in "Miss Dorothy Phillips, mi esposa," but instead conceives a plan to murder her. He believes that by annihilating the original body he can make her filmic double corporeal. This exchange of life force is a clear play on Poe's "The Oval Portrait"—explicitly cited in the text—in which Poe's character, a painter obsessed with his art, literally draws the life out of his young wife. Somehow the painter magically transfers the heroine's soul onto the canvas itself, consequently annihilating her and thus making their relationship a vampiric one. However, in Quiroga's story, Don Rosales wants to do the reverse; instead of drawing the life out of the heroine in order to place her animated body onto a canvas, Don Rosales wants to extract the movie star's vitality out of the moving-picture frame so that he can possess the specter in a material human form. That is to say, he is in love with the specter, the actress's double, and he wants to materialize the image, not the "real" Hollywood starlet.

Don Rosales is so convinced that his theory is valid that he apparently goes to Hollywood to murder the actress and somehow succeeds in his fevered plan. To Grant's surprise, the experiment goes as intended, and her double emerges from the screen, now embodied, to join them in their soirees; however, she is no longer a beautiful actress but rather a bewitching skeleton whose hollow gaze constantly follows and persecutes them. Ironically, just as they have drawn her out of the screen, she begins to suck the life out of them, and she, too, like Don Rosales, becomes a metaphoric vampire. As a result of her seductive aura or some other mysterious force, both men begin to show signs of madness and soon realize their inevitable demise. Don Rosales dies, and Grant will surely meet the same fate.

This brief story is jam-packed with all things Gothic and, although the title of the story is "The Vampire," it represents a more modern riff on the age-old vampire story as conceived by Stoker and Murnau. The narrator's explicit reference to Poe's "The Oval Portrait" is important because Poe's story has already been analyzed, not surprisingly, as a vampiric tale, given that the obsessed painter is like a destructive vampire that demands too much, including the life of its victims.[44] Quiroga not only entertains and expresses his amazement with cinema in his story, but he also articulates certain anxieties having to do with this new technology. His reaction is paradoxical; he imagines the many gratifying possibilities that film can create, *and* he envisions monstrous realities thanks to this new invention—this, in a sense, also makes his work tacitly science fiction.

"El espectro" is another story that references the spectral qualities inherent in film, and it also describes the dark, unfortunate events that can come about as a result of this new technology and its obsessed fans. Guillermo Grant, his corporeal life extinguished and now existing as a specter, narrates the story of how he and his partner, Enid, died in a movie theater and their ghosts now travel the world watching films. The narrator explains that he was once a dear friend of the famous Hollywood actor Duncan Wyoming (a well-known movie star when Quiroga wrote this story), whom he decides to visit, and this is where he meets his beautiful wife, Enid. He lives with them for some time, becoming torn between his desire for Enid and his loyalty to his friend.

Much to Grant's secret delight, Wyoming becomes ill and soon dies, allowing Grant to freely pursue Enid. Wyoming's untimely death suggests that somehow Grant drew the life force out of him through his unremitting gaze—as happened in both "El vampiro" and "The Oval Portrait." Now living as a couple in New York, Enid and Grant eagerly attend the premiere of Wyoming's last moving picture, released posthumously. They are so mesmerized and haunted by the film that they return night after night to see Wyoming on the big screen. Yet Wyoming's spectral double becomes so embodied after each subsequent viewing that they both imagine that Wyoming can actually see them sitting together.

On one of their final visits, Wyoming seems to break through the film screen in order to harm them. Even though they are both fearful, it is as if they are under some sort of spell and they nevertheless attend the movie theater once again—but this time Grant carries a gun. By some unexplainable force, Wyoming, according to Grant, crosses the screen and kills both Enid and himself. Grant's specter is confused by how the events transpired because he believed that he was aiming at the screen and directly at Wyoming's head, but somehow he was actually aiming at his own temple. There is a clear play on the doppelgänger here: somehow Grant has become Wyoming's double, and, in true doppelgänger fashion, the death of Wyoming also brings about Grant's death because they are one and the same.

This story is similar to that of "El vampiro" in that the protagonist's obsessive, desirous gaze can give as well as take away life through some mysterious transmuted energy force. In a manner similar to the way Don Rosales was able to exhume the body of the Hollywood actress from the screen, Grant and Enid seem to do the same with Wyoming's body. In both instances, the presence of a double means certain death for the characters, who have become obsessed—perhaps even bewitched—by the moving images on the screen. Quiroga's "El vampiro" and "El espectro" emphasize how he was fascinated by the role of both the spectator and specter created by cinema. This dual role is significant when one looks at the origin of these words: the word *spectator* is from the Latin word *spectare* and refers to the act of watching, and the word *specter* means ghost, appearance, or to look at.[45] Thus, this looking at the filmic ghost that is, in turn, looking at the movie viewer is one of the unifying themes in "El vampiro" and "El espectro," one in which the cinematic specters can seemingly seduce and draw the life out of audiences from beyond the screen.

Quiroga's story "El puritano," although not as vampiric as the previous two stories mentioned, also features spectators fixated with movies. The ghosts of famous actors and actresses have a social gathering each night in a theater that still plays the films in which they starred. The narrator mentions one striking movie star in particular who committed suicide because a movie investor, Dougald Mac Namara, did not pursue her as most men did. Mac Namara is in love with the starlet, but because he is married and has a son, he suppresses his true desire—hence his moniker *the puritan*. Yet after the actress dies, Mac Namara still continues to attend the cinema to admire her figure on the screen, finally committing suicide himself. The story ends with the union of both specters living blissfully in the afterlife.

Quiroga's description of the pleasurable prolonged gaze encouraged by film, or cinematic voyeurism, anticipates what feminist film theorists would problematize and study more fully later in the century.[46] Gawking openly or secretly peeping at the image of another is certainly shunned and considered deviant in the material world, yet in film the spectator is invited to gaze at length at the human form on the screen, and notions of deviance and lawlessness have no real bearing. In Quiroga's stories, however, cinematic voyeurism is not innocuous but rather is a moral offense with punitive consequences: characters who become obsessed with the moving images either die or become crazed. Thus, in Quiroga's stories spectatorship is a treacherous pastime in which moving pictures, conferred at times with vampiric qualities, suck the very life force out of viewers who desire too much. Quiroga's body of work fixates on death and madness; and the film apparatus offered him another source to broach these themes.

Vicente Huidobro

The interplay between contemporary film trends and supernatural themes especially coalesces in Huidobro's "novela-film" *Cagliostro*, which is a Gothic-themed novel that playfully attempts to be a German Expressionist film. Huidobro, a Chilean poet and prose writer who contributed artistically on both sides of the Atlantic, was one of the fundamental figures of the Latin American avant-garde who used cinematic language in his own creations. In 1916 he moved to Europe and settled in Paris, where he interacted with the latest cultural innovators, among them Guillaume Apollinaire, André Breton, Luis Buñuel, and Pablo Picasso, among other artists.[47] Building on the aesthetics of the time, Huidobro contributed to the avant-garde by initiating his own movement called Creacionismo. According to him, the poet was deemed a demigod, a divinely inspired Creator through language, which was similar to the many ways avant-garde artists approached their works.[48] Huidobro was first drawn to Surrealism; however, as illustrated by René de Costa, Huidobro rejected Surrealism's penchant for automatism and the unconscious creation. He was opposed to the idea that artists should become receivers of oneiric and unconscious forces, thereby relinquishing their primary role as creators.[49] That is to say, Huidobro privileged deliberate and conscious writing rather than subconscious or automatism proposed by the Surrealists.

Influenced by Apollinaire, Huidobro is also known for his imaginative and visual poetry, as found in his caligramas.[50] However, Huidobro, an admirer of modernity, went beyond the visual poetry and was also interested in steeping other literary genres with cinematic techniques. In particular, this ambitious attempt is found in *Cagliostro* in which Huidobro pretends to create a moving picture through words. After Huidobro was awarded a prize for his *Cagliostro* screenplay, Buñuel remarks on how Huidobro's verses and script are cinematic: "De todos los poetas, ¿no es el creacionista el que se halla más cerca de lo fotogénico, el de poesía más cinegráfica? Sus versos actúan por grandes planos como el cine"[51] (Of all the poets, is not the creationist the one who most closely finds the photogenic, of the most cinematic poetry? His verses act like great takes found in film). Huidobro later transfigured this same script into a novel inspired by the cinema of the time.

Huidobro was not only interested in the newness that modernity could provide literature, but he also wanted his works to reach a broader readership and this is perhaps the reason that he first imagined *Cagliostro* as a movie script.[52] As a poet, his works were mostly limited to a small circle of the educated elite, yet he longed to reach a broader audience by creating a work that could attract mass audiences as only cinema could; however, this text was transformed into a pioneering vanguard novel.[53] In the introduction to this unusual text, he states: "He querido escribir sobre 'Cagliostro' una novela visual. En ella la técnica, los medios de expresión, los acontecimientos elegidos, concurren hacia una forma realmente cinematográfica"[54] (I have wanted to write a visual novel in 'Calgiostro.' In it, the technique, the medium of expression, the chosen happenings, allude toward a form that is truly cinematic). True to his vanguard sensibilities Huidobro adopted an anti-realistic film aesthetic in his novela-film instead of a Hollywood model, in which several descriptions in his text replicate images associated with German Expressionist films.

Critics René de Costa, Gabriele Morelli, and Edmundo Paz Soldán discuss the novel's cinematic qualities, especially as they relate to the German Expressionist film *The Cabinet of Dr. Caligari*. In the novel there are many descriptions that are verbal representations of filmic techniques found in these types of movies. He describes scenes in which he emphasizes the chiaroscuro illumination. He also describes the characters' dramatic facial expressions and striking eyes, which is particularly exemplified by Lorenza, the female victim, whose eyes become larger, revealing her increasing terror as Cagliostro, the villain, comes closer to her.

In addition to associating Huidobro's novel with Wiene's film, de Costa and Morelli also reference *Nosferatu* as a filmic model for the text's creation. In doing so, they connect this work, perhaps inadvertently, to the Gothic tradition because *Nosferatu* is the first screen adaptation of Bram Stoker's *Dracula*. Based on the images that Huidobro describes in the novel, it is apparent that he was well versed in the conventions associated with horror films and Gothic literature; however, he uses these stock characters and situations to explore his own aesthetic preoccupations and to create something new. Instead of eliciting fear through horrific images as the Expressionist films had done, he elicits humor through his playful representation of the cinema and its spectators. In other words, his novel is a parody of a well-established type of fiction, and in order for this parody to work, the spectators/readers must be well aware of the conventions having to do with film and Gothic works.

As I discussed in detail at the beginning of this book, because the Gothic, like any popular genre, relies on the repetition of certain conventions, the plot becomes quite predictable, and the characters fall into predetermined types. Gothic texts typically have a villain, a hero—sometimes ineffectual—and a damsel in distress in a fear-eliciting setting. The Gothic background usually includes ominous storms, trapdoors, live burials, vampires, and werewolves. The element of fear is present; although primarily felt by the characters in the novel, it is also meant to generate fear in the reader as well. Many of these conventions appear in Gothic-inspired films, and they also emerge in Huidobro's *Cagliostro* but with a significant difference: instead of provoking fear, he amuses the audience through his playful portrayal of the Gothic.

The title of the work itself is the name of the villain, which is also common in Gothic literature and Gothic film—*Dracula*, *Dr. Jekyll and Mr. Hyde*, *The Monk*, *Nosferatu*, and *The Picture of Dorian Gray*, for example. More precisely, Cagliostro echoes certain Gothic attributes in terms of characters, ambience, and plot. As in many Gothic works, *Cagliostro* is set in the distant past, in eighteenth-century France on the verge of the revolution, and a villainous character with supernatural powers is holding a beautiful young heroine captive. He is a magician who can raise the dead, heal the sick, and see into the future; however, like many Gothic villains, he becomes corrupt and uses his supernatural powers for evil and personal gain.

A terrifying description of live burial—a favorite of Gothic writers—can also be found in the descriptive images in *Cagliostro*. Like many other Gothic heroines, Huidobro's is trapped in the villain's house and is literally entombed in the walls of the house, preventing her escape. Cagliostro hypnotizes Lorenza to keep her subdued, and he even uses her in some of his illicit dealings. In this way she is similar to Caligari's somnambulist, Cesare, who is kept in a coffin in a constant hypnotic state and is only awakened to carry out Caligari's evil tasks.

There is a Gothic ambience in the descriptions of Huidobro's story. The novel opens with the villain riding through a stereotypically Gothic storm that is brimming with large black clouds.[55] This already eerie atmosphere is heightened when he describes the historical werewolves and roads constructed of legends.[56] The description of Cagliostro's arrival at the secret meeting is a literary rendition that corresponds to the scene in *Nosferatu* in which Nosferatu travels in an unusually fast-paced carriage at night to meet his guest and future victim, Hutter.[57] In this same way, Cagliostro begins with a mysterious horse-drawn carriage that is rushing through a winding forest during a nocturnal, portentous storm. The man driving the carriage, Cagliostro, is cloaked in a black cape, and only his phosphorescent eyes pierce the darkness:

> La extraña portezuela del extraño carruaje cruje al abrirse lentamente y un hombre cubierto con una capa que no deja ver sino ojos saca la cabeza de la noche de la carroza a la noche del cielo a fin de saber que sucede. . . . Sus ojos fosforescentes como los arroyos que corren sobre las minas de mercurio; sus ojos de repente han enriquecido la noche, ellos son la única luz en el fondo de su propia existencia. Miradlos bien porque esos ojos son el centro de mi historia y han atravesado todo el siglo XVIII como un riel electrizado.[58]

> [The strange door of the strange carriage creaks as it opens slowly. A man covered in a cape shows only his eyes when his head peers out of the carriage to find out what is happening. . . . His phosphorescent eyes are like streams that run through mercury mines; his eyes have suddenly enriched the night; they are the only source of light in the depths of his own existence. Look at them closely because those eyes are at the center of my story that has crossed the eighteenth century like an electric rail.]

The playful language also evokes images found in Expressionist films.

The same luminous eyes that Huidobro constantly mentions can also be found in film—such as when the camera focuses attention on Count Orlok's evil gaze, made even brighter by the dark painted shadows around his piercing stare. Similarly accentuated eyes, made emphatic by special lighting and makeup, also appear in *The Cabinet of Dr. Caligari*, on Cesare. The mercurial glare, so emphasized throughout Huidobro's novela-film and in many other Expressionist films, will later be copied by the Hollywood filmmakers in the 1930s; one must only recall Bela Lugosi's arresting gaze as he portrayed the quintessential Gothic monster Dracula, and how that film played up his dramatic and hypnotic eyes.

Perhaps the most Gothic-like quality of *Cagliostro* is the description of supernatural acts, also found in many Expressionist films. Several gruesome scenes appear in the text. For example, the villain conjures an image of a duel from the past in which the bloody head of the deceased man floats by, frightening the widow, who faints when she sees the image of her dead husband.[59] A cinematic trick relying on such a startling image would normally be used to shock spectators of a film, and Huidobro tries to mimic this through words. In another scene, the narration appears to flash-forward to the French Revolution in a vivid description of the gruesome severed heads that will be brought about by the invention of the guillotine.[60] In yet another scene, there is a doubling of the magician: a spirit walks out of his body, seemingly materialized, and then leaves and disappears into the sky.[61] A cinematic superimposition of images, created by the use of double exposure, is a frequent editing technique utilized since the beginning of film, and Huidobro's incorporation of such a doubling makes his narration all the more cinematic.

Paz-Soldán describes doubling as "the movie trick par excellence,"[62] but this "movie trick" is also one of the defining characteristics of the Gothic as well—many Gothic villains are split selves who have a shadowy doppelgänger running amok. Furthermore, when Paz-Soldán mentions the doppelgänger in the pre-Expressionist film *The Student of Prague* (1913), he is also implicitly describing the Gothic characteristics found in *Cagliostro*. As I already described, the image of the double, the divided self in constant battle, is a common Gothic trope—as seen in Shelley's *Frankenstein* and Stevenson's *Dr. Jekyll and Mr. Hyde*, among many other works—and this doubling has been projected onto the big screen many times over. For example, in the German film *The Student of Prague* (1913), a young man sells his soul to a sorcerer in return for material gain. He sees his other self, summoned from the other side of the mirror and taken by the necromancer. Similarly, in Dreyer's *Vampyr*, the camera also uses this editing technique when Allan Gray sees his own double emerge from his body. In other words, the double is a prevalent Gothic literary *and* filmic trope.

Although the novela-film *Cagliostro* features well-known Gothic characteristics, this is by no means a Gothic novel. Huidobro's text is metafictional and self-referential; it consistently reminds the reader that it is a book pretending to be a film. In this way, Huidobro plays with the conventions found in popular fiction and movies, such as those found in Gothic and German Expressionist films, but subverts the reader's expectations. Such subversion is not a surprise given that as an avant-garde artist he would have consistently aspired to create something new that could somehow alter the reader's conception of reality and provoke shock. De Costa affirms that this work was conceived to amuse: "The novel, like the movies it emulates, was conceived as entertainment."[63] However, this novel is also implicitly critiquing how spectators can become unaware of their material space when immersed in a film's plot.[64] Furthermore, he is attentive in showing the material properties of fiction making.[65]

Huidobro pokes fun at the reader by constantly showing the artifice of his own design. He asks the spectators/readers to pretend that they are in a movie theater, yet he constantly interrupts this imagined scenario by taking the reader out of the "visual" experience. The first line of the novel begins with these words: "Suponga el lector que no ha comprado este libro en una librería, sino que ha comprado un billete para entrar al cinematógrafo"[66] (Reader, suppose that you have not purchased this book in the bookstore, but rather a ticket to enter into the movie theater). Presumably, readers should imagine that they are seated in a theater, but Huidobro soon disturbs this illusory world that he had instructed the reader to imagine. Although he gives horrific details of events in his descriptions, the reader can never fully be affected by the ghastly tale because, unexpectedly, the narrator will make observations that break the narrative continuity. For example, in a scene in which he describes the arrival of a horse-drawn carriage, he says: "La carroza llega delante de nosotros, muy cerca, a algunos metros de nuestros ojos. . . . Mi feo lector o mi hermosa lectora deben retroceder algunos metros para no ser salpicados por la ruedas de este misterio que pasa"[67] (The carriage arrives before us, very close, a few meters from our eyes. . . . My ugly male reader or my beautiful female reader, you must step back a few meters so that you will not be splashed by the wheels of this mystery that crosses by you). He tells readers that they are supposed to be spectators sitting in a theater watching the film and even describes the perspective from which they are "seeing" the moving image, yet he also breaks with the semblance of truth by telling the reader directly that she or he is beautiful or ugly. Following the ideas set out in his manifestos, he privileges artists' predominance, and he, in a certain sense, enters the novel to remind the reader that this is a work of fiction about fiction constructed by an author. His work is different from Quiroga's film-inspired stories. Quiroga's characters, like spectators, are drawn in, becoming disembodied when they watch movies, while Huidobro invites readers/spectators to do the opposite by constantly reminding them of their bodily presence.[68]

The Gothic strokes found in Quiroga's and Huidobro's texts are some of the first examples of filmic appropriation that highlight Gothic features in Latin American cultural production. Given the popularity of German Expressionist and Gothic films internationally, it is quite likely that authors from Latin America, especially cinephiles, saw the films described here, whether while traveling abroad or in their own countries' cosmopolitan centers. Even if authors in Spanish-speaking countries tried to steer away from Gothic literature because they believed these works lacked literary merit, their familiarity with Gothic themes through cinema is illustrated by their many film reviews and literary works published during the 1920s and 1930s.

PART 2
CULTURAL ANXIETIES AND AESTHETIC CRITIQUES

PART 2
CULTURAL ANXIETIES AND AESTHETIC CRITIQUES

CHAPTER 3

LIVE BURIALS AND DEATH-DEFYING BEAUTIES

Gothic writers are known for evoking terror by describing live burials in detail, especially when they involve female heroines. Characters frequently find themselves immured in fortress walls or incarcerated and left to die in subterranean dungeons at the hands of madmen. These imprisoned bodies are suggestive of the novels' oppressive atmosphere and also may allude to a context beyond the text associated with significant historical and political events. The Latin American authors, discussed in this chapter, at times describe gruesome live burials that are evocative of Gothic aesthetics that speak to authoritarianism or other forms of tyranny, while other authors complicate and subvert Gothic literary representations by using poetic metaphors and erotic language to describe slow deaths and live interments in ways that drain them of their usual fear-instilling quality. In some of the texts briefly mentioned here, the authors represent live burials in terms of their negative aesthetics (dreadful, horrific, gory), as in the case of Alejo Carpentier's *El reino de este mundo* (1955), whereas others totally change these horrific portrayals from disturbing happenings to peaceful and poetic ones. In *La amortajada* (1938) (The Shrouded Woman) by María Luisa Bombal and *Pedro Páramo* (1955) by Juan Rulfo, live burials speak to claustrophobic environments that allegorize the limited position of women under oppressive patriarchy, common to Gothic literature; however, female heroines also speak through death and from beyond the grave, showing how the afterlife has been imagined as a space of self-realization, offering them deliverance from suffocating systems. Some of the characters analyzed here do not express fear because they are buried sentient corpses; rather, they lyrically describe their state in which they feel liberation and even pleasure, thus turning the well-known live burial trope on its head.

Artful Live Burials

Regardless of the aesthetics utilized to describe painful deaths and live burials, premature entombments are certainly universally considered one of the most horrific punishments a person can endure, and female characters are usually the ones who suffer this type of punishment in Gothic literature.[1] In her book *Femicidal Fears*, Helene Meyers writes through the Gothic, "a literary site where fear of female annihilation is a plot convention,"[2] and many times these slayings are carried out through live entombments. In Ann Radcliffe's novel *The Mysteries of Udolpho* (1794), the protagonist, Emily, finds herself entrapped in a dark, subterranean torture chamber in which her aunt had previously been subjected to horrors that Emily apparently will also have to endure. In Matthew Lewis's Gothic novel *The Monk* (1796), the villain Ambrosio gives Antonia a potion that puts her into a living-dead state; he then buries her alive. Holly Furneaux, in her insightful article "Gendered Cover-Ups: Live Burial, Social Death, and Coverture in Mary Braddon's Fiction," describes how Jane Austen's *Northanger Abbey* (1818) parodies the representation of female live burial that is so common in Gothic romances.[3] Although women are most often the ones to suffer this punishment in Gothic literature, there are also stories featuring male premature internments, as illustrated in John Galt's short story "The Buried Alive" (1821). The main character, who is suffering from a mysterious disease similar to "locked-in syndrome," can neither speak nor move. Trapped in his own body, the character describes how he is mistakenly pronounced dead and is subsequently entombed—even though he can still feel and hear: "I heard the sound of weeping at my pillow—and the voice of the nurse say, 'He is dead.'—I cannot describe what I felt at these words.—I exerted my utmost power of volition to stir myself, but I could not move even an eyelid. After a short pause my friend drew near; and, sobbing and convulsed with grief, drew his hand over my face, and closed my eyes. The world was then darkened, but I could still hear, and feel, and suffer."[4]

He describes how his body is placed in a coffin and lowered into the earth, magnifying his suffocating and desperate feelings. Galt's narration also demonstrates the ways in which live burials can often represent multiple forms of entrapment; the victim is not only trapped in his own body without the ability to move or speak, but he is also enclosed in a coffin doomed to be buried even deeper. Galt's story first appeared in 1821 in *Blackwood's Magazine*, a popular British literary journal known for publishing grisly tales that were influential in the works of Charles Dickens, the Brontë sisters, Nathaniel Hawthorne, and Edgar Allan Poe.[5] Galt's story and other contemporaneous tales were popular at a time when there was a pervasive fear of being prematurely buried because of the hasty interments of cholera victims in eighteenth- and nineteenth-century Europe.[6]

Inspired by stories featured in *Blackwood's Magazine*,[7] Poe in "The Premature Burial" (1844) describes live entombment as a particularly distressing event, and the narrator recounts his experience in graphic detail. Poe often resorts to these ghastly punishments in his literary works and, not surprisingly, he has since become associated with such descriptions of premature interments. In his short story "Berenice" (1835), the eponymous heroine is buried after a prolonged sickness, but a servant, after hearing mysterious screams, discovers her unburied, still-alive body near the grave. The story also suggests that her crazed husband, Egaeus, who is obsessed with Berenice's perfect teeth, had exhumed her from the grave in order to extract her teeth. "The Oval Portrait" (1842) represents yet another type of live burial, in which a painter mysteriously transfers his wife's image and soul onto a picture frame, and thus she becomes, in a sense, trapped in the tableau vivant that her husband has created. In "The Cask of Amontillado" (1846), Montreso, the protagonist, has been repeatedly insulted by his friend and foe, Fortunato, and decides to punish him. Montreso lures Fortunato deep into the vaults of the Montreso family crypt where he buries him alive in the walls of the catacomb. Poe also describes live burials in his tale "The Fall of the House of Usher" (1839), in which Roderick Usher buries his sister, Madeline, not realizing that she is still alive. Even when he suspects that she is not dead, he does nothing to save her and allows her to suffer in her coffin. When her body is finally exhumed, her bloodied robe reveals her terrifying struggle. Although there are more examples, the few mentioned here underscore the many ways in which Poe's characters, especially women, suffer premature entombments, both literally and metaphorically.

The representations of live burials transcend the Gothic representations of the eighteenth and nineteenth centuries and are also imitated in other art forms, such as film. In 1928, US directors J. S. Watson Jr. and Melville Webber created a short film adaptation of Poe's "The Fall of the House of Usher." In that same year, *La chute de la maison Usher*, directed by Jean Epstein and written by Luis Buñuel, premiered. This French film coalesces two of Poe's famous works, "The Fall of the House of Usher" and "The Oval Portrait," in which Madeline's entrapment is multiplied on the screen. In the first few scenes of this film, Roderick Usher obsessively paints the image of his sister-wife Madeline, showing how his love for art surpasses his love for her. As he paints the image of Madeline, she is slowly being drawn into the frame and transferred onto the canvas. Once her painted figure is complete, Madeline dies. Her death leads to yet another live burial sequence—an image that is highly dramatized on screen. When the coffin is sealed, Roderick watches in horror as they take her casket to the place of her sepulcher. The director further emphasizes the image of the trapped heroine by using the camera to intently focus on the silent woman trapped behind the painting and later in the coffin. Unlike Poe's "The Oval Portrait," the portrait in this film is not oval but square, and resembles a movie-screen frame. Thus, this film imagines multiple entrapments; because Madeline's body is trapped in the portrait, coffin, crypt, and ultimately the film frame, her live burial is thus magnified and multiplied on the screen.

In the German Expressionist film *The Cabinet of Dr. Caligari* (1920), Cesare, who is under the control of Dr. Caligari, murders several people in the town. Cesare, similar to a vampire, is kept in a coffin in a living-dead state. In that sense, all vampire films explicitly show live burial by the monster's body slumbering in the coffin every night—as in the case of Count Orlok, Dracula, or Dracula's wives. Anyone bitten by a vampire will certainly suffer a doubly horrifying fate: becoming a member of the undead at night, and perpetually resting in an oppressive tomb by day. Those who venture into the vampire's castle will most likely be imprisoned in it and left to fend off other vampires; this is what happens to Jonathan Harker, who in Bram Stoker's *Dracula* (1897) realizes he is trapped and says, "The castle is a veritable prison, and I am a prisoner!"[8] Harker's dire situation is portrayed in almost every film adaptation based on Stoker's novel, whereby the castle virtually becomes a structurally enclosed burial chamber. Bodily entrapment at the hand of vampires is also dramatized in Theodor Dreyer's film *Vampyr* (1932), in which the ineffectual hero, Allan Gray, is buried alive in two ways by the vampire's henchmen. Although he is conscious of his surroundings, he is trapped in his own body, unable to move or speak. While he is laying face up and wide-eyed in the coffin, through a glass pane he sees the villains screwing down the lid of the coffin and then carrying him to the churchyard where he will be interred. At times the camera's point of view shifts from outsider to insider, and the spectators can see the villains sealing the coffin from the perspective of the trapped victim. This scene is reminiscent of Galt's and Poe's representations of live burials in which the characters can still hear, feel, and suffer. There are many more examples, but these emphasize the popularity of visually representing entrapped bodies and live burials in multiple ways, especially in early cinema based on Gothic works.[9] Most significant are the Latin American writers' conjuring of live burials and through these representations speaking to oppressive social and political situations.

Live Burial in Latin American Novels

Eve Sedgwick, in *The Coherence of Gothic Conventions*, states that live burial is a conventional and popular punishment in Gothic literature that also offers "a more general description of the novels' physical ambience."[10] In parallel fashion, the live burials described in Alejo Carpentier's novel underscore the oppressive authoritarian spaces in which the characters find themselves, as well as the novels' atmosphere in general, which is also similar to how Gothic writers represented their environments.

Alejo Carpentier, one of Latin America's most esteemed authors known for his neo-Baroque style and his notions of the Marvelous Real, spent almost ten years in France collaborating with the Surrealists. He soon became disillusioned with them and returned to Cuba where he began to develop a type of writing that was rooted in local culture and history. Carpentier was critical of the Surrealists; he believed that their works were contrived and nothing like *lo real maravilloso* that he identified in Caribbean and Latin American culture and history, which he felt could inspire a more authentic form of writing. In his prologue to the novel *El reino de este mundo* (1949) (The Kingdom of This World), he not only critiques Surrealists' approaches but he also criticizes the Gothic when he describes the genre's predictable conventions. Of this, he says, "el rey de la *Julieta* de Sade, el supermacho de Jarry, el monje de Lewis, la utilería escalofriante de la novela negra inglesa: fantasmas, sacerdotes emparedados, licantropías, manos clavadas sobre la puerta de un castillo[11] (the king Sade's *Julieta*, Jarry's Supermacho, Lewis' monk, the horrifying machinery of the English Gothic novel: ghosts, immured priests, lycanthropes, hands nailed to the castle door).[12] Carpentier's words could mean that the Gothic machinery is horrifying, and they could also suggest that the Gothic easily produces horror; regardless, what is significant in Carpentier's words is his referencing ghosts, live burials, werewolves, and castles—specific tropes found in Gothic novels like Lewis's *The Monk*, among others—which underscores his familiarity with Gothic literature. Of course, many Surrealists were also acquainted with this imagery, yet Carpentier wanted to transcend these artificial imaginings, preferring more genuine literary expressions based on the local historical past. His novel in particular evokes layered realities influenced by African cosmography, pre-Columbian myths, regional folklore, and oral histories, yet his work is also informed by live burials as found in Gothic texts.

In *El reino de este mundo*, Carpentier describes the political situation that sparked the successful slave revolt that resulted in Haiti's independence from France. The unfolding of these Haitian historical events is narrated from the perspective of the protagonist, Ti Noel, a former slave who witnesses the successive toppling of one regime by another. He sees how each new authoritarian leader perpetuates similar injustices, thus underscoring the inherent depravity of power in which former slaves and the poor are most often the victims. Although Carpentier's novel is based on historical events, he also includes supernatural happenings inspired by African beliefs brought to the island by slaves. The characters in the novel seek guidance from and speak to the spirit-beings called *Loas*, concoct magical brews, and shape-shift. Carpentier also mentions Vodou priests, known as *houngans*, and even tacitly refers to the Haitian zombie myth about enslaved animated corpses forced into labor who can only recover their will and soul by consuming salt.[13] The narrator says the following about the living dead: "Otros afirmaban que el houngán, llevado en una goleta, estaba operando en la región de Jacmel, donde muchos hombres que habían muerto trabajaban la tierra, mientras no tuvieron la oportunidad de probar la sal"[14] (Others stated that the *houngan* had got away on a schooner, and was operating in the region of Jacmel, where many men who had died tilled the land as long as they were kept from tasting salt).[15] His brief mention of the zombie figures shows how he was drawn to mysterious stories rooted in Haitian local folklore and culture.[16]

Even though Carpentier was turning away from European models to seek a more genuine homegrown style, he still evoked Gothic aesthetics; in particular, in *El reino de este mundo* he narrates a case of an immured priest whose spirit returns to haunt the totalitarian ruler. In this way, Carpentier creolizes a well-known Gothic literary feature by coalescing it with remarkable Haitian historical events and the Vodou religion, couching it in the Gothic-inspired language of live entombments and hauntings. In the chapter titled "El emparedado" (The Immured), the narrator describes how a monk, Cornejo Breille, has been entombed alive in the walls as punishment for wanting to leave Haiti, which is under the rule of Henri Christophe. The monk's painful cries could be heard for days in the city, which affected the citizens in a profound way because they could not save him, perhaps because they would also face a similar fate.

> Porque aquel capuchino que estaba emparedado en el edificio del Arzobispado, sepultado en vida dentro de su oratorio, era Cornejo Breille, duque del Anse, confesor de Henri Christophe. Había sido condenado a morir ahí, al pie de una pared recién repellada, por el delito de querer marchar a Francia conociendo todos los secretos del rey, todos los secretos de la Ciudadela, sobre cuyas torres encarnadas había caído el rayo varias veces ya.[17]

[For that Capuchin immured in the Archbishop's Palace, buried alive in its oratory, was Corneille Breille, the Duke of Anse, confessor of Henri Christophe. He had been condemned to die there, at the foot of a newly plastered wall, for the crime of having wanted to go to France knowing all the secrets of the King, all the secrets of the Citadel whose red towers had already been struck by lightning several times.][18]

Drawn by revenge after dying in such a cruel way, the specter of the Capuchin monk returns to haunt and persecute King Christophe during Mass. He, like many specters, returns to make things right;[19] however, he not only emerges to make an injunction, but he also returns to seek revenge publicly. The priest, queen, and churchgoers react with fear when they first see the specter dressed in a bloodied robe. He stares fixedly at the king to terrorize him; as if casting a spell, he leaves the king speechless and paralyzed. The king is trapped in his own body because he can't move or speak after being confronted by the specter. The situation is made even more ominous when the narrator describes how the specter's damning words toward the king vibrate like organ music throughout the sanctuary, shaking the church's stained-glass windows. During this supernatural scene, lightning strikes the cathedral tower, splitting all the bells. In the background, the narrator also mentions the African drums beating like ill omens as this frightful spectacle unfolds. The king dies soon after and his corpse is buried in the mortar of the citadel, becoming "one with the stone that imprisoned it."[20] Ironically, Henri Christophe's body will also be entombed in the structure, similar to the way in which the monk's body was immured.

The buried bodies possibly allude to something else as well. The suffocating feelings elicited in *El reino de este mundo* mirror the political situation in which many of the citizens, especially former slaves, were confined under the authoritarian regime. They were unable to speak or travel freely without being re-enslaved or punished. This same live entrapment wherein citizens' voices are suppressed under authoritarian regimes is also found in other texts. For example, in Augusto Roa Bastos's novel *Yo el supremo* (1974) (I, the Supreme), discussed in chapter 4, the dictator regularly displays unnecessary cruelty against his enemies by imprisoning them in subterranean dungeons in complete darkness. He too is a totalitarian ruler who silences his detractors, which could be understood as another type of interment in which citizens cannot speak freely. Carlos Fuentes's *Vlad* (2010), also discussed in chapter 4, is yet another example of an authoritarian leader who practices horrific means of torture against detractors, including live burials; yet Vlad, ironically, is punished in the same manner. In the novel, an innocent-looking girl, Minea, who is really an ancient vampire, rescues Vlad the dictator from a grave where he was buried alive. Even though she saves him, she also blinds him and transforms him into a vampire monster like herself, condemning him to a dark and buried existence. Some authors appropriate the live-burial trope and use the horrific event for other reasons, even expunging its fear-provoking qualities entirely. In particular, the following discussed texts suggest Gothic settings and features, yet the authors dramatically change what one usually expects from this genre of literature.

Playful Live Burials?

Despite the spine-tingling qualities usually associated with live burials, not all of them are narrated to provoke the same emotional response; that is, the terror and taphephobia usually associated with live burial scenes are not really the point of their conjuring. Authors through lyrical and ludic language ironically disassociate these gruesome happenings from the way they have frequently been portrayed, as illustrated in Vicente Huidobro's novela-film *Cagliostro* (1934)—a parody of German Expressionist films, discussed in chapter 2. His text features a live burial, but due to the novel's playful language the event is hardly frightful. In the introduction to Huidobro's novel, the narrator asks the readers to pretend that they are in a theater viewing a film and not, in fact, reading a novel. The novel is also self-referential in the way that the narrator frequently reminds the reader that this is a work of fiction about fiction, thus limiting readers' ability to fully engage with the filmic story they are supposedly seeing "on the screen." In Huidobro's novela-film, a parody of *The Cabinet of Dr. Caligari*, the villain and protagonist, Cagliostro, keeps the female heroine, Lorenza, sedated and enclosed in a coffinlike trunk that is hidden behind the walls of his home. Similar to what

Dr. Caligari did with Cesare, Cagliostro hypnotizes Lorenza, and she is occasionally allowed to exit the burial chamber so that she can carry out Cagliostro's illicit tasks. Lorenza wants to escape, but Cagliostro is obsessed with her and keeps her close so that he can admire her beauty. She later realizes the oppressive and inescapable existence she is enduring under Cagliostro, which drives her to commit suicide rather than continue her buried existence. Even after Lorenza opts out of life, Cagliostro still yearns for her and abducts her corpse; the ending suggests that he will resurrect her through his magic, damning her again to live burial. The narrator vividly describes the first time Lorenza's body ascends from entombment: "Del interior del baúl empieza a subir con gran lentitud una especie de plataforma acolchonada, recubierta de terciopelo negro. Encima de la plataforma, que sigue subiendo, aparece el cuerpo de Lorenza como una muñeca dormida y vestida de blanco. Cagliostro la contempla con indecible ternura"[21] [From the trunk's interior a large cushioned platform, covered in black velvet, begins to emerge slowly. On top of the platform, which continues to emerge, Lorenza's body appears, as if she were a sleeping doll all dressed in white. Cagliostro contemplates her with unspeakable tenderness]. Her live entombment at the hands of a villain seems cruel, yet Huidobro's description somehow negates Cagliostro's horrific actions: the language evokes the image of something else—a virginal sleeping beauty that stirs feelings of tenderness in Cagliostro, a view that the reader-spectator would seem to share. Huidobro subverts the usual representations of death and live burials through his poetic metaphors and playful self-referential language, which disengage the reader from fully appreciating the horrific details that are being "projected" in Huidobro's cinematic novel.

Another example of a live burial that does not convey feelings of terror can be found in Xavier Villaurrutia's avant-garde novel *Dama de corazones* (1928) (Dame of Hearts). The author erotically speaks of the body but also creates a new type of subjectivity in which the dead expresses a particular presence. In Villaurrutia's work, the main character can hear and feel despite being seemingly dead, which recalls Galt's character in "The Buried Alive," who can also hear and feel his own burial process; however, the mood created in Villaurrutia's novel is quite different because the language of desire and illusion supplants feelings of dread.

A Mexican author, Villaurrutia formed part of a literary movement known as the Contemporaneos, a group that first initiated Mexican artists' interest in Surrealism.[22] The vanguard group also published a literary magazine of the same name from 1927 to 1929 in postrevolutionary Mexico. These authors sought literary inspiration in their predecessors, such as authors affiliated with the Ateneo de México (an association of writers and philosophers who promoted intellectual and artistic culture) as well as European and North American poets, including Poe and Walt Whitman.[23] The Contemporaneos were not necessarily seeking to represent social reality, including themes having to do with Mexico's recent war-torn years; rather, they were concerned with literary creation and aesthetics, especially with adopting strategies associated with the avant-garde.[24] As Rosa García Gutiérrez explains, the avant-garde had a profound effect on the Hispanic world, and one could trace modernist characteristics in Villaurrutia's work, such as in his references to film and in the novel's fragmentary style.[25] At the same time, Villaurrutia employs stream-of-consciousness passages and dreamlike sequences as well as other literary techniques associated with Surrealism.

García Gutiérrez also comments how Villaurrutia saw the death theme as one of Mexico's preoccupations, which is certainly evident in his works.[26] Death becomes a poetic inspiration that does not necessarily provoke fear or dread, as exemplified in his book of poems *Nostalgia de la muerte* (1938) (Nostalgia of Death) and in the short novel *Dama de corazones*. In the novel, the main character, Julio, returns to visit his aunt and cousins in Mexico during his vacation from Harvard University. His visit is narrated oneirically; Julio alternates between stages of consciousness that reveal his unsettled mind and his erotic desire for Aurora and Susana, his cousins. What is important in Villaurrutia's prose as it relates to this chapter is the way that Julio employs lyrical language to speak of his own imagined death. Julio says: "Ahora, estoy muerto. Descanso. Escucho"[27] (Now I am dead. I rest. I hear). In the case of *Dama de corazones*, Julio reflects on the slow passing of time; of death he says, "Morir es estar incomunicado felizmente de personas y las cosas, y mirarlas como la lente de la cámara debe mirar, con exactitud y frialdad. Morir no es otra cosa que convertirse en un ojo perfecto que mira sin emocionarse"[28] (To die is to be happily disconnected from people and things. It is to see them, as a camera should, with preciseness and coldness. To die is no other thing than to transform oneself into a perfect eye that sees without emotion). In this dreamlike passage, the author asks the reader to view death and the body as something else—in this case, a camera lens.

Not only does Julio speak about his experience as a dead man; he also describes how he is in a coffin and is being carried to the cemetery: "Ahora me llevan ¿adónde? Al cementerio. No se han olvidado de cerrar la tapa del ataúd. Ignoran que no estoy dentro de él. Sigo el cortejo"[29] (Now they are taking me, where? To the cemetery. They have not forgotten to close the lid of the coffin. They ignore that I am not inside. I follow the procession). This fragment of his death and burial is then interrupted with other thoughts and events of his visit; thus, it is not entirely clear whether his ghost or he, as a material person, is walking beside his coffin with the crowd toward the burial site. For a while, it seems that he might be truly dead, but then, suddenly, he is alive again and the moment of death is negated. Julio never actually died; rather, he had imagined his death and burial procession in a dreamlike sequence. Villaurrutia, who published this novel in 1928, made an important contribution to works that deal with death and live burials: he had his character articulate a subjective presence to describe his own illusory death and burial—not in terms that provoked fear or despair but rather in terms that were quixotic, sensual, and ludic. Villaurrutia's novel further contributed to how death themes were evolving as a particular artistic preoccupation in works created by other authors in Mexico.[30] Octavio Paz's 1950 essay "Day of the Dead" discusses Mexico's familiarity with and playful approach to death as seen in these commemorative celebrations.[31] Similarly, in Elena Garro's 1957 theatrical play *Un hogar sólido* (A Solid Home), she uses humor to describe loquacious sentient corpses buried in the family crypt who reminisce about their past as they await the resurrection.

More Female Entrapments

Characters who could speak of their deaths subjectively and in more erotic terms would emerge many years later in *Pedro Páramo*, written in 1955 by one of Mexico's most esteemed authors, Juan Rulfo. The theme of death is pervasive in this novel, given that most of the characters found in the town of Comala are wandering apparitions that, at times, materialize into their former selves, who then communicate and interact with the living. When Juan Preciado travels to Comala in search of his father, Pedro Páramo, he does not understand fully that he is interacting with ghosts until it is too late and he too, like the others, becomes a murmuring ghost and sentient corpse buried in the town's cemetery. In spite of it being a haunted town that is steeped in mortality, there are passages in which death is represented as something else, perhaps art. Philippe Ariès, in *The Hour of Our Death*, argues that nineteenth-century Romantic representations of death coalesce with notions of beauty; as such, death hides behind a mask of beauty and becomes an illusion of art.[32] Examples of corpses that denote art and beauty have since become a common and appealing literary trope, and Rulfo does this with his aesthetic and poetic descriptions, the moribund body and death of the female heroine, Susana San Juan.

Rulfo's description of Susana recalls how female bodies—especially deteriorating ones—are characterized as sleeping beauties, thus veiling the idea of imminent decomposition and decay. In Rulfo's novel, the villain, Pedro Páramo, has throughout his lifetime ached to possess Susana. She is his singular object of affection and he still longs for her even as she lies dying:

> —Susana—dijo. Luego cerró los ojos.—Yo te pedí que regresaras . . . —. . . Había una luna grande en medio del mundo. Se me perdían los ojos mirándote. Los rayos de la luna filtrándose sobre tu cara. No me cansaba de ver esa aparición que eras tú. Suave, restregada de luna; tu boca abullonada, humedecida, irisada de estrellas; tu cuerpo transparentándose en el agua de la noche. Susana, Susana San Juan." . . .—Ésta es mi muerte—dijo.[33]

> ["Susana," he said. He closed his eyes. "I begged you to come back. . . ." "An enormous moon was shining over the world. I stared at you till I was nearly blind. At the moonlight pouring over her face. I never grew tired of looking at you, as the vision that you were. Soft, caressed by the moonlight, your swollen, moist lips iridescent with

stars, your body growing transparent in the night dew. Susana. Susana San Juan." . . . "This is death," he thought.]³⁴

He does not describe a dying body but rather a beautiful woman who is like the moon and stars, fading into the mist. His reaction to her death recalls the notions of death and beauty found in Poe's essay "The Philosophy of Composition." Poe states that melancholy is the ideal poetic tone, and the most melancholic moment is the death of a beautiful woman: this moment is "when it most closely allies itself to *Beauty*: the death then of a beautiful woman is unquestionably the most poetical topic in the world, and equally is it beyond doubt that the lips best suited for such topic are those of a bereaved lover."³⁵ Similarly, Pedro, the grieving lover, expresses melancholic and poetic words at the same moment Susana is at death's door.

Even though Pedro is madly in love with Susana, and in fact plotted her father's death so that he could finally possess her, his love is unrequited. Instead, she becomes trapped in Pedro's home and retreats into the world of fantasy, oblivious to the world that he has constructed for her. Susana, who is described as mad, is imprisoned under the villain's force, yet she refuses to surrender to him and escapes into an oneiric space. She is portrayed as if she were in a living-dead state, always recumbent in her bed and buried in between the sheets that the narrator describes as her sepulcher.³⁶ She dreams of her dead husband, Florencio, and she also imagines an erotic existence with nature, especially water. This erotic pleasure related to water is made clear when she states:

> Volví yo. Volvería siempre. El mar moja mis tobillos y se va; moja mis rodillas, mis muslos; rodea mi cintura con su brazo suave, da vuelta sobre mis senos; se abraza de mi cuello; aprieta mis hombros. Entonces me hundo en él, entera. Me entrego a él en su fuerte batir, en su suave poseer, sin dejar pedazo.³⁷

> [I went back. I would always go back. The sea bathes my ankles, and retreats; it bathes my knees, my thighs; it puts its gentle arm

around my waist, circles my breasts, embraces my throat, presses my shoulders. Then I sink into it, my whole body. I give myself to its pulsing strength, to its gentle possession, holding nothing back.]³⁸

Later in the passage, she describes how she went to the sea often as a way to purify herself. In this way, water seems to be both a spiritual and an erotic experience for her, as well as a utopic space of escape and absolution. She does not flee from the castle, nor does she commit suicide, as other Gothic heroines might have done; she escapes inward, toward the interior spaces of her mind, remembering and fantasizing.

Most important, whether Susana is alive or dead, her physical body and positioning remain the same throughout the novel: she is always reclined either on her bed or in the casket, dreaming—ultimately causing Pedro's demise. She escapes from him by escaping into a dream world and ultimately destroys him through her premature death. In the Spanish version, Pedro expresses Susana's passing as "mi muerte"—his own death—thus experiencing her death as his own. Because of his profound grief, he loses interest in his vast and fertile lands, which soon begin to wither as he too begins to wane. Completely disillusioned, he spends the rest of his days staring at the road along which Susana's body was carried to the cemetery, yearning to return to her.³⁹

After Susana dies, she is buried in the churchyard where other buried corpses, Juan Preciado and Dorothea, hear her lament. Susana remembers her mother's wake and burial; she describes how joyful and beautiful that morning appeared to her and how she did not mourn and grieve, as she would have been expected to. She recalls how she used to sleep cuddled in her mother's arms in her bed. While she remembers those happy moments with her mother, she notes that she is no longer resting on that nurturing bed but rather in a coffin lying face up because she is dead:

Estoy aquí, boca arriba, pensando en aquel tiempo para olvidar mi soledad. Porque no estoy acostada sólo por un rato. Y ni en la cama de mi madre, sino dentro de un cajón negro como el que se usa para enterrar a los muertos. Porque estoy muerta. Siento el lugar en que estoy y pienso.⁴⁰

[Here I lie, flat on my back, hoping to forget my loneliness by remembering those times. Because I am not here just for awhile. And I am not in my mother's bed but in a black box like the ones for burying the dead. Because I am dead. I sense where I am, but I can think.]⁴¹

In the novel, the beautiful morning and mourning are narrated lyrically, especially when read aloud; however, the poetic words become unsettling when readers realize that these lovely memories are being recounted by a corpse who has been buried for many years. The border between life and death, which usually remains separate, becomes intertwined in a way that can be disconcerting. This passage is also an example of a live burial because Susana is portrayed as a speaking and sentient body who is buried in the cemetery, who can still feel and think.

Susana's voice is not the only one whispering from the grave; Juan Preciado, who dies in the town of Comala, also speaks, even though he is, presumably, dead. Yet he is not alone; Dorothea, another town resident and stranger to Juan, died at the same time as he did and by happenstance they have been buried in the same grave. While Juan's corpse is cradling Dorothea's, she explains the circumstances of their communal burial:

Después que te encontramos a ti, se resolvieron mis huesos a quedarse quietos. "Nadie me hará caso," pensé. Soy algo que no le estorba a nadie. Ya ves, ni siquiera le robé el espacio a la tierra. Me enterraron en tu misma sepultura y cupe muy bien en el hueco de tus brazos. Aquí en este rincón donde me tienes ahora. Sólo se me ocurre que debería ser yo la que te tuviera abrazado a ti. . . .—Ya déjate de miedos. Nadie te puede dar ya miedo. Haz por pensar en cosas agradables porque vamos a estar mucho tiempo enterrados.⁴²

[After we found you, my bones determined to find their rest. "No one will notice me," I thought. "I won't be a bother to anyone." You see, I didn't even steal a space from the earth. They buried me in the grave with you, and I fit right in the hollow of your arms. Here in this little space where I am now. The only thing is that probably I should have my hands around *you*. . . . "You don't have to be afraid. No one can scare you now. Try to think nice thoughts, because we are going to be a long time here in the ground."][43]

Certainly Susana, Juan, and Dorothea are examples of live burial: they no longer belong in world of the living; rather, they are speaking and self-aware dead bodies that are entombed, waiting for something, perhaps salvation or the Christian resurrection of the saints. Even though they are underground, they are not afraid of the suffocating situation, which is very unlike the typical terror tales in which characters experience a horrific awakening. For example, in Galt's work, the character finds that he is buried alive and doomed to suffer a terrible death. He also vividly explains the hideous changes that his body will suffer from the moles, rats, and worms, all of which suggest suffocation and terror. It is evident that he longs to be rescued and return to the good life that he once had, when he was successful doctor esteemed by many.

Galt's description of live burial is quite different from Susana's buried existence: Susana finds peace in her moribund state by dreaming of Florencio and the landscape; even when she dies and is buried, she continues to ruminate about her life so as to pass the time. As the passage given earlier emphasizes, Susana seems more concerned with resisting feelings of loneliness than struggling to escape from the tomb. Similarly, Dorothea and Juan are seeking ways to make their stay underground less boring or painful by remembering pleasant moments in their lives. They seem to have suffered and feared the most when they were alive, and now, when buried underground, they are more at peace. When Dorothea tells Juan, "You don't have to be afraid. No one can scare you now," she stresses how when they were alive they lived in fear. She suggests that their existence was unbearable under the austere regime of Pedro Páramo and that the only form of peace for many characters in the novel was to escape into the world of madness, fantasy, and even death. As such, in the afterlife, Pedro's wickedness can no longer reach them, making death their only safe haven.

Rulfo's description of live burials is unlike the way Gothic writers approached these premature interments and may have to do with the specific context in which this novel was written. Although live burial provokes struggle and despair in Gothic victims—Antonia, Emily, Fortunato, and Madeline, for example—it does not elicit the same feelings in Susana, Dorothea, or Juan. They may have felt terror while they were alive, yet becoming sentient buried bodies is comparably less horrific. In this way, death and live burials might also be another way in which Rulfo was making a social critique of Mexican postrevolutionary society, not by directly stating his disappointment with the status quo but by commenting on oppression and violence through the characters' physical bodies. These poetically narrated live burials suggest that existing as a buried body is more peaceful than living under an oppressive regime.

Improbable Revenants

So far this chapter has explored the works of male authors and their representation of death and live burials; while women novelists similarly employ the live-burial trope and describe the female dead body, they tend to do so differently.[44] In her novel, *La amortajada*, María Luisa Bombal has readers reconsider the female body through her protagonist, Ana María, who can still feel, think, and hear despite being dead. In this way, Bombal is implicitly questioning the way in which female bodies have been represented in literature by having Ana María speak through and out of death, which is different from Villaurrutia's and Rulfo's descriptions of sentient dead bodies. Villaurrutia and Bombal were contemporaries and they both describe premature interments in their works and use a subjective presence with sensual language in distinctive ways. Villaurrutia's description of live burial is more illusive, while Bombal's is more material in that the female corpse is at the core of the narration. Bombal's work also differs from Rulfo's novel. Scholars have already underscored the ways Rulfo's character Susana San Juan was inspired by Bombal's protagonist, Ana María (e.g., Marchiselli, Rodenas). Both characters are recumbent and in a deathlike state, remembering their past loves while experiencing a deeply sensual connection to nature. In Rulfo's work, it is mostly from Pedro Páramo's perspective that readers understand his desire and longing for Susana, as opposed to the narrator's description of Ana María's death experience, through which we understand how she sees her own dead body.

Ana María's circumstances and the feelings of entrapment resonate with what many female Gothic writers have already represented in their novels. Diana Wallace argues that the most powerful metaphor in feminist theory is also at the heart of Gothic fiction: "The idea of woman as 'dead' or 'buried (alive)' within male power structures which render her 'ghostly.'"[45] This Gothic metaphor could also be used to describe the ways death and live burial are used in Bombal's work; she employs live burials to reveal the female character's spectral quality because the character is voiceless and metaphorically buried alive under a patriarchal order. Given these many affinities between female Gothic writers and Bombal's work, it seems fitting to reframe her novel within what female Gothic writers have already noted, which provides another way of reading Bombal's novel.

Because there were so many female Gothic writers and female readers, Ellen Moers coined the term *female Gothic* to distinguish these works thematically.[46] Some of these important female writers include Ann Radcliffe, Mary Shelley, and the Brontë sisters, who all frequently questioned the confined roles of women in their writing. The female Gothicists used this antirationalist tradition to reproduce and challenge the patriarchal order, many times conveying this horror through their characters' bodies.[47] At the same time, female Gothic writers were implicitly addressing contemporary issues and cultural anxieties;[48] this seems to parallel the angst expressed by Bombal's character Ana María, who describes her claustrophobic situation and expresses how she feels trapped and dead inside. Bombal's work shares many aspects with female writers of the Gothic, so often preoccupied with the supernatural, live burials, and split selves. It is not unusual that Bombal should incorporate the many tropes born out of the Gothic tradition in her novel because she was not only a great admirer of the Gothic but also a film lover. As discussed in chapter 2, she was a devotee of Theodor Dreyer's work, whose film *Vampyr* was partially based on *Nosferatu* and the vampire tale "Carmilla." However, what brings *La amortajada* closer to the Gothicists is that Ana María is in a liminal state of being, trapped in her body and unable to move or speak.

The first Gothic gestures can be found in Bombal's debut novel, *La última niebla* (1935) (The House of Mist), in which nebulous and foggy settings characterize the novel's atmosphere and the heroine's mental state. The nameless narrator feels like she is dead because of her oppressive marriage to her husband, Daniel, even though she is a newlywed. She especially apprehends her lifeless existence when she contemplates the corpse of a young woman at a wake:

> Me acerco y miro, por primera vez, la cara de un muerto. Veo un rostro descolorido, sin ni un toque de sombra en los anchos párpados cerrados. Un rostro vacío de todo sentimiento. Esta muerta, sobre la cual no se me ocurriría inclinarme para llamarla porque parece que no hubiera vivido nunca, me sugiere de pronto la palabra silencio.[49]

> [I come closer and I look at, for the first time, the face of a dead person. I see her pale face, without even a touch of shadow over her broad closed eyelids. A face void of all feeling. This dead woman, who I would not even dare to lean over and call because she seems to have never have lived at all. All of a sudden she suggests the word *silence*.][50]

Later in the story, she describes how she runs outside because she is afraid of the corpse's immobility and wonders whether that very same dead body might really be her, leading her to question her own existence. As if to convince herself that she is still among the living, she screams, "Yo existo, yo existo—digo en voz alta—y soy bella y feliz"[51] (I exist, I exist—I say out loud and I am beautiful and happy!). Although she speaks audibly to convince herself that she does indeed exist, the readers know that she is unhappily married and only entered into this union because it was expected of a woman of her social class. As critic Lucía

Guerra-Cunningham argues, the protagonist's life is one of enclosure and restriction:

> Restringida al espacio cerrado del hogar y sin poseer el impulso necesario para romper con los límites físicos y existenciales que la sociedad de la época asignaba a la mujer, la heroína opta por la pasividad y el ensueño, únicas vías de evasión y rebelión dentro de los esquemas establecidos por el orden burgués.[52]

> [Restricted in the enclosed space of the home and lacking the necessary impetus to break with the physical and existential limits that society has imposed on women of that epoch, the heroine opts for passivity and illusion, which is the only way to evade and rebel against the schemes established by the bourgeoisie].

In order to exist in a life deemed appropriate for her, she escapes to a world of fantasy, imagining that she has another lover. She might be losing her mind, as it is unclear whether this man actually exists; however, imagining a passionate romance propels her to continue living.

The claustrophobic feelings that the heroine expresses in Bombal's first novel also emerge in her subsequent work, *La amortajada*, but in a much more grave manner because the heroine is already dead. Ana María is trapped in her body in a living-dead state and aware of her surroundings. Most significant, the female subject is able to witness her death, wake, and burial. The title *La amortajada* is derived from the verb *amortajar*, meaning "to enshroud a cadaver," and refers to the dead body of the protagonist, who, according to the narrator, can still see and feel despite being dead. While lying face up at her wake, she observes and hears family and lovers bid her farewell. This echoes Galt's work, in which the character is also present in his body despite being declared dead. He can hear his friends speak of their sorrow and he can even feel a teardrop on his face. Similarly, in her living-dead state, Ana María is present in her body and hears her family's sorrow. Yet she does not express feelings of despair; rather, she calmly observes her surroundings and even seems to enjoy her own wake; in this sense, she is like Villaurrutia's character Julio who, like a camera, can focus on his environment.

She is notably unlike other Gothic victims, who express panic at finding themselves trapped in their bodies and unable to speak. She does not express feelings of dread or recognize the "hideous form of awakening and a dialogue between worlds that should remain disengaged."[53] Instead, this new liminal state allows her to experience and even appreciate her life differently. As Guerra-Cunningham explains, in death she has a better understanding of her life, which is exemplified when the narrator ponders: "¿Era preciso morir para saber ciertas cosas?"[54] (Must one die to know certain things?). In Ana María's entrapped living-dead state, she fluctuates between observing, dreaming, and remembering. She remembers her life with former lovers, she hears the voices of her loved ones attending her wake. At the same time, she also hears a voice from the afterlife that summons her to cross over. While she reminisces about her past, some moments bring her pleasure, but other memories are sorrowful and oppressive.

She recalls a distant erotic past with her lover Ricardo, a man who gave her torturous pleasure through his abuse. He is sensually described as a dark, virile man with shimmering skin, a man who provoked pleasurable pain and terror in her. She says of him, "reinabas por el terror"[55] (You reigned by terror). In her memories of their childhood together, she remembers how they frolicked in the sun while he chased her and lashed her naked legs with a whip. At the same time, he excited her with frightful ghost tales at night, in particular one of a mysterious man who lived in the forest. This creature dressed in black, had a pocket full of bats, and commanded rats and mice, among other creatures[56]—an obvious allusion to the vampire figure, who represents the living dead and erotic existence, which is a situation that Ana María also experiences.

Ana María describes female dissatisfaction in a society that does not allow her to communicate or realize her desires fully. Men have many spheres of self-realization, whereas women must find meaning through marriage and in the confines of the home. Lying face up, she ruminates on women's limited lives as compared to the many options men possess:

Pasaron años. Años en que se retrajo y se fue volviendo día a día más limitada y mezquina. ¿Por qué, por qué la naturaleza de la mujer ha de ser tal que tenga que ser siempre un hombre el eje de su vida? Los hombres, ellos, logran poner su pasión en otras cosas. Pero el destino de las mujeres es remover una pena de amor en una casa ordenada, ante una tapicería inconclusa.[57]

[Years passed, years in which she withdrew within herself and became, day by day, more narrow and petty. Why, oh why must a woman's nature be such that a man has always to be the pivot of her life? Men succeed in directing their passion to other things. But the fate of so many women seems to turn over and over in their heart some love sorrow while sitting in a neatly ordered house, facing an unfinished tapestry.][58]

As the quote suggests, Ana María's home had become an unhappy, miserable space to which she retreated. As Guerra-Cunningham suggests, this belief that women essentially live truncated lives in which desires are suppressed, leaving them with a half-lived existence, results in dissatisfaction that leads the characters to live an intense inner life.[59] Female characters also become disconnected from their bodies, occupying divided selves where the exterior behavior does not correspond with their true desires. She expresses feelings of despair and suffocation with no relief: "Es que todos los que han nacido para amar viven así como ella vivió?, ¿ahogando minuto a minuto lo más vital dentro de sí"[60] [Are all those born to love compelled to live as she did, compelled to drift toward self-destruction, so smother minute after minute within themselves all that is most vital in their own being?].[61]

When Ana María was alive she endured a buried existence and the slow and agonizing passing of time. Her marriage to Antonio is loveless, which leads her to live an even more interred situation because she cannot express herself physically with him; he is always absent, traveling frequently to his second house in the city, where he has other lovers. She becomes a divided self: a dutiful yet miserable wife. Of her painful duties as a wife, she says: "Tener que peinarse, que hablar, ordenar y sonreír.

Tener que cumplir el túnel de un largo verano con ese puntapié en medio del corazón"[62] [To have to do her hair, to speak, to give orders, to smile. To have to go through the horror of a long Summer, bearing that kick in the middle of her heart!].[63] Although later she admires the beauty of her corpse, in her isolated life she seems to have abandoned any enjoyment of her physical body.

Stifled in her adult life and in marriage, ironically it is in death where Ana María finally finds beauty and pleasure. In the novel, the protagonist mentions that she feels *melancolía* in her living-dead state.[64] Her use of the word *melancholy* recalls Poe's thoughts about female death, beauty, and the poetic words that flow from the mouth of the bereaved lover; however, the male gaze has been subverted here. It is Ana María, according to the narrator, who examines her own corpse and poetically describes her own death in lyrical terms that denote beauty. Ana María is not the object of contemplation and subject to the male gaze, as found in other works; rather, she has agency by the very act of describing her own body and mortality. While she contemplates her dead body, she comments that her elegantly combed hair gives her an air of mystery and charm. She feels that all her wrinkles have vanished and that she is as pale and beautiful as ever.[65] Paradoxically, seeing her dead body does not horrify her; instead, she is filled with immense delight. She is a living-dead woman who finds bodily pleasure in the afterlife.

Ana María also has an extremely intense relationship with the landscape, specifically with water, which is mentioned throughout the text. When Ana María's body is carried toward the churchyard where she will begin her final descent, the narrator vividly describes the many layers of earth that finally end in total aquatic submersion. As the novel nears its end, Ana María's body becomes intertwined with currents: "Una corriente la empuja, la empuja canal abajo por un trópico cuya vegetación va descolorándose a medida que la tierra se parte en mil y mil apretados islotes. . . . La naturaleza entera aspira, se nutre aquí de agua, nada más que de agua"[66] (Down the watery channel, the current pushes and pushes through a tropical region where the vegetation fades in color as the earth parts into thousands and thousands of serried islands. . . . And the stream still pushes her slowly on, and with her it drags along enormous tangles of plants on the roots of which travel entwined gentle water snakes).[67] In this manner her body is interlinked with nature and water, alluding to an idealized mythic embodiment that will exist in the afterlife.[68]

This erotic awakening in death in relation to water is also found in the nineteenth-century vampire tale "Carmilla." Sheridan LeFanu's work was not only an important model for Stoker's novel *Dracula*; it was also one of the inspirations for Dreyer's film *Vampyr*, which critics have argued also stimulated Bombal's literary work. Because of such interweaving influence, it is relevant to underscore the relationship between the water imagery found in both *La amortajada* and "Carmilla." In this highly erotic tale, the aristocratic vampire Carmilla, like many vampires, spends time buried in her family crypt, yet she also lurks in the forest, looking to seduce and feed off young women. The victim's vampiric transformations are described in terms of water. Her first victim, Bertha Rheinfeldt, describes the bite: "Lastly came sensations. One, not unpleasant, but very peculiar, she said, resembled the flow of an icy stream against her breast."[69] Laura, her second victim, likens her own descent to the vampire underworld to Avernus the entrance to hell—and one of its rivers.[70] She also recalls how "certain strange sensations visited me in my sleep. The prevailing one was of that pleasant, peculiar cold thrill which we feel in bathing, when we move against the current of a river."[71] Finally, Carmilla the vampire describes her own night of initiation into the vampire world: "'I remember everything about it—with an effort. I see it all, as divers see what is going on above them, through a medium, dense, rippling, but transparent.... I was all but assassinated in my bed, wounded here,' she touched her breast, 'and never was the same since.'"[72] All of these anecdotes of vampire bites are intertwined with images of water, streams, and submersion and share an uncanny similarity to Ana María's own experience of death and submersion—they are all death experiences linked to water and highly erotic and pleasurable experiences found in the afterlife.

Like Ana María, Carmilla the vampire (who has been dead for more than one hundred years) also expresses how life for women signifies live burial, and that there is freedom only in the afterlife. Carmilla states, "Girls are caterpillars while they live in the world, to be finally butterflies when the summer comes but in the meantime they are grubs and larvae."[73] For Carmilla, worldly existence for women is synonymous with the claustrophobic existence in a cocoon, and only in death and in communion with nature do women find freedom. The ideas that Carmilla expresses are similar to the feelings that Ana María has when she remembers her life; she too describes her life in terms of being trapped and seems to feel freedom only when she dies. Yet Ana María differs from Carmilla in that she has no desire to return. As Ana María's body is descending into death, the narrator states that she has the power to get up: "En la oscuridad de la cripta, tuvo la impresión de que podía al fin moverse. Y hubiera podido, en efecto, empujar la tapa del ataúd, levantarse y volver derecha y fría, por los caminos hasta el umbral de su casa"[74] (In the darkness of the crypt, she had the feeling that she could move at last. And she could actually have pushed up the lid of the coffin, arisen and returned, erect and cold, over the paths to the threshold of her house).[75] This is what most characters in the Gothic tradition seem to want: to return to a satisfying life that they once knew. For example, all Galt's character desired was to lift the lid of the coffin and resume his former life. This resurrection from the dead would be the natural instinct of the vampire as well; however, Ana María does not become a revenant. She does not rise from the grave like Carmilla or Dracula; she surrenders herself to the reincorporation into the cosmos. The earth will reabsorb her decomposing body, where perhaps another realization in another existence can provide respite for a suffering soul. In death Ana María will find fulfillment, not in the patriarchal order but rather in a space outside the world of the living. Before her final incorporation into the death space, she states: "Había sufrido la muerte de los vivos. Ahora anhelaba la inmersión total, la segunda muerte: la muerte de los muertos"[76] (For she had suffered the death of the living. And now she longed for total immersion, for the second death, the death of the dead).[77] The word *anhelaba* means "to yearn for," which is important because she finds no consolation in returning to be near the living but instead longs for death in order to surrender to Mother Earth. As such, there seems to be no consolatory view of existence in the realm of the living.

Several passages in *La amortajada* express suffocating feelings associated with female live burial. Most significantly, Bombal, through her novel, implicitly asks readers to reexamine the female corpse in literary creation, which critiques patriarchy and creates another imaginary space of contestation and realization. Nevertheless, the novel ends pessimistically, with Ana María finding no sense of fulfillment in life and willingly surrendering to the unknown; Bombal's work suggests that women are better off dead. Of course, death as an imagined safe space is problematic because it does not really provide a viable alternative for women and it conveys a rather desperate situation. Guerra-Cunningham comments on this bleak ending: "Si la única forma de recuperar la esencia natural y cósmica se encuentra en la muerte, implícitamente se ha anulado todo posibilidad de salida en el contexto individualizado de la sociedad en un momento histórico específico"[78] (If the only way to recuperate the natural and cosmic essence is found in death, implicitly all possibility of escape is annulled in the individual context of society in a specific historical moment). However, idealizing the death space does reveal how women, like Ana María, felt about their options as women.

Bombal uses Gothic imagery to express female anxiety of being figuratively buried alive or trapped in their own bodies without the ability to speak, which is also how many female Gothic writers conveyed their protagonists' literally buried bodies. However, the author also subverts what most buried victims desire: deliverance, freedom, and life. In Bombal's work, her character prefers death, burial, and cosmic incorporation in the afterlife, which suggests that, at least for Ana María, living is a worse fate than death. Similarly as a buried sentient body, whether buried in her sheets or underground, Susana San Juan speaks through death and beyond the grave, temporarily defying death. The texts reveal how these heroines prefer to escape into oneiric or other spaces, hardly yearning to return to the material world. They are the most improbable of revenants.

CHAPTER 4

VAMPIRES CLOAKED IN METAPHOR

Since at least the nineteenth century, violent rulers have inspired the creation of literary vampires, and, correspondingly, vampiric qualities have been bestowed on powerful rulers: Vlad the Impaler was one of the models in the creation of Bram Stoker's vampire, which he set in present-day Romania, a place where Vlad ruled and caused terror with his gory war tactics. Napoleon III, a French emperor who was known for his blood thirst and penchant for feeding on the wealth of weaker nations, has at times been depicted in vampiric terms.[1] Similar to the way rulers create oppressive regimes in the material world, literary vampires also produce terrorizing environments, and these fictional settings might also reveal prevailing societal and political anxieties. Timothy Beal, Donna Haraway, Jeffrey Jerome Cohen, and Sara Potter have already argued that monsters are inherently demonstrative. Thus, the vampire monster can both reveal and signify something beyond itself, or, as Joan Gordon and Veronica Hollinger succinctly posit in *Blood Read: The Vampire as Metaphor in Contemporary Culture*, "the vampire stands before us cloaked in metaphor."[2] By framing the novels within this idea of metaphor, this chapter analyzes how Augusto Roa Bastos's and Carlos Fuentes's vampiric entities speak to the corrosive effects of power and the societal nightmares they engender. Roa Bastos's *Yo el supremo* (1974) (I, the Supreme) and Fuentes's *Vlad* (2010) feature ubiquitous villains who are violent, powerful, and, most important, do not die. Unlike the modernistas (discussed in chapter 1), who at the turn of the nineteenth century usually featured female vampires and passive male victims, Roa Bastos and Fuentes create authoritarian male protagonists who are reminiscent of Bram Stoker's Dracula and Vlad the Impaler.

Roa Bastos attributes extraordinary vampirelike powers to the main character, El Supremo, to underscore the horrors of the dictatorship that plagued Paraguay, while Carlos Fuentes features a vampire who is attempting to invade and overtake the Mexican nation, a country that is already in state of crisis as a result of the ongoing violence and political instability linked to the drug underworld. The social tribulations that plague the country come closer to Gothic terror as found in fiction whereby citizens experience fear, anxiety, horror, and unprecedented bloodshed under the dominion of ominous forces.

Piecing Together Paraguay's Vampire

Roa Bastos is one of Paraguay's most esteemed authors and has received many accolades from Latin American critics who consider *Yo el supremo* to be his masterpiece. Because of his political views and his writings, Roa Bastos suffered personally under oppressive governments. He had to leave Paraguay in 1947 and continued to be persona non grata after the publication of *Yo el supremo* because dictator Alfredo Stroessner (1912–2006), who was in power from 1954 through 1989, perceived *Yo el supremo* to be a direct attack on his regime.[3] Even though, on the surface, Roa Bastos's novel is situated in the distant past, his work critiques the political situation and figures of his times. When Roa Bastos wrote this historically based novel, he was already exiled in Argentina, a country on the verge of experiencing its own dictatorship in which thousands would disappear or die between 1976 and 1983. His novel treats both the past and the present, and, unknowingly, also foretells the terrors that would continue into the future in Latin America.

In a 1998 interview with Silvia Lemus, Roa Bastos described his novels *El fiscal* (1993) and *Yo el supremo* as united by a common theme—"the probing of evil." Roa Bastos also stated that he wanted to transcend direct political discourse in order to study the profound human soul, where the monsters reside. Furthermore, he referred to Hieronymus Bosch's fifteenth-century painting *The Garden of Earthly Delights* as a source of his inspiration. One of the panels of the triptych depicts sinners in hell suffering unusual tortures at the hands of demons. By exploring these dark beings, Roa Bastos finds the images to create his own legendary monster—a metaphor of power and dictatorship—exemplified in El

Supremo, who is represented as an abusive leader and as a living-dead entity with extraordinary abilities.

The vampire and its ubiquitous powers are representative of El Supremo's persona and reign, emphasizing the sinister quality of dictators that continued to emerge in Paraguay. The abusive form of government propagated by José Gaspar Rodríguez de Francia (1766–1840), known as Dr. Francia and *El Supremo*, did not die with him; rather, it was transmuted and perpetuated through different bodies and exemplified by the cruel regimes that characterized Paraguay's early nineteenth century and still plagued the nation in the 1970s under the Stroessner dictatorship, which was in power at the time Roa Bastos was writing this novel. This perpetual cycle of dictatorship recalls what Raymond McNally and Radu Florescu state about the vampire's eternal return in *The Essential Dracula*: "Nothing begins, nothing ends. Nothing ever really dies; merely transforms itself into another form of existence. But it is a terrible kind of existence."[4] Just as vampires return, dictatorships reappear; when it seems that one regime had been ousted, a new one emerges in its place.

Roa Bastos summons the underworld to express the abuses suffered under the Paraguayan dictatorship by bestowing vampiric qualities on *El Supremo*, who became the first leader of Paraguay after the country won its independence from Spain. Like other notorious dictators corrupted by power, he proclaimed himself "Perpetual Dictator of the Republic of Paraguay" and remained in power until his death. In the novel, Roa Bastos amalgamates historical, fictional, and mythological characters to devise his own extraordinary literary figure. Upon careful study, a meaningful connection between the historical character and the image of the vampire as articulated in the Gothic emerges, thereby opening the text to other possibilities of interpretation. Because the Gothic world of vampires and doppelgängers is obscure in the novel, it is imperative to highlight the most significant instances that bear an implicit relationship with the Gothic and, specifically, with Stoker's *Dracula*, thus revealing the way the author draws from various sources to create his own mythic entity.

Anachronistic Historical Fiction

The Gothic literary tradition, as mentioned in the introduction, is typified by the presence of evil characters, mysterious settings, and the supernatural, all of which serve to defy reason and logic—inciting the questioning of reality itself. Most important, it aims to elicit an emotive response, mainly fear, in the reader. The Gothic is also fixated on representations of the past, especially premodern ones. In a certain sense, the Gothic is tangentially similar to historical novels given that they narrate events from former times; however, they are different in the way that Gothic writers privilege the illusion of the past over historical accuracy. The setting in bygone times underscores what critic Jerrold Hogle remarks about the historical ambiguity found in the Gothic, which frequently projects modern concerns onto a deliberately vague and fictionalized past.[5] This prevalent anachronistic approach to the past is different from the aims of a traditional historical novel. For example, in the nineteenth century, Sir Walter Scott, who is most often associated with this genre of literature, introduced fictitious characters into made-up plots, yet the writing was characterized by and admired for its chronological preciseness and accurate historical depictions.

Thus, the many anachronisms found in the Gothic could explain why this literary genre has been criticized for its historical inaccuracy. Richard Albright, in his article "No Time Like the Present," emphasizes the anachronisms found in Gothic literature; citing Terry Castle's notes in *The Mysteries of Udolpho* (1794), he describes how Ann Radcliffe uses vague historical markers and temporally incongruous objects. For example, the characters drink coffee and use forks a century before those items were introduced to Europe.[6] That is, the authors were interested in creating narratives that could enhance feelings of dread and wonder, whereby historical trueness became secondary. Roa Bastos produces a similarly incongruous world through his purposeful misplacement of events, creating a mythic and obfuscated past. Moreover, readers familiar with the nation's history would likely become unsettled by the obvious and purposeful "errors," thus provoking more questions as to the reasons behind Roa Bastos's time-manipulating literary strategy.

The events depicted in Gothic novels are not only anachronistic, at times; the characters themselves often exist out of sequence as well. Entities belonging to another epoch reappear into the present, obscuring chronology. Oftentimes the supernatural characters found in the Gothic transgress the linear bounds of time, such as in "The Vampyre" (1819) by John Polidori, *Dracula* (1897) by Bram Stoker, and *Interview with the Vampire* (1976) by Anne Rice. These vampires, who seem ageless, emerge from ancient times and continue to live in the present. Whereas birth, aging, and death are indicators of a mortal's life, the vampire's eternal youth and revenant status break with what is understood to be a usual lifespan. The vampires might have had one physical death or many feigned deaths and just as many returns. Thus, their perpetual reappearances in the past, present, and future muddle markers that situate one event in relation to another. That is to say, through their many possible incarnations, vampires exist without relation to time and, in a sense, become atemporal. This ability to exist beyond the bounds of time also characterizes the dictatorial figure, who, when overthrown, is often replaced by a newer, and sometimes more malicious, ruler or regime—the same creature in a different body, which echoes Paraguay's history, a country that had experienced a series of dictatorial rulers since its independence.

Roa Bastos's novel *Yo el supremo* is steeped in the anachronistic and includes characters that transcend time, which is similar to the Gothic approach to historicity and chronology. This temporal dissonance is found in Roa Bastos's novel at the level of historical facts and at the level of language, as the author himself states: "Como no pretendía elaborar una narración histórica o biografía situada y fechada cronológicamente, comencé anulando las coordenadas de tiempo y espacio en busca de una dimensión intemporal o, mejor dicho, atemporal"[7] (Since my aim was not to elaborate a historical or biographical narration situated and dated chronologically, I began to erase coordinates of time and space in search of a timeless dimension, or, better said, an atemporal one).

As this quote suggests, Roa Bastos creates a new way of representing historical writing to frame Dr. Francia and Paraguay. Instead of reconstructing a past that mimics historical fiction or nonfiction, in which the placement of the events in chronological order is usual and expected, he opted to rewrite the past in a genre of fiction in which causality and chronological time could be undermined. He also stated that, through this fictional world, he wanted to recapture mythic images from the distant past and bring them to the present, which is similar to the way he presents El Supremo, a persona who can transcend time to exist in the contemporary. Such examples emphasize how Roa Bastos's approach to historical representations bears an implicit relationship with what Gothic writers have often done. That is, their works often feature characters from a previous time period that continue to exist in the present, which can also be said about the reemergence of dictatorships throughout history that behave like virtual revenants—bodies that return from the dead.

Roa Bastos's novel is also an implicit critique of realism and the reality that historical writing intends to tell. *Yo el supremo*—narrated in a fragmented way—represents a piecing together of past events as inspired by various historical sources. However, the incorporation of "real" historical documents in *Yo el supremo* does not result in a more "real" historic novel; rather, he creates a novel steeped in fantasy, which bears an uncanny resemblance to how Stoker's Dracula novel is pieced together. In particular, the reconstruction of history by assembling a collage of documents is similar to *Dracula*, in which the editor and one of the characters in the novel, Mina Murray (Jonathan Harker's fiancée), compile letters, diary notes, and sound recordings and then transfer these sources into typewritten documents, dated and organized in chronological order so as to give testament to the supernatural events that have transpired. Mina says the following about the documents: "How these papers have been placed in sequence will be made manifest in the reading of them. . . . There is throughout no statement of past things wherein memory may err, for all the records chosen are exactly contemporary, given from the standpoints and with the range of knowledge of those who made them."[8]

The novel is a piece of fiction that is attempting to feign truth. Correspondingly, in Roa Bastos's text, a fictitious editor or *compilador* has assembled a variety of documents in the construction of the novel: bookkeeping ledgers, newspaper clippings, diary notes, official archives, and passages from well-known history books. Supposedly, the editor of the novel has taken these fragments and has incorporated them into the text in an attempt to give unity and credibility to the events narrated. The fictitious editor even provides footnotes explaining certain inconsistencies in the history he is trying to reconstruct. Yet the editor's fictitious notes are confusing, and the insistence on historical authenticity only helps to add to the novel's illusory quality. So, while Mina's fictional notes aim to present a supernatural story as a factual one, the compilador's factual documents produce the opposite effect, causing the events to become even more unreal and befuddled, whereby the overwhelming amount of documents make the project unmanageable.

In the introduction to Roa Bastos's novel, Milagros Ezquerro mentions the paradoxical relationship between the historically based novel and the truth it pretends to represent: "Evidentemente, el propósito de Augusto Roa Bastos al desarrollar este 'interjuego' intertextual no es el de lograr una verosimilitud histórica, o una pintura fiel de la Dictadura Perpetua como se podría creer considerando la utilización del material histórico"[9] (Evidently, Augusto Roa Bastos's purpose of unfolding this intertextual "intergame" is not aimed at historical verisimilitude, or to paint the Perpetual Dictatorship faithfully as one would surmise, given the use of historical material). That is to say, in the novel Roa Bastos speaks of actual historical figures and even weaves in official and historical documents into his fiction, but he does not create a chronologically ordered realistic or historical novel, which a reader might expect from a novel immersed in facts. Roa Bastos instead disorganizes chronology and calls attention to the mythic and the supernatural as illustrated by El Supremo and other ominous characters mentioned in the text.

The process of writing history is a central theme in Roa Bastos's novel, but, as previously mentioned, the novel does not conform to the usual form of historical writing. Yet he exploits a particular genre of historically based novels, thereby emphasizing the frailty of historical truth, which can be manipulated by those who dictate them. In this way, the past is reimagined so that those in power can remain so, which is implied when El Supremo returns from the grave to dictate his own history. The concern with historical discourse and its misrepresentation is directly discussed in the novel by the main character, El Supremo. In it, the fictional character, who is himself dead and is in the process of dictating his memoirs to his scribe, Patiño, criticizes and disapproves of the various well-known historical works that have been written about Paraguay and his own dictatorship. He criticizes the nineteenth-century travel letters written by foreigners, such as John and William Parish Robertson's *Letters on Paraguay* (1838), Francia's *Reign of Terror* (1839), and Johann Rudolph Rengger and Marcelin Longchamp's *The Reign of Doctor*

Joseph Gaspard Roderick de Francia in Paraguay (1827). These texts forged exotic and terrorizing images of Paraguay in the nineteenth century for European readership that showed the dictator to be ruthless, cruel, and monstrous. These travel letters and historical accounts at times even suggest that Dr. Francia had supernatural powers. El Supremo also disapproves of later historical texts having to do with his regime after his death, as found in Julio César Chaves's *El supremo dictador: Biografía de José Gaspar de Francia* (1964). Dr. Francia died in 1840, so obviously, being published in 1964, it would have been impossible for him to have read Chaves's work, which is yet another example of the anachronisms in the text. Although Chaves's book was a revisionist historiography that tried to redeem aspects of Dr. Francia's governance, the protagonist still finds it deficient. El Supremo criticizes the conflicting versions of his life because, as the dictator argues, none of the representations are accurate.

By referring to various historical texts written about him over two centuries, the dictator also emphasizes the impossibility of narrating history when he states the following: "Ninguna historia puede ser contada. Ninguna historia que valga la pena ser contada. Mas el verdadero lenguaje no nació todavía"[10] (No story can be told. No story worth the telling. But true language hasn't yet been born).[11] Roa Bastos, through the main character, a vampiric dictator, underscores this impossibility of giving a totalizing view of historical events with which even El Supremo himself struggles to dictate and reconstruct. Moreover, the narrator emphasizes the way facts can be manipulated to create multiple versions of the same history and how figures can be malevolent or heroic depending on the selection of the events that are emphasized. The piecing together of disparate fragments also mirrors the ways regimes in power construct their image of self, who so often seek to legitimize their rise to power by the construction of "official" and "truthful" narratives that demonstrate their heroism or other self-important qualities and may even claim that their rise is predestined and an act of providence.

In *Yo el supremo*, Roa Bastos not only shares this interest in the remote past and the undoing of customary historical representation and chronology but he also incorporates other usual Gothic features such as supernatural events, mysterious settings, and the emblematic doppelgänger.

This duality embodies the two sides of the dictator: he is the patriotic man responsible for leading Paraguay to independence from Spain while protecting the country from foreign incursions; paradoxically, this founding father is also the power-hungry evildoer who crowns himself "Perpetual Dictator" and commits abhorrent crimes against his own citizens. In *Yo el supremo*, the split-self is repeatedly mentioned as the protagonist's defining quality. He speaks of himself as "Yo/Él" (I/Him), and at the same time he explicitly says that he is a double: "Yo he nacido de mí y Yo solo me he hecho Doble"[12] (I was born of myself and *I* alone have made myself Double).[13] The duplicity not only applies to his personality; it also applies to his state of being: he is both dead and alive. The split-self links him to the world of the living dead and brings him into the realm of monsters and doubles as fabricated by Gothic works such as *The Strange Case of Dr. Jekyll and Mr. Hyde* (1886) by Robert Louis Stevenson and *The Picture of Dorian Gray* (1890) by Oscar Wilde. These novels feature doppelgängers—protagonists who can be good and evil, human and monster, self and other. Vampires such as Dracula also embody the notions of the double because the vampires are the reincarnation of a former souled-self. In *Splitting the Difference*, Wendy Doniger corroborates the vampire's double quality when she states that they "double as themselves in the coffin and in the flesh."[14] Furthermore, vampires will create even more monster-doubles.

As the narration unfolds, it is apparent that El Supremo also has a literary double in Dracula. Both El Supremo and Dracula, have a voracious appetite for power that is unyielding, and this hunger is a metaphor for the political megalomania that defines dictators. Dracula, through his consumption of blood, not only receives eternal life to continue his reign of terror, he is also able to infect many and, in effect, double and exponentially perpetuate his offspring. This hunger instigates his move from Transylvania to London, where he has plans to conquer new territory and convert more victims. Similarly, El Supremo, who is also a living-dead being, represents another ravaging dictator who becomes more powerful through the bloodshed of many of his victims. The omniscient narrator, as if cursing the dictator to terrible death, describes how his buried body will decompose, states that he will suffer an insatiable hunger: "Terrible apetito. Tan terrible, que comerte el mundo, el universo entero, todavía sería poco para calmar tu hambre"[15] (A terrible appetite. So terrible that eating up the whole world, the entire universe, would still not be nearly enough to appease your hunger).[16] Is this hunger what initiates his return to dictate his own history? These words could also emphasize the devouring nature of power that characterizes many authoritarian regimes and its dictators, as is the case for El Supremo.

The dictator also has questionable relationships with unsavory characters, who seem to emerge from the Gothic underworld. The vampire frame is initially established in Roa Bastos's novel with the description of a mysterious man, Don Mateo Fleitas, who has an enigmatic and ominous relationship with El Supremo that is never clearly explicated in the novel. Patiño, the Supremo's scribe and servant, describes Fleitas and his home as follows: "Encerrado en su casa, como en un calabozo, en la más total obscuridad, vive don Mateo Fleitas. Nadie lo ve durante el día. . . . Cuando la luna no sale, sale don Mateo. Envuelto en la capa de forro colorado que Su Excelencia le regaló"[17] (Don Mateo Fleitas lives shut up in his house, as in a dungeon, in utter darkness. Nobody sees him during the day. . . . When the moon doesn't come out, Don Mateo does. Enveloped in the cape with the red lining that Your Excellency gave him as a gift).[18]

Fleitas, who according to the footnotes in the novel lives to be 106 years old, keeps nocturnal hours similar to those of bats. He also dresses in the same characteristic cape as Count Dracula. The mysterious Fleitas has a hypnotic effect on Patiño when he first meets him. Patiño explains how he is suddenly transported to Fleitas's house, seemingly defying time and space, as described in the following: "Ni me di cuenta que habíamos entrado al rancho. . . . Apagó todas las velas menos el cabo más gastadito con esas uñas de kaguaré; las del pulgar y el índice sobre todo, Señor, ganchudas y filosas como una navaja"[19] (I didn't even realize we'd entered the hut. . . . He snuffed out all the candles except the stubbiest one with those nails of his of a hairy armadillo; the thumb and index one especially, Sire, as sharp and curved as knife blades).[20] Patiño's physical description of Fleitas is not only reminiscent of the vampire Nosferatu as depicted in films, but it also concurs with Stoker's description of Dracula as given by the main character, Jonathan Harker, on his encounter with the monster: "The nails were long and fine, and cut to a sharp point. As the Count leaned over me and his hands touched me, I could not repress a shudder."[21] Similarly, Patiño describes the eerie feeling provoked when Fleitas places his hand on his shoulder and he feels Fleitas's razor-sharp fingernails dig into the fringes of his poncho.[22] Being in the presence of this man in a confined and dark space frightens Patiño; he is also made more anxious when he discovers Fleitas's unusual hobby of raising bats, so often evoked as vampires' animal double, as illustrated in *Dracula*.

Fleitas has an unusual relationship with bats, often reminiscent of vampire literature, and tacitly links the dictator with the vampire folklore. Fleitas, a nocturnal man who lives in a dungeonlike home, has an ambiguous friendship with El Supremo. While the circumstances of their alliance are never clearly defined in the novel, it reveals that Fleitas has received a gift—a cape lined in red—from the dictator, and that Fleitas plans to reciprocate this gesture with his own mysterious and magical cloak.

Fleitas, who is dedicated to breeding bats, is weaving an enchanted blanket made of bat fur for El Supremo. According to Fleitas, who has spent ten years weaving this ominous blanket, the gift cannot only make El Supremo invisible but, most important, it can also protect and cure him, which is made clear when Fleitas states: "Este 6 de enero . . . yo mismo voy a ir a llevarle mi regalo porque me han contado que nuestro Karaí anda medio sin ropa y medio enfermo. Esta manta lo va a abrigar y lo va a curar"[23] (This January sixth . . . I'm going to bring him my gift myself because I've been told that our Karaí has almost no clothes and is quite ill. This blanket is going to keep him warm and cure him).[24] The cloak can hide him, heal him, and protect him, which could be understood as a sign of the allegiance El Supremo inspires in some of his subjects.

Through his magical blanket, Fleitas can also provide the ultimate protection and cure for the ultimate ailment—death. This is conveyed when Fleitas proclaims that his bats can heal El Supremo: "Pero dejando aparte la colcha que no es de discutir, yo malicio que uno de estos mis animalitos podría aliviar los males de Su Excelencia"[25] (But aside from the bedcover, which I won't even discuss, I suspect that one of these little creatures of mine might remedy His Excellency's ills).[26] The ambiguous friendship between Fleitas, who has all the indications of being a vampire, and El Supremo further links him to the vampire. Perhaps Fleitas has turned him into one through the healing power of his bats.

The bat's supernatural ability to heal is made more explicit when Fleitas relays an anecdote having to do with the miraculous recovery of a moribund Dominican friar who was bitten by a bat, known as *mpobi* in Guaraní, on his deathbed. The narrator says the following about the monk's recovery: "Lo encontraron vivo, alegre, casí güeno, leyendo su Breviario en la cama. Gracias al mpobí-médico el fraile volvió muy pronto a su natural"[27] (They found him alive, chipper, almost well, reading his breviary in his bed. Thanks to the medic mbopí, the friar was very soon his usual self again).[28] This episode that Patiño narrates is important because it describes how a bat bite allows victims to transcend death, which is a common belief in European folklore but not necessarily part of Guaraní beliefs. The relationship between Fleitas and El Supremo establishes the Gothic themes that are woven throughout the text. Most important, it indicates an alliance that El Supremo has with the vampire-like Fleitas.

Both Dracula and El Supremo also share an affinity for rats. Similar to the bat metaphor, rats in both of these novels simultaneously reveal the subhuman way the citizens are treated and the way they are transformed to be part of the dictator's army. The dictator displays cruelty against his detractors by imprisoning them in subterranean dungeons in complete darkness and experimenting with them. John Parish Robertson, a historian, who also doubles as a character in Roa Bastos's novel, describes the hair-raising sounds that result from the dictator's experiments: "Desde el exterior, posiblemente desde los patios o corrales traseros, comenzó a llegar el creciente rumor de unos chillidos como de roedores hambrientos . . . que venían de una cueva subterránea, por no decir de ultratumba"[29] (From the outside, perhaps from the enclosed yards or pens in the back, the sound of shrill squeals, as of hungry rodents, began to reach my ears . . . they seem to me to be coming from some subterranean cave, if not from beyond the grave).[30]

These macabre experiments are mentioned in fictitious footnotes in which the editor describes how El Supremo maintains a rat nursery. The fictitious editor explains that the dictator uses the knowledge gained from the rodents' behavior to control his citizens, as the following quote reveals: "Todo esto, digo, Rvdo. Padre, lleva a sospechar que el diabólico Dictador ensaya allí, es esta suerte de borrador en vivo, sus métodos de gobierno con los que está bestializando a nuestros paysanos"[31] (All this, I tell you Rev. Father, leads one to suspect that the diabolical Dictator tries out there, is that sort of rough draft in vivo, those methods of government of his through which he is bestializing our peasants).[32] The use of animal-related language is a metaphor for the Paraguayan population that is at the mercy of totalitarian regimes. This reference to *bestializando* emphasizes the underworld in association with the dictator and also refers to the cruelty that he applies to his citizens.

The power to rule over rats and other animals bears a resemblance to vampire beliefs because vampires can shape-shift into rats and other animals. The rat motif appears frequently in *Dracula*. On the one hand, the rats epitomize Dracula's victims, exemplified when Jonathan Harker mentions that he feels like a rat in Dracula's castle. On the other hand, they represent Dracula's subhuman army. The dominance of rats is made clear by the words of one of Dracula's demonic servants, Renfield: "Rats, rats, rats! Hundreds, thousands, millions of them, and every one a life. . . . I got up and looked out, and He raised his hands, and seemed to call out without using any words. A dark mass spread over the grass, coming on like the shape of a flame of fire. And then He moved the mist to the right and left, and I could see that there were thousands of rats with their eyes blazing red, like His only smaller."[33]

Dracula's army is analogous to Dr. Francia's manipulation of his own "subjects" and supporters. Clearly, the rat metaphor is significant in both these novels given that the rats are compared to citizens, who can be controlled and manipulated to serve. These references to fear, bats, and rats, negative aesthetics that characterize the Gothic, in Roa Bastos's political allegory also help emphasize the way in which terror is one of the most salient powers perpetrated by dictatorial tyranny—fear is multiplied and relished by those in power.

Culturally Conditioned Vampires

Guaraní folklore and culture are an integral part of Paraguay, and several of the mythical elements in this novel correspond to this culture's worldview as interpreted by Roa Bastos, an expert in Guaraní culture. Critics, such as Rubén Bareiro Saguier and Sibylle Fischer, have made abundant contributions connecting the Guaraní mythic elements and language in *Yo el supremo*. Nevertheless, Roa Bastos goes beyond the direct Guaraní boundaries and local folklore by incorporating vampiric features usually associated with the Gothic. Roa Bastos not only draws from historical sources but he also incorporates indigenous beliefs, local folktales, and European literary features for his own aims: to critique the continued resurrection of authoritarian figures, who in turn bury free and democratic societies. The amalgamation of historical sources and local and transatlantic traditions is similar to Bram Stoker's work, reflective of the coalescing of various traditions. As mentioned in chapter 1, Stoker, in creating his quintessential vampire, was not only informed by European and eastern European folklore, but he also drew from American legends, specifically mentioning the American vampire-bat species.

Stoker dedicated a great amount of time to investigating sources in the creation of his most important work. He consulted historical documents, reviewed fifteenth-century maps, and learned about Romanian superstitions, among many other sources.[34] This detailed research led to the creation of his monster, which was partially modeled after the autocrat Dracul, the prince of south Romania, who became infamous in history as a result of his bloody and horrifying war tactics against Turkish invaders. His severity earned him the name of Vlad Tepes (Vlad the Impaler), which alludes to the many impalings that he ordered after torturing his victims.

Vlad Tepes is a contradictory historical figure. On the one hand, he was a fierce protector of his kingdom against invaders, which later elevated him to hero status by some. This hero status was celebrated centuries later by Romanian dictator Nicolae Ceaușescu, who proclaimed Vlad Tepes a national hero and commemorated the five-hundredth anniversary of his birth in 1976 by producing a special postage stamp in his honor.[35] On the other hand, his pleasurable indulgence in torture and violence, as described in history books, also makes him a legendary monster. McNally and Florescu emphasize the contradictory duality of Vlad Tepes: He was a psychopath, torturer, and inquisitor, and also a modern statesman who justified his actions for the benefit of the state.[36] This historical and monstrous historical figure inspired the fictional Dracula. More specifically, the fictional Count Dracula shares the aristocratic lineage associated with this prince of Romania, as well as the desire for territorial expansionism. As mentioned previously, Dracula buys property and moves to London to expand his terror beyond the Transylvanian border. Thus, Stoker's fictitious character is a hybrid creature derived from a historical figure, Dracul, as well as from popular vampire folklore.

Stoker's cultural and historical tapestry is similar to the crafting of *Yo el supremo* and its message about revenant authoritarian figures—metaphoric vampires. In reference to his leadership, El Supremo displays cruelty against his detractors by imprisoning them in subterranean dungeons in complete darkness under grotesque circumstances. El Supremo's methods of punishment recall some of those used by Vlad Tepes; both seem to have had a predilection for spearing their enemies in public places as a form of dissuasion. In *Yo el supremo*, the dictator annihilates five thousand Payaguá Indians and then has their bodies impaled and displayed en bloody masse: "Un malón como de cinco mil de éstos fue reprimido a fines de 1816. Todos fueron lanceados y colocadas sus cabezas sobre picas a cincuenta varas unas de otras formaron un cordón escarmentador a lo largo de muchas leguas de frontera"[37] (A surprise attack by some five thousand of these latter was successfully fended off at the end of 1816. They were all run through with lances and their heads, placed on pikes fifty yards distant from each other, formed an exemplary cordon stretching across many leagues of the invaded frontier region).[38] The Payaguá Indians were victims of an extermination campaign because they were hostile warriors and considered to be a threat to the nation. Their extermination by the nation's leader underscores the violence an authoritarian regime will undertake to construct an image of a nation that clearly delineates the citizens who are deemed to belong, while singling out those who must be forced into extinction.

As mentioned previously, Dracul, the historical figure who was considered a hero by some of his citizens and a vile despot by others, is comparable to El Supremo. His cruelty is in disharmony with his political engagement and national pride, which he demonstrates by being the most fervent protector against foreigners and foreign invasion, such as by the Triple Alliance (Brazil, Argentina, and Uruguay). The paradox is evident in the case of the historical figure Dr. Francia, who in many early history books was portrayed as a despot, but in subsequent revisionist narratives pertaining to his administration he was credited with creating an egalitarian society and economic stability that was subsequently lost after the invasion by the Triple Alliance in 1865. The narrator situates El Supremo within the time period of the war with the Triple Alliance, but it is important to note that this historical battle does not coincide with Dr. Francia's actual reign, which ended with his death in 1840. This again recalls the prevalent anachronisms in Roa Bastos's texts, which are similar to Gothic novels' general disregard for historical preciseness. Clearly, Roa Bastos was making deliberate rhetorical choices that also reveals how this fictional dictator transcends time.

As the novel progresses, more instances of El Supremo's supernatural powers emerge that link him to Dracula. Therefore, it is important to highlight the various elements found in vampire folklore as used by Stoker in order to establish the connection with El Supremo. McNally and Florescu in their book *The Essential Dracula* summarize the most salient features associated with the vampire. Below are the most relevant ones that also describe some of El Supremo's powers: "Count Dracula never eats nor drinks. He possesses enormous strength, he can see in the dark and he can become large or small. . . . He goes through the fog by instinct. . . . Count Dracula can control wolves and rats. Painters cannot paint him; his likeness is always of someone else. . . . He cannot be photographed; photos come out bluish or like the image of a skeleton."[39] Roa Bastos evokes many of these same characteristics in his creation of the vampire-inspired villain, as shown in the next few examples. However, the most important characteristic they share is the duality that defies natural laws—that is, of being both alive and dead.

These characters, who are both living-dead entities, have an unusual relationship with mirrors, which can both expose and create vampires. According to folklore, as described by McNally and Florescu, vampires do not have a soul, and because the mirror is the reflection of the soul, their image cannot be reproduced. Mirrors reveal vampires in their absent reflection, yet mirrors also produce vampires, which is why, in many cultures, mirrors are covered in the presence of a corpse. McNally and Florescu state the following: "According to Orthodox Christian belief, the soul does not leave the body to enter the world until forty days after the body is laid in the grave. . . . If the dead body is reflected in a mirror, the reflection helps the spirit leave the body and becomes a vampire."[40] The aforementioned description of the vampire's relation with mirrors becomes important when the narrator recalls the dictator's funeral ceremony, in which El Supremo's corpse is infinitely reflected, emphasizing the ubiquitous quality of dictators and the way their power can be duplicated, expansive, and far-reaching.

During the ceremony, El Supremo's dead body is reflected in a mirror, which initiates him into the sinister world of the living dead. The event surrounding the wake before his final burial is described as follows:

El día 19 se celebraron las honras fúnebres. Se levantó un cúmulo de tres cuerpos revestidos de espejos. . . . Estaba el cúmulo iluminado con 84 candelas, una por cada año de vida del Supremo Dictador. Muchos, por no decir todos, notaron su aparición entre los reflejos que se multiplicaban sin término a semejanza de su infinita protección paternal.[41]

[On the nineteenth the funeral rites were held. A cumulus three cuerpos high, adorned with mirrors, was erected. . . . The cumulus was illuminated with eighty-four candles, one for each year of the Supreme Dictator's life. Many persons—if not all—noted his apparition amid the endlessly multiplied reflections, the very image and likeness of his infinite paternal protection.][42]

As the quotation suggests, the body of the dictator is reflected endlessly, and many witnessed the apparition of the dictator, which, of course, would condemn his soul.

Just as mirrors have the power to create vampires, they also have to power to reveal them. According to vampire lore, once a body has become a vampire, because he has become soulless, his image can no longer be reflected. If an image is reflected, it is usually that of a skeleton. This inability to see their bodies reflected appears in a passage when the dictator asks Patiño to face the mirror to describe what he sees:

¿Qué ves en ese espejo? Nada de particular, Excelencia. Fíjate bien. Bueno, Señor, si he de decirle lo que veo, lo mismo de siempre. El retrato de Napoleón a la izquierda. ¿Qué más? El retrato de su compadre Franklin a la derecha. ¿Qué más? La mesa llena de papeles. La punta recortada del aerolito con el candelario encima. ¿No ves mi cara? No, Señor; únicamente la caravela . . . digo la calavera. . . . Vuélvete. Mírame, Levanta la cabeza, levanta eso ojos rastreros. ¿No sabrás alguna vez mirar de frente?[43]

[What do you see in the mirror? Nothing in particular, Excellency. Take a good look. Well, Sire, if I must tell you what I see, the same thing as always. The portrait of Señor Napoleon on the left. What else? The portrait of your compadre Franklin on the right. What else? The table full of papers. What else? The clipped-off tip of the aerolith with the candle-stick on top. Don't you see my face? No Sire; only the debt's head. What debt's head? I mean the death's head that Your Excellency has always had on the table underneath the piece of red flannel. Turn around. Look at me. Raise your head, raise those creeping eyes. When are you going to learn to look at what's right before your eyes?][44]

As described in this quotation, the dictator's figure does not appear in the mirror even though the dictator and Patiño were sharing the same visual space. Patiño can see the skull in the mirror, but not El Supremo's reflection. This anomaly could be explained through vampire superstitions because it is believed that the apparition of a skeleton in a mirror can occur in the presence of a vampire—the body is synonymous with the shadowy death that they represent. This appearance of a skeleton could also be interpreted as the deaths that many suffered in Paraguay under the dictatorship of Dr. Francia. Most suggestively, there is a picture of Napoleon, who, similar to Napoleon III, his nephew, were at times portrayed as vampiric entities.[45] In Paul Féval's novel, *La vampire* (1865), Napoleon Bonaparte "owes his success and survival to a predatory vampire."[46] Thus Roa Bastos's intentional mentioning of him calls to mind the ravaging hunger for power that characterizes authoritarian leaders.

Dictators do not see themselves for what they are, nor do they allow themselves to be examined or scrutinized. And dictators' disassociation with reality perpetuates fantasies of self, which is exemplified when El Supremo complains that none of the images that have been painted of him have really managed to represent him truly; in fact, he hardly recognizes himself: "Los que se ocuparon del aspecto exterior de mi persona para denigrarme o ensalzarme, no han logrado coincidir en la descripción de mi vestimenta. Menos aún en la de mis rasgos físicos"[47] [Those who occupied themselves with the outward appearance of my person in order to revile me or exalt me never managed to agree on the description of my attire. Less still on that of my physical appearance].[48] He also criticizes the painting that Englishman Don Juan Robertson made of him: "Por esto te mandé quemar el mamarracho pintado por el inglés en que me hizo aparecer bajo extrañ imagen, mezcla confusa de mono y niña mal humorada, chupando la inmensa bombilla de un mate, que nada tenía de mate Paraguayo (That's why I ordered you to burn the grotesque portrait painted by the Englishman in which he showed me in a very strange guise, a confused mixture of a monkey and a sulky girl, sucking on the immense sipper of a maté [sic] vessel that wasn't at all Paraguayan).[49] In a similar fashion, he refers to all the paintings of him with disapproval, whether painted by foreigners or local artists, claiming that they never reflect him truly. This inability to capture his image is directly related to the phenomenon in vampire folklore; however, it also reifies the challenging endeavor that writers have to truly represent history because these depictions are always somehow lacking, somehow inaccurate, and may even be false representations. Similar to El Supremo and the vampire image, what is reflected in paintings is always of something else.

There are many mysterious instances woven throughout the novel that link El Supremo to the vampire figure—in particular, when the novel mentions that the historical figure's remains were inexplicably exhumed from the grave and never recovered. The removal of remains from or the disruption of a gravesite is especially suggestive because, according to popular folklore, this points to the possibility that the corpse has turned into a vampire. Furthermore, in the fictional appendix of the novel, titled "Migración de los restos de El Supremo"[50] (Migration of the Remains of El Supremo),[51] the narrator describes the unusual circumstances surrounding his bodily remains. An eerie incident involving the apparition of a vampirelike character next to the tomb of El Supremo further provokes the mysterious association with Dracula. The narrator says, "De allí se desprendió envuelto en su capa y un inmenso chambergo, tal un inmenso murciélago en forma humana"[52] (From there he flew forth to meet him, enveloped in his cape and an immense broad-brimmed hat, like a giant bat in human form).[53] It is unclear why the character emerges in the form of a vampire, but this juxtaposition of a caped, batlike human next to the grave of El Supremo certainly suggests a vampiric imagery subtlety woven throughout the novel.

Van Helsing, a vampire hunter in Stoker's novel, states the following when he speaks of the undead, which is relevant to this discussion: "When they become such, there comes with the change, the curse of immortality; they cannot die, but most go on age after age adding new victims and multiplying the evils of the world; for all that die from the preying of the Un-Dead become themselves Un-Dead, and prey on their kind."[54] As Van Helsing suggests, vampires prey on their own kind while expanding their power and territory, which mimics vampires' behavior but also describes dictators. This plague of authoritarian characters existed long before Dr. Francia and did so after him: Caligula, Vlad Tepes, Hitler, Stalin, Stroessner, Videla, and Pinochet, among many others. These dictators, so often characterized as madmen, justify the bloodshed for the benefit of the state, but in effect they silence many through imprisonment, torture, and death. In the material world dictators create Gothic spaces characterized by terror, horror, torture, and bloodshed.

Dr. Francia is one metaphoric vampire in the long genealogy of monsters, and this lineage does not end with his death. The power is transformed to another place and another time, making the dictator figure a timeless revenant. As Roa Bastos states, *Yo el supremo* is the probing of evil, and the Gothic tradition certainly plays a role in the articulation of his monster. Specifically, Dracula emerges from the pages of the novel to underscore the oppressive and infectious power of the dictatorships that have persisted not only in Paraguay but also anywhere in the world and throughout history. The interplay of mutual and multiple reflections mirrors many images in which Dracul, Vlad Tepes, El Supremo, and Dr. Francia begin to collapse into one another, and it becomes difficult to distinguish the characters that belong to fiction and those that belong to history. The monsters and dictators converge into one atemporal figure that embodies the evils that seized Paraguay during almost two centuries and that would, unfortunately, also affect other countries in Latin America.

Vlad's Summer Holiday in Mexico

The novel discussed in the previous section features Gothic imagery and an implicit and hidden vampire. However, Carlos Fuentes, in his short novel *Vlad*, does not just tacitly allude to Dracula; he virtually resurrects Dracula and brings him to Mexico City. Fuentes appropriates Gothic features in his work for his own aims, and one such aim is that of critiquing contemporary Mexican society and politics. *Vlad* first appeared in the short-story collection *Inquieta compañía* (2004) and was later reprinted as a short novel in 2010, which was then translated into English and published in 2012. The back cover of the novel succinctly underscores one of the novel's themes: "More than a postmodern riff on 'the vampire craze,' *Vlad* is also an anatomy of the Mexican bourgeoisie, as well as our culture's ways of dealing with death." Yet this novel also addresses gloomy forces that are threatening the nation. As the title suggests, *Vlad* refers to the historical Romanian authoritarian figure Vlad Tepes, or Vlad the Impaler, one of the models upon which Stoker's Transylvanian Count Dracula was fashioned. In no uncertain terms, Fuentes's novel doubles and transforms previous literary characters as found in Gothic texts and *Dracula* specifically.[55] Similar to Roa Bastos, Fuentes evokes the vampiric figure to articulate anxieties associated with contemporary Mexican culture, while concurrently alluding to mythic and historical figures of the past that have been foundational in the forging of national identity.

In *Vlad*, a young, middle-class couple, Asunción and Yves Navarro, are mourning the death of their young son, Didier, whose body was never recovered after the boy was pulled into the ocean by a riptide in Acapulco. Asunción deeply laments the drowning death of her son and longs to search for her lost child's body at all costs; however, the father decides to abandon the search and accept his son's death. He explicitly says to Asunción, "Yo pedí serenidad, resignación y ofendí a mi mujer cuando le dije: No lo quiero volver a ver. Quiero recordarlo como era"[56] ("I don't want to see him again," I begged, to Asuncion's deep offense, "I want to remember him the way he was").[57] After this, they never speak of the boy's corpse again. Yet Yves's harsh words and the absence of the dead body—so necessary in the mourning process—creates distance between them, leaving their relationship vulnerable to estrangement and infidelity.

After the death of their son, they focus on their surviving ten-year-old daughter, Magdalena, and appear to have regained some sort of normalcy in their daily routines. Yet Asunción's hidden, turbulent feelings will seemingly invite the monster to cross their threshold, luring them into his terrain of terror. Vlad singles them out specifically because he wants a playmate for his precocious ten-year-old daughter Minea, and chooses Magdalena because she bears an uncanny resemblance to Minea. He also picks the Navarro family because he wants Magdalena as his vampire wife so that he can reach his ultimate goal and overrun the country.

Following a plotline similar to that found in the novel *Dracula*, Yves (like Jonathan Harker in *Dracula*) is in charge of finalizing a real estate transaction that will allow the count to move from the Balkans to a cosmopolitan place; in this case, instead of relocating to London, the count will relocate to Mexico City. He desires to leave his homeland because he has exhausted its resources, and he is looking for more victims. Fuentes's Count Vlad Radu eventually arrives in Mexico with, Minea, to establish roots in his newly adopted city. However, things are not quite as they appear. Readers later discover that Count Radu[58] is really Vlad the Impaler and that Minea is not ten but rather centuries old. Most surprisingly, the innocent-looking Minea is also the original monster that initiated Vlad into the vampire world sometime in the fifteenth century after having rescued him from a grave where he was buried alive.

Religious and Female Transgressions

Vlad, similar to Dracula and other vampires, becomes an interloper and outsider who transgresses boundaries. Vlad threatens the nation. As mentioned in chapter 1, William Hughes describes how the vampire's "practices constitute an intervention into the integrity of race and nation or an invasion to the sanctity of home and family."[59] Vlad invades and destroys family and home; just as he has destroyed one home, he will continue with others and ultimately infect the entire country. One way that Vlad intervenes in the home and nation is by undermining edifying national symbols having to do with the nation's religious figures, especially as they relate to women. He corrupts the normative notions of the family and unveils the underbelly of human sexuality that in many ways contests the values of the Catholic Church, which represents another foundational institution in the imagining of Mexican identity.

Fuentes evokes a devil-like entity, Vlad, a vampire, who is the most blasphemous of creatures when cast within Catholic religious tradition. More specifically, the vampire defies death, resurrecting in Christ-like fashion; however, he is not a symbol of salvation but rather an agent of damnation. The vampire is also soulless and therefore a godless body. In other words, the body is preserved to partake in erotic nocturnal pleasure and murder, while the soul is nonexistent. The vampire figure takes the blood of its victims, bringing perdition, which represents the opposite of Christ, whose blood is transmuted and consumed for the soul's salvation, according to Catholic ideology.

Vlad's duplicitous deeds will be carried out with the help of women, who are represented as both long-suffering mothers and treacherous women in the novel. In many passages, Fuentes describes the way that the Navarros, a bourgeoisie family, behave in a manner befitting their social class, especially as seen in the female character Asunción. In the Mexican context, women's behavior, according to religious dogma, ought to be modeled after the Virgin Mary: chaste, modest, virtuous women who are guardians of the family. Susan Migden Socolow's work on women in colonial Latin America points out that women were believed to have no control of their sexuality and had to remain confined in some sort of interior space or building and were expected to live an "honest and sheltered life."[60] The ideas that were established in colonial times are still prevalent even in contemporary culture, which Fuentes ostensibly addresses in the novel.

The family appears outwardly to live a typical and happy middle-class life in Mexico City. Yves—who is characterized as naïve and oblivious to the obvious threats—imagines that he has a stable relationship with his wife in spite of their tragic loss. She tries to perform the role of dutiful wife, but her secret desires erupt, propelling her to follow another man. Asunción confesses to Yves that she will run away with Vlad and coldly states, "Tu amor repetitivo me cansa, me aburre tu fidelidad, llevo años incubando mi receptividad hacia Vladimiro, sin saberlo"[61] (Your repetitious love is tiresome; your faithfulness, a bore. I've spent years preparing myself for Vladimiro, without knowing it).[62] Yves misunderstands the family dynamics and Asunción's superficial behavior, not realizing that her true desires would be fulfilled elsewhere.

Asunción is responsible for negotiating with Vlad regarding Magdalena's introduction to the vampire world. Vlad offers eternal life to the couple's ten-year-old daughter by promising to convert her to a vampire. Vlad will not only turn Magdalena into a monster like himself; he will also take Asunción with him. In so doing, he will have both the mother and daughter as lovers, yet another example of the ways in which vampires transgress notions of the family.

Asunción's pact with the devil-like Vlad is a blasphemous choice when cast in a Catholic setting, especially considering the origin of Asunción's name, the Assumption of Mary. On the Feast of Assumption, a holiday specifically mentioned in the novel, believers celebrate the miraculous ascension of the Virgin Mary's body into the heavens. Fuentes undermines this very holy imagery because Asunción has made a pact with the count and has secured a more sinister type of eternal life for herself and her daughter. Most pointedly, at the end of the novel, bats fly out of a Gothic-esque house and, as their bodies cross the sky, Yves imagines that those celestial bodies are Vlad accompanied by his wife and daughter, Asunción and Magdalena. In this final passage, Fuentes transposes the image of the Virgin Mary in the heavens with images of flying bats, whereby a most holy moment and symbol is transgressed and made profane.

National Allegory through the Female Body

Fuentes's confers on Asunción negative qualities involving national betrayal and murderess mothers that are drawn from both colonial and pre-Columbian myths. In effect, he evokes mythic and polemic female characters; specifically, he calls upon the Mexican female trinity, La Virgen de Guadalupe, La Malinche, and La Llorona, to speak to the nation's past history of conquest, betrayal, independence, invasion, and human sacrifice. Most important, the nation, allegorically represented through the female body, has been seduced and occupied by more portentous foreign forces.

Asunción, as her name suggests, is on the surface similar to Mexico's Madonna, and her role is supposed to be that of protector of the family. As such, it would be expected that she would have restored order in the supernatural world by casting out vampires from the home and, metaphorically, from Mexico. Yet she is not represented as a national heroine who vanquishes the foreign other that is threatening the sanctity of home and nation; rather, she willingly betrays and surrenders her family to Vlad. The Virgin Mary in the Mexican context is reincarnated as La Virgen de Guadalupe and receives the most fervent veneration. She is the synthesis of the Indian goddess and the Virgin Mary, and since Mexican independence she has been a symbol of national identity. William Taylor asserts that after her miraculous apparition in 1531, she became Mexico's new mother and restorer of "order in the supernatural world as well as in the here and now"[63]—and Asunción represents a perversion of an important national symbol.

While devoted and chaste women might remind readers of one of Mexico's archetypes, La Virgen de Guadalupe, traitorous women in the Mexican context also evoke another well-known symbolic entity, La Malinche. La Malinche, also known as Malintzin and Doña Marina, was Hernán Cortés's interpreter, guide, and mistress. She played an important role in the conquest of the Aztec empire in the sixteenth century and has since been considered the archetypal traitor and someone without honor. Yet she also bore Cortes's son, a mestizo child of both Indian and Spanish ancestry, thus concurrently becoming the symbolic mother of the Mexican nation. As such, La Malinche is characterized as both mother and traitor, which has since become a common literary trope often evoked by writers; Octavio Paz's essay "El laberinto de la soledad" (The Labyrinth of Solitude) is an emblematic example of the discourse involving La Malinche and her influence in the construction of Mexican identity.[64] Fuentes returns to the traditional national mother paradigm, in which women are framed within this Guadalupe-Malinche dichotomy. Thus Asunción is portrayed as both a suffering mother and a duplicitous figure who has made an unsavory arrangement with an invading power. If Asunción—as an allegory for the nation—is the reincarnation of La Malinche, then she is aiding a foreigner, and Vlad has taken the place of Cortés in this latest literary articulation of subjugation.

Similar to the Guadalupe-Malinche paradigm, the Malinche-Llorona dichotomy also becomes important in the understanding of Asunción's character. Asunción, like La Llorona, is in many ways a weeping mother who is still mourning the death of her drowned son, Didier. La Llorona figures in popular folklore and oral tradition, and many versions of this mythic woman exist. Most often she is described as a young mother who has drowned her children. Burdened with remorse, her spirit wanders near rivers searching for them. Children are often warned against going out alone at night because La Llorona, who is a type of monster, might appear and abduct them.

Such devouring murderesses also reveal the tacit relationship that Asunción has not only with La Llorona but also with the pre-Columbian goddess Cihuacoátl. Luis Leal, in "The Malinche-Llorona Dichotomy: The Evolution of a Myth," argues that La Malinche was equated with La Llorona, but the latter is a character from pre-Hispanic times inspired by Mexican goddesses.[65] Depending upon the context, at times these goddesses are described as devouring mothers and as women who weep and desire to eat the hearts of men.[66] Asunción did not harm Didier, but she does offer her daughter and family to Vlad, which has sacrificial undertones. Because these female deities are associated with sacrificial rituals, Asunción might also be considered under the rubric of devouring mother, who sacrifices her own. Luis Leal states that "when La Malinche was identified with La Llorona, and therefore with Cihuacoátl and sacrifice, it was easy to present a negative image of her in history and literature."[67] The unjust quality of betrayal and devouring mother conferred on La Malinche is prevalent in national mythmaking, which Fuentes exploits in his articulation of Asunción.

Just as other writers have allegorized the nation through polarized female characters, Fuentes continues with this tradition to speak of other ominous forces that are penetrating the nation, both figuratively and literally—which recalls Octavio Paz's treatise on La Malinche in relation to the word *chingar*. She is the mother of the Mexican nation, but also one who was violated.

> ¿Quién es la Chingada? Ante todo, es la madre. No una madre de carne y hueso, sino una figura mítica. La Chingada es una de las representaciones mexicanas de la Maternidad, como la Llorona o la "sufrida madre mexicana" que festejamos el diez de mayo. La Chingada es la madre que ha sufrido, metafórica o realmente, la acción corrosiva e infamante implícita en el verbo que le da nombre. Vale la pena detenerse en el significado de esta voz.[68]

> [Who is the *Chingada*? Above all, she is the Mother. Not a Mother of flesh and blood but a mythical figure. The *Chingada* is one of the Mexican representations of Maternity, like *La Llorona* or the "long-suffering Mexican mother" we celebrate on the tenth of May. The *Chingada* is the mother who has suffered—metaphorically or actually—the corrosive and defaming action implicit in the verb that gives her her name. It would be worthwhile to examine that verb.][69]

By characterizing Asunción as both a traitorous and long-suffering mother, Fuentes seems to be saying, "Nos están chigando los chingones," or we are being violated, invaded, yet again, but by new, more modern entities.

Past Invasions

In *Vlad*, Fuentes revisits some of the common themes played out in his previous works, including references to cyclical history, the return of the repressed, and hauntings. Similar to Roa Bastos's *Yo el supremo*, Fuentes evokes the past to speak of the present. Thus, past historical invasions become important in understanding the author's articulation of the hostile forces that are threatening the nation in the present. In terms of history, Fuentes repeatedly mentions French language and culture. The main character, Yves, speaks French and his parents are from France. Their son is named Didier, a French name. Vlad and his henchman, Don

Eloy Zurinaga, studied together at the Sorbonne in Paris. The pervasive inclusion of francophone culture is purposeful. Perhaps he intends to remind readers that Mexico has had a complicated relationship with France—one of both admiration and loathing. Mexico has had its share of invasions instigated by France, including the Pastry War in 1838 and the Battle of Puebla in 1862. In 1864, Napoleon III commandeered the country and named Archduke Fernando Maximilian and his wife, Carlota of Belgium, emperor and empress of Mexico. Mexico was not only invaded militarily; it was also appropriated financially when many of the natural resources were in the hands of foreign investors, especially under the regime of Porfirio Díaz. In *Vlad*, the narrator mentions that one of the characters lives in an old mansion built during Díaz's administration. One of Díaz's aims was to modernize and "Frenchify" Mexico, which many citizens resisted, especially after the Mexican Revolution when nationalism flourished and foreign influence was shunned. Conceivably, Fuentes wants to remind readers that invasions have been part of Mexico's history as represented by multiple French invasions and foreign financial intervention in Mexico when Porfirio Díaz was in power. Fuentes also recalls the Spanish Conquest by alluding to La Malinche, symbolic mother of the Mexican people, and to La Virgen de Guadalupe, patron saint of independence and the protector of the nation. Yet, by recalling past incursions and betrayals, Fuentes is also alluding to another new and sinister presence in the nation.

New Vampiric Entities

In *Vlad*, the vampire crosses the threshold to invade, seduce, and destroy the family and home, yet this domestic space also allegorizes the nation, which is being threatened by not only old rivals such as France, but new and ominous forces as well. If a vampire can express anxieties about contemporary culture, as critics have already postulated, who are the powerful entities threatening the nation when Fuentes writes this story? Arguably, the novel could express the nation's crisis brought on by neoliberal policies that began soon after the North American Free Trade Agreement (NAFTA) was set in motion.[70] Fuentes has already used the Malinche trope to discuss the nation in his short story "Malitzin de las maquilas" (1995). Rolando Romero succinctly demonstrates the way

Malitzin allegorizes contemporary ills related to Mexico's neoliberal economy in a more globalized world that aims to create a fluid interchange of products between borders in order to create financial opportunities between nations.[71] Ironically, it has also created an increasingly fluid drug trade, leaving Mexico vulnerable to foreign drug lords, who are dumping even more drugs—such as pseudoephedrine from China, Russia, Germany, India, among other countries—that fuel the drug economy.[72]

In *Vlad*, Fuentes channels contemporary anxieties in response to the apparent hijacking of the country by narcotraffickers in cahoots with foreign dealers, who have caused the most unprecedented violence in Mexico since the Mexican Revolution (1910–1920). His novel specifically addresses Mexican politics and its weakness against foreign assault when the narrator describes how Vlad can easily maneuver in Mexico City. Vlad says the following: "¡Y en México, una ciudad de veinte millones de nuevas víctimas, como las llamaría usted! ¡Una ciudad sin seguridad policiaca! Viera usted los trabajos que pasé con Scotland Yard en Londres! . . . ¡Veinte millones de sabrosas morongas!"[73] (And she was in Mexico, a city with twenty million new—as you might call them—victims! A city without police protection! You wouldn't believe the trouble Scotland Yard put me through in London! . . . Twenty million delectable blood sausages!).[74] Clearly, Vlad is extremely excited to have a found a new territory to invade without restrictions, and this underscores Mexico's vulnerability to outside forces. The weakness of the police force that Vlad mentions plays out in very tangible ways in Mexican society. Ineffective controls have allowed for mass drug trafficking, unchecked gang violence, and the enrichment of the *Capos*, or drug lords, at the high cost of human lives. The violence endemic to Colombia earlier in the century has now migrated into Mexico, an international drug-trafficking hub from which drugs are sent mostly to the United States, one of the largest consumers of these drugs.[75] The country, government, and some of its citizens have unwittingly made an unfortunate pact and become intertwined with the vampiric drug lords, thus adding another chapter of extraordinary violence to the nation's history.

It could be argued that the drug culture has many affinities with the violence portrayed in vampire lore. The word *lord* suggests nobility and people of power with influence over other people. The drug lords, like vampires, seek new victims to seduce and infect. Thus, they have created a virtual army through "enforcer gangs" that help them maintain their stronghold. Indeed, the vampire imprints his victims with a bite; in a similar manner, drug lords and their gang members—their henchmen—also infect and possess their victims. The drug lord's need for red "blood" could metaphorically refer to the green dollar. As such, consumers exchange monies for the exhilarating feelings that only drugs can provide, becoming addicts and craving more, which is akin to the vampire's insatiable hunger.

Drug lords often expand their realm of power by controlling their subjects through fear, bloodshed, and even torture. They have intimidated and assassinated reporters, politicians, lawyers, and judges who have attempted to defy them, and the weak security has allowed cartels to continue their double-dealings with impunity. Recalling Van Helsing, "they cannot die, but most go on age after age adding new victims and multiplying the evils of the world";[76] similarly, the Capos behave like revenants, who, when ousted, are continually replaced with others. There is always someone ready to usurp the available niches.

As many have argued, the vampire has the ability to figuratively express concerns about one subject under the guise of something else. In the case of Fuentes's *Vlad*, the monsters expose the darker side of suppressed feelings as exemplified by Asunción. Fuentes also reminds readers of past invasions by making many references to historical events, which underscores concerns about vulnerabilities in national security, thereby suggesting that Mexico, *la patria*, might again be in the midst of another menacing subjugation fueled by foreign powers; other countries supply raw materials needed for drug making to Mexico, while the United States contributes by being its most singular and significant consumer. One of the unfortunate results of globalization has been that the citizens are now being devoured by the terrorizing drug culture that has befallen Mexico.

Vlad represents a rewriting and subversion of the novel *Dracula* whereby Fuentes plays with the well-known vampire trope to critique contemporary Mexican social order; however, Fuentes also subverts the mollifying endings found in many Gothic texts. Perhaps most significantly, while the vampire monster is killed in Stoker's work and Jonathan Harker's betrothed is saved, in *Vlad* there is no such conciliatory ending. The monster is not killed, and the women follow the vampire into a dark underworld. It is a rather bleak ending that offers little hope in terms of returning to some previous or imagined order. Most tragically, the drug crisis has gotten even worse since this novel's publication in 2010. Similar to Roa Bastos's novel, Fuentes's treatment of the past and present also forebodes a more cruel future.

CHAPTER 5

THE DOPPELGÄNGER

Split-Selves, Animal-Doubles, and Spectral Couples

The doubles reviewed in this book's previous chapters feature split-selves, spectral couples, animal-doubles, along with many forms of twoness that create tension in the stories, portend death, and often become the root of a character's demise. The expression of duality in Latin American fiction has a close relationship with the notion of the doppelgänger, which is usually associated with German Romanticism and is also a defining quality of Gothic and fantastic literature.[1] This final chapter analyzes how Latin American authors react to, rival, and/ or alter usual representations of the literary doubles as articulated in the fiction of the eighteenth and nineteenth centuries.[2] In particular, the texts discussed here include authors who transform notions of twoness by amalgamating them with regional folklore and Amerindian myths as illustrated in Alejo Carpentier's *El reino de este mundo* (1949) (The Kingdom of This World), Julio Cortázar's "Axolotl" (1952), and Carlos Fuentes's "Chac Mool" (1954) and *Aura* (1962). These authors created doubles whose earthly existence is represented as cyclical and one that does not necessarily articulate life and death as opposing binaries. They search beyond Western culture's more traditional religious conceptions of the life/death paradigm, drawing from Mesoamerican and other worldviews in which human existence becomes more mutable and cyclical—death can simultaneously signify rebirth, continuity, or transmutation rather than a definitive rupture with the earthly realm.

Carpentier transcends traditional Western artistic models and innovates his prose by taking from Haitian culture and African and Taíno mysticism.³ His novel demonstrates the way in which local folklore, history, and customs become sites of inquiry, thus contributing to a new theoretical and artistic tradition. In particular, his work undermines the literary animal-double's usual association with evil, as found in the Gothic, and instead he describes shape-shifting in positive terms. That is to say, he emancipates animal-doubles from their customary monstrous association and presents them as vehicles of transcendence, knowledge, and liberation. The passage described in more detail below represents a stark departure from the section described in chapter 3, in which Carpentier employs Gothic aesthetics to describe a horrific case of live burial and hauntings.

While Carpentier creates doubles with liberating qualities, Fuentes and Cortázar generate lurid ones by summoning pre-Columbian deities and customs. The characters are not who they pretend to be but are, rather, spectral duplications and reembodiments of previous historical, literary, and mythical figures; these uncanny revenants, virtual doppelgängers, demand sacrificial victims to secure immortality—an obvious reference to certain pre-Columbian rituals—thus altering the usual literary representations that feature split entities. Especially in "Chac Mool" and *Aura*, the doubles ask for small offerings and, eventually, a human life in order to live beyond the bounds of time, thus restaging Mesoamerican sacrificial ceremonies to the gods.

The first part of this final chapter examines the way doubles have been evoked in various Latin American texts as either ill-omened or liberating forces, while the latter part of this chapter more intently analyzes Fuentes's innovative doubles in *Aura*. His novel in particular presents several instances of copying and doubling illustrated by the characters and the *nouvelle*. That is to say, the characters behave as virtual doppelgängers, and the text itself echoes recognizable plots. In his essays and interviews, Fuentes openly describes the backgrounded texts he emulates, which include Gothic-inspired novels and films; even Gothic-like historiography. And through this constant conjuring of doubles and the repetition of certain themes, the author implicitly underscores that absolute novelty is an impossibility. His pervasive doubling of previous works of art into his own literary works suggests that he privileges duplications with variation, thus questioning absolute originality. In this sense, the relationship between duplicated texts and the authentic one corresponds to the relationship between the monster-double and human. Just as authentic bodies become annulled when confronted by their copy—their other—complete originality of the new text can be undermined when faced with its literary predecessors, which are discussed in more detail below. However, before describing the way certain consecrated authors, credited with transforming Latin American letters in the 1950s and 1960s, utilized and innovated doubles, a brief summary of the literary doppelgänger's most salient feature will provide a frame to guide the analysis.

The Literary Doppelgänger

The literary world of the doppelgänger embodies excess, mystery, contradictions, and the impossible. Doubles destabilize fantasies of stable subjectivity; they can represent the return of the repressed, the monstrous, or the Devil. Sigmund Freud, citing Otto Rank in his treatise on the uncanny, states that humans first created the double when they imagined an immortal soul. The invention of a second self was also a way to avoid the destruction of the ego by envisaging an eternal spirit; however, what promised immortality also "becomes the uncanny harbinger of death."[4] In literature, characters embroiled with doppelgängers do not usually secure immortality but rather its opposite. More often than not, when the uninvited other emerges, the protagonist attempts to destroy the menacing second-self in order to recover the former singular and more authentic one; however, protagonists realize that they cannot exist without their other, and the annihilation of the double almost always means the death of the host subject.

Characters might feel haunted by an interior self that is motioning or even forcing them to behave differently and perversely, or they might have an identical exterior and material *other* that is creating havoc in the character's formerly contained and manageable world, or, as René Girard succinctly states in *Violence and the Sacred*, "The subject watches monstrosity that takes shape within him and outside of him simultaneously."[5] The protagonist's double might have a similar name, a common birthday, or some other comparable feature that seems more than coincidental, as in the case of Edgar Allan Poe's "William Wilson" (1839).[6] A character may be uncannily identical to his *other*, or he can be diametrically different, physically or morally. In *The Picture of Dorian Gray*, the deceptive Dorian Gray appears youthful, handsome, and ageless, while his countenance in the painting, his virtual doppelgänger, continually transforms to reflect the opposite—a faithful portrait of his malevolence. At times, singular subjects metamorphose into another; Dr. Jekyll, a smart and reasonable man, transmutes into a more untamable beastly creature, similar to a lycanthrope.[7]

John Paul in *Siebenkäs* (1796) coined the term *Doppelgänger* to describe people who can see themselves.[8] And this mirrored other mysteriously becomes detached from the subject, thus creating a crisis and putting an end to uniqueness. In many cases, the characters feel persecuted and diminished by their other self or, as Andrew J. Webber in *The Doppelgänger: Double Visions in German Literature* succinctly states, "specular replications can halve/annul the identity it shapes."[9] More often than not, when the doppelgänger emerges, the protagonists become destabilized as they see their wholeness dislocated. Furthermore, this double is not simply a ghost or specter but a more substantive creature that aims to ruin and take over the host subject's domain. The interloper or double who breaches the material world "cannot simply be written off as a phantasm: it insists upon its place in the real."[10] That is to say, the other is often represented in tangible terms, an interloper who wants to usurp and overwhelm the host subject, and whose presence often signifies death for both of them.

Latin American examples in which the death of the other implies the death of the protagonist, and vice versa, include the Uruguayan writer Mario Benedetti's "El otro yo" (The Other Self), which appears in *La muerte y otras sorpresas* (1968) (Death and Other Surprises). In his story, a young man, Armando, lives with his other, who is described as refined, sensitive, intelligent, and poetic, while Armando is his polar opposite: he is ordinary, ill-mannered, and simple-minded. The narrator describes how he feels self-conscious and compelled to behave more properly when his more sophisticated second self is present. The melancholic double commits suicide, causing Armando to momentarily feel relief and free to behave authentically. Yet he soon realizes that his friends can no longer see him, suggesting that he himself no longer exists. In true doppelgänger fashion, the death of his other also implies the end of Armando.

Benedetti's story recalls the many film versions of *The Student of Prague*, partially based on Poe's "William Wilson," in which the character attempts to annihilate his malicious other by shooting him in the heart, but the central character quickly discovers that he has fatally shot himself. A similar plot unfolds in Horacio Quiroga's "El espectro," as described in chapter 1, in which the protagonist, Guillermo Grant, aims his handgun at an actor on the screen, his other self, not entirely grasping that he is actually pointing the firearm at his own temple when he pulls the trigger. Benedetti and Quiroga are examples of how authors might employ the double in a more characteristic way, whereby the death of one simultaneously brings about the death of the other.

A character's other might also be their opposite in terms of gender, suggesting that they are twinned souls; one cannot live without the other, as illustrated in the case of the modernista "La vampira" (1897) by Leopoldo Lugones, as discussed in chapter 1. In the story, the nameless female protagonist has a type of interior doppelgänger: her dead husband. Because he partially possesses her, she is unable to fully accept the attention of other suitors. In the story, an unsuspecting lover tries to woo the young widow, yet she, overtaken by her husband's anima, murders him. The female/male double will become relevant when analyzing *Aura*, in which the female character, Consuelo, is obsessed with bringing back her deceased husband, General Llorente, her second self.

Latin American literary works at times feature destructive others that iterate plots characteristic of the literary doubles found in classic Gothic and other fantastic texts. However, these authors also distort, undermine, and transform the usual articulations of the literary doppelgänger by combining them in Mesoamerican traditions associated with animal-doubles and human sacrifice. The hybridization of these texts speaks to a particular national identity—and one that is itself also a mixture: African, indigenous, and European. In other words, authors draw from the local folklore, regional myths, and pre-Columbian traditions, innovating and transcending the way literary doubles have usually been portrayed.

Animal-Doubles

The power to assume an animal body forms a part of creation stories, mythology, and popular folklore around the globe. Animal transmutations may include animal familiars, bush-souls, lycanthropes, nahuales (naguales), and shape-shifters, for example.[11] The book of Genesis suggests that Satan, who in the Bible is described as the ancient serpent and deceiver of the world, shape-shifted to tempt Eve.[12] Not surprisingly, animal-doubles many times signify the Devil and evil. They are the witch's ally, labeled as "familiars," usually a cat or rabbit that carries out unsavory deeds. Animal-doubles are a Gothic cliché, as seen in the most representative case of Bram Stoker's *Dracula*, whose vampire can transform into a bat, rat, or even a wolf (but only during a full moon), and in the werewolf literature of the nineteenth century.[13] Often, when authors endow their villains with metamorphic abilities that allow them to take an animal form, they create an even more beastly and visceral character.

Latin American authors at times combine pre-Columbian myths, indigenous religious beliefs, and the Gothic, as in the case of Froylán Turcios's *El vampiro* (1910), introduced in chapter 1, in which the malevolent priest is able to transform into a vampire bat to haunt and kill, thus representing the darker side of nahualismo. Depending on context, the nahual can be a benevolent animal companion, guardian, deity, or it can be associated with evil. A nahual is sometimes called upon to prevent evil from entering a community or may be summoned for astrological divination.[14] A person, usually a shaman, is able to transform into an animal, but deities also have the ability to assume animal forms.[15] In *Magic, Witchcraft, and Curing*, John Middleton describes the nahual as follows: "In broad and general terms, the kinds of meanings most frequently associated with nagual in ethnographic literature can be classed under two headings: the 'companion' or 'guardian' spirit and the 'transforming witch.'"[16] Authors might call upon the more positive and/or negative qualities associated with the nahual to create innovative split entities.

Julio Cortázar is often cited for featuring doubles in his stories, whose characters at times become transmuted into something entirely different, as in the case of "El hijo del vampiro" (1937), as discussed in chapter 1, in which the vampire Duggu Van impregnates his lover, Lady Vanda. During her pregnancy, her body transforms from the female body into a young male one. More specifically, she is reborn as her own son; hence, she is metamorphosed into a creature who is simultaneously mother and newly minted vampire-son. In "Axolotl," first published in 1952 and later appearing in *Final del juego* (1956) (End of the Game, and Other Stories), the author returns to the theme of metamorphoses and calls upon the nahual to create his story.

Cortázar invokes nahualismo but adds more foreboding Gothic traits, as illustrated in "Axolotl," in which a nameless character retrospectively narrates the way he has been converted into an animal and is virtually buried alive. The narrator, whose sanity is put into question from the start, initially states that he is an axolotl—a type of salamander found only in Mexico. The narrator then proceeds to describe the circumstances that brought about his animal transformation. However, the narrator's identity and state of mind become suspect. Is the reader witnessing the imaginings of an unstable and alienated person who believes that he has turned into an axolotl? Is the narrator the former human, who is now somehow trapped? Or is the narrator the axolotl in human form? This purposeful ambiguity, of course, reveals why this story has often been celebrated for its fantastic qualities; however, Gothic language also informs the story.

The axolotl already embodies notions associated with miraculous regeneration, doubling, and the shadowy aspects of the cosmos, which only adds to the mythic and awe-inspiring qualities of the axolotl that Cortázar weaves throughout the story. The axolotl has the incredible ability to regenerate its body parts, even sections of a damaged brain and spinal cord. The axolotl's ability to regrow its cells has fascinated research scientists, who hope that the axolotl's genetic features will contribute to developing treatments that may help amputees and people with brain injuries, for example.[17] The Aztecs were well aware of the axolotl's renewing power and used it as a food source and for its homeopathic healing properties. The axolotl is associated with the deity Xolotl, which is described as a deformed deity with doglike features who guides souls to the underworld. Eloise Quiñones Keber, in "Xolotl: Dogs, Death, and Deities in Aztec Myth," analyzes the many qualities associated with Xolotl and his multifaceted position in the Aztec pantheon. According to myth, the Xolotl can transform into other entities associated with twinned things. The Xolotl promises to offer himself up for sacrifice so that the sun could be given life; however, going back on his word, the deity attempts to flee by first transmogrifying into a two-stalked maize plant, a double agave plant, and finally into an axolotl.[18] The myth surrounding the Xolotl, a type of trickster, reveals how he can transcend the earthly realm and travel to the underworld; he can also transform into animate and inanimate entities, including the axolotl.

Cortázar utilizes animal transmutations inspired by the nahual, but he also turns nahualismo on its head by inverting the power dynamics between man and beast. In the story, the narrator describes the axolotls' mesmerizing effect on him when he first sets eyes on them in an aquarium in Paris. Mysteriously drawn to the axolotls, he visits them daily so that he can study them more closely. He feels a deep connection with the creatures, imagining that one axolotl in particular can read his thoughts and vice versa. All the same, this obsession leads to his demise; as he stares into the axolotl's eyes, beguiled, he magically becomes an axolotl, and conversely, the creature takes possession of his human body. Could this be the return of Xolotl? The story leaves the reader to interpret multiple possibilities, including that of animal transformations associated with the nahual.

However, the nahual's role in Cortázar's story is reversed. The man does not shape-shift to disguise himself or seek knowledge, as a shaman might do, but rather the animal has the power to transform into a human being by using an innocent character as his host. The person does not deliberately shape-shift into an animal, but rather the axolotl, the beast, has the power to vanquish human agency, leaving the host subject submerged, trapped, and voiceless—or, as the victim states, "buried alive" in an aquarium, his virtual prison. The narrator describes how he has become trapped in the animal body, while the axolotl is free to leave and take on the narrator's persona, describing his terrible fate in terms of live burial: "Sólo una cosa era extraña: seguir pensando como antes, saber. Darme cuenta de eso fue en el primer momento como el horror del enterrado vivo que despierta a su destino"[19] (Only one thing was strange: to go on thinking as usual, to know. To realize that was, for the first moment, like the horror of a man buried alive awaking to his fate).[20] The description of live burial—a frequent Gothic motif—is indicative of the oppressive atmosphere created in the text and also addresses the ways in which characters might feel trapped in their specific social environment or might sense dread because they cannot behave as their true selves.

Critics have already emphasized that the story expresses existential angst and/or might address anxieties with Peronismo authoritarianism—one of the reasons Cortázar was exiled in Paris.[21] However, the aspect of the story relevant to this discussion specifically is the manner in which Cortázar portrays doubles as portentous, and those mixed up with them usually end up dead or somehow transfigured in a terrible way, which corresponds to the way doubles are usually imagined as something negative. While particular authors like Cortázar might create ominous doubles, echoing pre-Columbian myths, other writers endow animal-doubles with more liberating qualities.

Liberating Doubles

In the passage from *El reino de este mundo* described in chapter 3, Carpentier illustrates a gruesome case of live burial informed by Gothic aesthetics; notwithstanding in the passage described here, he returns to and reaffirms concepts of the Marvelous Real to describe extraordinary events that transpired in Haiti during their transition from colony to sovereign state. He features two characters who can shape-shift; however, these figures are not presented as ominous but rather promising agents of change: animal-doubling can signify liberation, thus representing an appropriation and rupture with a literary tradition featuring doubles. In Carpentier's *El reino de este mundo*, he grounds animal-doubles in African *and* indigenous beliefs. His animal transformations embody more positive qualities associated with deities and shamans, in which transmutations can provide a safe haven and knowledge or serve as a path to emancipation.

Carpentier states that when he was researching sources for his novel he found that people in Haiti still believed in the transformative power of Mackandal, a hero whose defiance instigated a slave revolt that eventually led to other uprisings, culminating in the Haitian Revolution that brought about the end of slavery on the island. In the prologue, Carpentier states, "De Mackandal el americano, en cambio, ha quedado toda una mitología, acompañada de himnos mágicos, conservados por todo un pueblo que aún se cantan en las ceremonias del Vaudou"[22] (The American Mackandal, on the contrary, leaves an entire mythology, preserved by an entire people and accompanied by magic hymns still sung today during voodoo ceremonies).²³ According to the stories of this community, well versed in Vodou religion, Mackandal had the supernatural ability to shape-shift into an animal in order to escape persecution and obtain information that would be helpful to the rebellion.

In the novel's prologue, Carpentier initially mentions a more ominous animal-double, the lycanthrope, but then he contests and undermines the monstrous qualities usually bestowed upon the popular "wolfman" figure. Carpentier states the following about Mackandal's transformative powers in terms of lycanthropy: "Pisaba yo una tierra donde millares de hombres ansiosos de libertad creyeron en los poderes licantrópicos de Mackandal, a punto de que esa fe colectiva produjera un milagro el día de su ejecución"²⁴ (I was in a land where thousands of men, anxious for freedom, believed in Mackandal's lycanthropic powers to the extent that their collective faith produced a miracle on the day of his execution).²⁵ His use of the word *licantrópicos* to speak of Mackandal's transformative powers becomes noteworthy because the figure resonates more with Indo-European and Hellenic mythmaking. *Lykos* is derived from the Greek word for wolf, which refers to a person who can turn into a wolf. Greek myths describe a wolf transformation resulting from divine punishment as exemplified by Lycaon, who was changed into a wolf by Zeus.²⁶ It was believed that lycanthropic victims suffered from wolf transformations because they had been bitten or scratched by a wolf, or because they had been cursed or given herbs by a witch that provoked their lupine transformation on nights with full moons.²⁷ The word *lycanthropy* also describes a type of mental illness in which people suffer the delusion that they can transform themselves into a wolf or other animal.²⁸ In Haitian culture, local folktales speak of the *Jé-rouge* (red eyes), a creature described as a type of wolf-man-vampire spirit that possesses humans at night, provoking them to behave like wolves with cannibalistic tendencies. This Haitian lupine figure can trick mothers into giving up their children.²⁹

Carpentier specifically reveals the European source that inspired his own articulation of lycanthropy, as the following epigraph in the novel's prologue indicates: "Lo que se ha de entender desto [sic] de convertirse en lobos es que hay una enfermedad a quien llaman los médicos manía lupina—*Los trabajos de Persiles y Segismunda*"³⁰ (What must be understood concerning this matter of being transformed into wolves is that there is an illness that the doctors call wolf madness—*Los trabajos de Persiles y Segismunda*).[31] By opening the novel with a reference to the Spanish writer Miguel de Cervantes's last novel, *Los trabajos de Persiles y Sigismunda*, published posthumously in 1617, Carpentier initially anchors the werewolf myth within the European tradition, not necessarily a Haitian one.[32] Cervantes's novel narrates the story of a Nordic prince and princess who are fleeing to Rome to get married. During their travels, the characters describe objectionable people in England and Sicily, among other places, who can magically convert into wolves. These wolf-people live in the woods, travel in packs, murder, and consume human flesh. While the existence of unreal creatures such as wolf-men would later become demystified in the modern era, Cervantes situates his novel in premodern and superstitious times when marvelous events could coexist, including the existence of wolf-men. Carpentier's novel primarily explores Vodou culture; however, by making references to European traditions he is also making equivalencies in cultural beliefs that were part of Old World and New World societies. In other words, when Carpentier cites Cervantes's *Persiles y Sigismunda*, he returns to a time when stories of werewolves and other miraculous events were accepted as part of the real.

Carpentier in *El reino de este mundo* situates his novel in colonial Haiti, when slaves believed in sacred animal transformations. However, unlike Cervantes's text, he changes the perception of wolf-men and strips them of their ill-omened qualities. That is to say, Carpentier's description of the shape-shifting powers of his protagonists, Mackandal and Ti Noel, bears scant resemblance to the fear-instilling and monstrous wolf-people that appear in Cervantes's novel. Carpentier's utilization of the animal-double functions differently from much of werewolf and other texts featuring ominous animal-doubles. This departure is innovative, given that the author initially frames the novel in terms of horrific versions of lycanthropy, as narrated in *Persiles y Sigismunda*, which have different connotations and more nuanced associations with monstrous transformations, witchcraft, and/or mental illness. Mackandal in the novel never specifically transforms into a wolf, as might be expected given the prologue's epigraph and the deliberate use of the words *manía lupina* and *lycanthropy*, but instead Mackandal's polymorphic abilities have more in common with notions of the bush-soul of West Africa and animal totems as found in other Native-American belief systems, in which animal spirits can serve as guardians of a clan or mystical guides.[33]

Mackandal behaves like a protector who will attempt to liberate the slaves, aided by his magical animal transformations. The narrator states that Mackandal can change into a bird, dog, insect, or goat as well as other animals as illustrated in the passage below:

> Todos sabían que la iguana verde, la mariposa nocturna, el perro desconocido, el alcatraz inverosímil, no eran sino simples disfraces. Dotado del poder de transformarse en animal de pezuña, en ave, pez o insecto, Mackandal visitaba continuamente las haciendas de la Llanura para vigilar a sus fieles y saber si todavía confiaban en su regreso. De metamorfosis en metamorfosis, el manco estaba en todas partes, habiendo recobrado su integridad corpórea al vestir trajes de animales.[34]

> [They all knew that the green lizard, the night moth, the strange dog, the incredible gannet, were nothing but disguises. As he had the power to take the shape of a hoofed animal, bird, fish, or insect, Macandal continually visited the plantations of the Plaine to watch over his faithful and find out if they still had faith in his return. In one metamorphosis or another, the one-armed was everywhere, having recovered his corporeal integrity in animal guise.][35]

Mackandal can at times take the form of an animal in order to hide from an enemy.[36] Mackandal, a type of high priest, a *houngán*, invokes ancestral Loas (spiritual intermediaries between humans and the gods) to obtain powers that will assist him in overthrowing the oppressive regimes enslaving them.

Native-American religious beliefs inform Carpentier's animal-doubles as well; however, they do not carry the portentous overtones bestowed on animal familiars in other folktales or literary traditions. Mackandal's animal transformations bear a tacit relationship with nahualismo, in which he is able to shape-shift in order to secure knowledge. This evocation of the Native American belief system is plausible given that, before the conquest and the forced trafficking of slaves, Taínos and other indigenous groups who had migrated from different parts of the American mainland inhabited Hispaniola. Their population diminished dramatically after the conquest due to European disease, epidemics, violence, and enslavement; hence, information about their culture and traditions is scarce.[37] Nevertheless, there is substantial evidence that indicates that, even with their reduced numbers, a syncretic relationship between local Taíno and African beliefs melded on the island, further stimulating Carpentier's innovative and syncretic literary versions of humans who can assume animal identities.

Mackandal can transfigure into an animal, but he also embodies notions of twoness in other ways. That is to say, the events narrated become double-visioned: depending on the witnesses' perspective, Mackandal is hero or villain, emancipator or persecutor, human or nonhuman, and holy priest or evil Vodou sorcerer. In Carpentier's novel, the slaves see Mackandal as heroic and as their supernatural protector; however, the slave owners see him as the opposite. For the landowners, he is a subversive entity who has spied on or harmed them, or has operated in other secretive ways to bring about the eventual downfall of slavery. And these two competing realities clash at the moment of Mackandal's execution. The following passage is often cited to emphasize the stark contrast between the two groups.[38]

En ese momento, Mackandal agitó su muñón que no habían podido atar, en un gesto conminatorio que no por menguado era menos terrible, aullando conjuros desconocidos y echando violentamente el torso hacia adelante. Sus ataduras cayeron, y el cuerpo del negro se espigó en el aire, volando por sobre las cabezas, antes de hundirse en las ondas negras de la masa de esclavos. Un solo grito llenó la plaza.
—*Mackandal sauvé!*[39]

[At that moment, Macandal moved the stump of his arm, which they had been unable to tie up, in a threatening gesture which was none the

less terrible for being partial, howling unknown spells and violently thrusting his torso forward. The bonds fell off and the body of the Negro rose in the air, flying overhead, until it plunged into the black waves of the sea of slaves. A single cry filled the square:
—"Macandal saved!"][40]

The slaves witness a miracle in which Mackandal's shackles fall off, and he flies into the air to join the slaves, causing the slaves to shout, "Mackandal saved!" The slave owners, on the contrary, witness another event: the execution of Mackandal as he is burned at the stake. So, while the slaves observe Mackandal's mysterious transformation and understand it as a message of hope, the landowners see the gruesome death of a dissident slave and a return to order.

> Los guardias se lanzaron, a culatazos, sobre la negrada aullante, que ya no parecía caber entre las casas y trepaba hacia los balcones. Y a tanto llegó el estrépito y la grita y la turbamulta, que muy pocos vieron que Mackandal, agarrado por diez soldados, era metido de cabeza en el fuego, y que una llama crecida por el pelo encendido ahogaba su último grito.[41]

> [The guards fell with rifle butts on the howling blacks, who now seemed to overflow the streets, climbing toward the windows. And the noise and screaming and uproar were such that very few saw that Macandal, held by ten soldiers, had been thrust head first into the fire, and that a flame fed by his burning hair had drowned his last cry.][42]

This incident, along with the previously quoted one, establish the two Mackandals: a human turned into supernatural emancipator who will continue to inspire the struggle for liberation or a malevolent entity and a slave with nonperson status who is now dead. One description depicts a horrific death reminiscent of witches being burned at the stake, while the other offers a miraculous story worthy of mythmaking.

Ti Noel, the narrator of the story, also shape-shifts but is in no way characterized as a malevolent transformation aiming to cause harm. His metamorphosis allows a path to access knowledge, which is more akin to the spiritual journeying that a shaman might experience. Throughout his life, Ti Noel witnesses the rise and fall of many regimes, only to be replaced by equally abusive systems. Because he is disillusioned, Ti Noel imagines that he can escape the cycle of oppression by metamorphosing into an animal. Unlike Mackandal, he does not transform in order to fight for the freedom of others; rather, "Cansado de licantropías azarosas, Ti Noel hizo uso de sus extraordinarios poderes para transformarse en ganso y convivir con las aves que se habían instalado en sus dominios"[43] [Tired of lycanthropic perilous animal transformations][44] [Ti Noël employed his magic powers to transform himself into a goose and live with the fowl that had made his domain their abode].[45] He finds the animal kingdom hierarchical and hostile, and he is immediately recognized as an outsider. This less-than-heroic escape to the animal kingdom allows Ti Noel to better appreciate Mackandal's bravery when for years he disguised himself as an animal to benefit the slaves.

Ti Noel's journey to the animal realm leads to an epiphany, in which he realizes that humans must be brave and continue their struggle and remain among the living or, as the narrator states, "el hombre sólo puede hallar su grandeza, su máxima medida en el Reino de este Mundo"[46] [man finds his greatest, his fullest measure, only in the Kingdom of This World].[47] His experience underscores how animal transformations can bring about knowledge and liberation, thus rescuing the animal-double from its usual malevolent status in literature. Carpentier initially invokes the malevolent lupine figure by citing Cervantes's novel, yet he strips animal transformation of its usual monstrous association, thus giving animal-doubles a new meaning in a new context that emancipates them from the more traditional articulations of lycanthropy. His doubles, like Fuentes's, are divine entities.

Eternal Doubles

Carlos Fuentes, informed by negative Gothic aesthetics, bestows ill-omened and divine qualities upon his split entities. As in many of his other texts, his characters are inspired by pre-Columbian and other transatlantic traditions forging innovative poetic representations. His texts are exemplary of the manner in which doubles bring about misfortune; however, he changes the usual qualities associated with the double because his doubles achieve immortality by annihilating the host subject, which is allusive of human sacrifice. In "Chac Mool" and *Aura*, Fuentes presents readers with the complex, albeit incongruous, aspects of human sacrifice that are simultaneously sacred and macabre. According to pre-Columbian worldviews, sacrificial victims, as divine offerings, could allow for the rebirth of the gods, the sun, and the moon, among other entities, yet these rituals also terrorized their victims and the outsiders who witnessed them. Miguel León-Portilla in "Those Made Worthy by Divine Sacrifice: The Faith of Ancient Mexico" explains the contradictory feelings evoked when chroniclers and observers both "expressed utter revulsion" and admiration for Aztec religious faith and devotion.[48] Human sacrifice in the Aztec context, unfathomable from a more modern perspective, was deemed imperative for maintaining balance in which "humans needed to acknowledge and even reimburse the forces that made life possible."[49] As the aforementioned critics reveal, sacrifice was not necessarily a punishment but rather a way to honor and nourish the gods, as well as a way to pay tribute with one of the most valuable vital fluids: blood. Therefore, human beings sustained by the land had to repay their debt to the deities by offering up their blood in exchange, sometimes by ritual bloodletting (piercing of body parts, for example) and at other times by surrendering a more meaningful offering, such as a human heart.

In *Aura*, Fuentes revisits the notions of human sacrifice that he had already explored in one of his most famous stories, "Chac Mool" in *Los días emascarados* (1954) (The Masked Days). The *chacmool* was the moniker invented by Augustus Le Plongeon to describe the Mayan sacrificial stone he unearthed in Chichen Itzá in the eighteenth century.[50] Although information related to this deity in Mayan culture has mostly disappeared, the chacmool is believed to represent the Mayan deity associated with rain and lightning and who also presides over water. These sacred stones possibly "symbolize fallen warriors who deliver offerings to the gods."[51] The chacmool figure inspired Fuentes's eponymous story, which is an obvious reference to human sacrificial ceremonies.

To briefly summarize the story, the protagonist, Feliberto, a forty-year-old man, comes from an affluent family that has seen better days, but he now leads a more modest life dedicating his time to one of his favorite hobbies, collecting Mexican Native art such as statues, idols, and pots—the Chac Mool figure being one that he eagerly purchases. When Feliberto appraises the stone figure he describes it as a marvelous replica, yet the stone copy is not as phony as the protagonist naïvely surmises but is rather a monstrous entity that will become more human and will usurp Feliberto's position and ultimately destroy him. In a sense, the Chac Mool has been invited into his home to function as an art showpiece; however, the stone artwork transforms into an interloper, a double who breaches the material world and insists on having a place in the protagonist's realm.[52] Feliberto escapes to Acapulco, both to save himself and to thwart his oppressor's complete metamorphosis; however, his plan fails and he drowns in the ocean, intimating that Chac Mool, who also controls the waters, has made good on his promise.

Tatiana Herrera Ávila, in *De lo mítico a lo profano: Chac Mool como monstruo* (From the Mythic to the Profane: Chac Mool as Monster) has already analyzed notions of divine sacrifice, the double, and the monstrous in the story. She also describes the way critics have usually framed the narration as fantastic and "*hasta gótico*," or even Gothic.[53] Herrera Ávila, among others, suggests that the story laments that indigenous origins have been forever lost and that attempts at the resurrection of pre-Columbian times result in monstrous representations:

> En este sentido, es exacto afirmar que Chac Mool es ominoso, y responde literalmente a esto, lo familiar que retorna como extraño, es, si se quiere ese pasado prehispánico del que ya no sabemos nada, y que en la modernidad impuesta en América, resulta monstruoso, precisamente por haber sido familiar, por haber sido nuestro, sin serlo ya.[54]

[In this sense, it is precise to affirm that Chac Mool is ominous, and responds literally to this; the familiar becomes strange. It is, if you will, the pre-Hispanic past of which we know nothing and that modernity, imposed on America, results in monstrosity, precisely for having been familiar, for having been ours, without it being so now.]

The return of the stone statue, whose past is mostly unknown, transmogrifies from deity that was once venerated into degraded version of his former self.

Personified, Chac Mool is described as an Indian man with sharp, pointy teeth who wears lipstick and whose wrinkled skin is haphazardly covered with face powder. More precisely, the narrator states, "Apareció un indio amarillo, en bata de casa, con bufanda. Su aspecto no podía ser más repulsivo"[55] (A yellow-skinned Indian in a smoking jacket and an ascot stood in the doorway. He couldn't have been more repulsive).[56] Chac Mool, a monstrous other, is out of place in a modern world in which he has lost his former claim to glory and now is an inferior and decrepit duplication. Feliberto, too, like Chac Mool, becomes alienated and obsolete, losing the dignified place he once occupied in society. Feliberto laments over his life, in which he ultimately finds himself financially and mentally destroyed. Even in death in the context of human sacrifice rituals, Feliberto underwhelms. He is not made worthy by divine sacrifice as a warrior might by approaching the sacrificial stone, but rather he attempts to escape, which bears a scant relationship to the pre-Columbian warriors who might have died heroically to feed the gods. This analysis becomes relevant when analyzing *Aura* because the nouvelle will revisit some of the ideas already presented in "Chac Mool," which again emphasizes the way Fuentes iterates other text's plots, including his own.

Aura

Aura especially replicates Gothic literary features and ghostly cinematic images, sometimes drawn from Gothic-inspired films. Echoing and reiteration are among the text's most striking features, and the idea of the double underscores how subjects are no longer unique, authentic, or original. Fuentes, well aware of the double's power to annul, split, and destabilize concepts of authenticity, returns many times to the theme of doubling and disassociated selves. In *La muerte de Artemio Cruz* (1962), published in the same year as *Aura*, Artemio Cruz, the protagonist, is able to ascend to power during and after the Mexican Revolution by usurping the place of others.[57] That is to say, others die so that he can live and gain power. The same notions of sacrifice that emerge in *La muerte de Artemio Cruz* and in "Chac Mool" will also appear in Fuentes's nouvelle *Aura*, in that human sacrifice allows for continued existence of another.[58]

Unlike Feliberto, who tries to save himself by escaping to Acapulco in order to avoid Chac Mool's punishment, *Aura*'s Felipe Montero willingly surrenders to divine sacrifice. This is yet another example of the way the author combines European folklore and pre-Columbian ideas of divine sacrifice, informed by negative Gothic aesthetics, in that situations simultaneously abhorrent and sacred are illustrated. In this Gothic-inspired nouvelle, Felipe Montero incarnates the typical ineffectual hero, the first character to appear. Felipe is a young historian who, in response to a newspaper advertisement, is hired by the aging widow Consuelo to complete the memoirs of her late husband, General Llorente. The novel invokes doubles on many levels: on the one hand, Consuelo becomes doubled when she creates a younger and more beautiful version of herself in Aura, presumably her niece, who will seduce a young victim, Felipe. Meanwhile, Felipe, who looks like Consuelo's dead husband, General Llorente, will need to surrender his body in order to bring the general back to life, her twinned soul, so that they can reclaim the love they once had.

Fuentes's consistent use of the double and parodying of previous works of art is also an aesthetic critique. He does not veil the use of the double in his works but rather overtly points to the texts that he is doubling, implicitly questioning notions of literary originality. In *Aura*'s epigraph, he mentions Jules Michelet's treatise on the witch in *La sorcière* (1862), (published in translation as Satanism and Witchcraft: A Study in Medieval Superstition) one of the backgrounded texts that is echoed, thus appropriating and transforming the usual image of the sorceress found in both historical writing and Gothic literature.[59] Critics have known to look for Michelet's witch because Fuentes openly refers to his work in *Aura*'s epigraph:

El hombre caza y lucha. La mujer intriga y sueña; es la madre de la fantasía, de los dioses. Posee la segunda visión, las alas que le permiten volar hacia el infinito del deseo de la imaginación . . . Los dioses son como los hombres: nacen y mueren sobre el pecho de una mujer . . . Jules Michelet

[Man hunts and struggles. Woman intrigues and dreams; she is the mother of fantasy, the mother of the gods. She has second sight, the wings that enable her to fly to the infinite of desire and imagination . . . the gods are like men: they are born and they die on a woman's breast . . . Jules Michelet]

The epigraph suggests that Consuelo should be understood within the articulation of the witch that Jules Michelet invented in his pseudo-historical treatise on witchcraft.

By rearticulating *Aura* through Michelet's lens, Fuentes also inherits the intrinsic Gothic undertones found in *La sorcière* and his other historical renditions, as argued by Julia Hell: "Michelet invents a form of writing history that reaches deep into the realm of the literary, indeed into the realm of the Gothic."[60] The historical account was written as if the narrator were actually present in medieval Europe, in communion with the witches. Through his fictional eyewitness accounts, he resurrects the past with his dynamic descriptions and even goes so far as to include dramatizations so that the reader may hear the dead speak; the effect is that the distant past is brought into the present, provoking the reader to experience the past vividly: "Using the inclusive 'we,' Michelet thus stages the historian's identification with the 'people' in his very writing, inventing a form of historiography that allows him to 'identify with, resurrect, and relive the life of the past in its totality.' Michelet himself named this form of writing history 'resurrection,' and this resurrectional historiography carries decidedly Gothic undertones that come to the fore in the story of his dreams."[61]

Michelet wrote *La sorcière* in a century when clear distinctions were being made between historical writing and fiction, and it was criticized by other historians for his unusual weaving of historical facts with fiction.[62] Michelet's work was appreciated for its imaginary and poetic prose more than for its historical accuracy because most of his facts have since been debunked. Even though his methods did not follow usual historical methods, and his work has lost its historical prestige, it has nonetheless had a profound effect on culture. His depictions have shaped many popular beliefs having to do with European witch folklore and rituals pertaining to the Black Mass, which Fuentes invokes in *Aura*. By referring to Michelet's work, Fuentes, like Carpentier and Cervantes, conjures premodern and superstitious times when unreal entities were believed to transcend the material world.

Returning to Premodernity

Just before crossing the threshold, Felipe takes one last look at the bustling and modern city, but upon crossing he steps into several historical pasts, both Mexican and European. One époque belongs to a time when General Llorente, the man whose memoirs he has been hired to translate, was young and served the French army during its occupation of Mexico in the mid-nineteenth century. General Llorente served when the Empress Carlota and the Emperor Maximilian ruled Mexico with the support of Napoleon III of France. This aristocratic couple met an unfortunate end: Maximilian at the age of thirty-five was executed, while the childless Carlota became insane living out the rest of her life locked away. Their tragic lives have made them into mythic figures in the Mexican imagination and, given Fuentes's predilection for myth, he reincarnates them in his depiction of General Llorente and Consuelo—an appropriation he openly cites as influential in creating these two characters.[63]

Yet Felipe also walks further back in time to a premodern era, both Aztec and European. The juxtaposition between the old and new is made evident when he enters the old, derelict mansion. Recalling this previous century, the exterior of the building is decorated with baroque stone and sandstone gargoyles, while the interior walls are covered by Gothic-style carved wood walls.[64] Similarly, the salon is decorated with what the character describes as Gothic chairs, Persian rugs, and antique lamps, while the drawn curtains are of green velvet.[65] The house is not lit by electricity but rather by the dim light of candelabras and candles, metaphorically alluding to the dark and nebulous realm that Felipe is entering. The mansion is also described as having dark corridors, musky odors, rotting wood, and rats, which recall the mysterious labyrinths, dark spaces, and negative aesthetics that inform the Gothic as found in "Carmilla" (1872), *Dracula* (1897), and *The Monk* (1796). The purposeful and explicit use of the word *Gothic* in the novel to describe the home's design also recalls the neo-Gothic architectural style that sought to revive the medieval style; thus, Felipe enters into the nineteenth century, concurrently and symbolically moving further back in time into the imagined premodern époque of Michelet's witches.

He also symbolically doubles back into a time before the conquest when he makes his way through the mansion to meet Consuelo for the first time. He is disoriented as he meanders through the dark corridors of the grand house, yet Consuelo guides him and instructs him to walk thirteen steps to reach the stairway, and then twenty-two steps to reach her room. Thirteen is an obvious ill-omened number, but the twenty-two steps become meaningful since it is an implicit reference to Tenochtitlan's Templo Mayor, an Aztec temple and place of human sacrifice. According to Aztec religion, the sacred Templo Mayor at the earthly level represents the axis point that divides the underworld from the heavens. There are twenty-two levels of the afterlife according to Aztec beliefs: thirteen levels of heaven, known as Omeyocán, and nine levels of the underworld, referred to as Mictlán.[66] Felipe must walk up twenty-two steps to reach Consuelo, which symbolically corresponds to the highest level of Omeyocán. The highest heavenly realm is also known as the place of duality in which Ometeotl, the creator of all creations, dwells.[67] In other words, Consuelo is like Ometeotl, the Aztec creator, who is also often described as a dual deity, a split entity that simultaneously embodies both Ometecuhtli and Omecíhuatl, gods representing both male and female forces. The purposeful mention of the numbers thirteen and twenty-two invoke the Aztec afterlife and gods that embody notions of twoness, further underscoring the way Fuentes amalgamates pre-Columbian and European religions in his fiction.

At first, the novel seems to be singularly focused on the European version of the witch, but Mesoamerican beliefs (described in more detail later), are subtly blended into the story. After stumbling through the dark labyrinth of her home, Felipe finally finds his way to Consuelo in a room upstairs, where she reclines in her bed next to her rabbit Saga, an obvious animal familiar. He is unsettled when she places her decrepit and cold hands on his for a prolonged time; her cold fingers register no temperature or, as he says, "dedos sin temperatura,"[68] which makes her more corpselike. There he will accept the contract with a frail, haggard, and toothless woman, but, by taking this contract, he is unknowingly surrendering his body and soul to her.

He is told that he will have to temporarily live in the ruinous mansion in order to translate her husband's memoirs. He unwillingly accepts the living arrangements, thus signifying the first concession or sacrifice he will make in his dealings with Consuelo. This small sacrifice will finally provide him with enough money to write his own important history book on Spanish discoveries and conquest of the New World.[69] Felipe's project privileges European versions of conquest and the most important achievements of the Renaissance while simultaneously ignoring pre-Columbian history; this lacuna will also affect his ability to comprehend sacrificial traditions. Furthermore, as a translator, his task involves a thorough understanding of another language in which he must intently interpret both sign and signifier, so that he can take an original and duplicate it into another—in a sense, doubling the text. Even though he is trained in interpretation and rewriting, it will become apparent that he is incapable of deciphering the real scheme behind the contract. Felipe, a Sorbonne graduate, is overconfident, perhaps even arrogant, in his self-perceived ability to understand his surroundings.

Felipe has foolishly constructed a definitive notion of his role, which is, as he will later discover, precariously situated in a vast and dangerous unknown. His profession is that of a historian, which is significant because his craft calls for the compiling and ordering of events that are usually logically written and chronologically arranged to elucidate the past, yet his faith in reason and order will blindside him. His practical plans to earn money unravel as soon as he crosses the ghostly mansion's threshold because he has inadvertently walked into a world of myth and magic where he will be unable to discern his surroundings or foresee his role as sacrificial victim. He realizes too late that his reliance on reason has led to a fatal misreading of his function in this supernatural plot. He does not realize that once he enters into the mythic space he can no longer comprehend nor control anything because he has simultaneously entered the Aztec mythic world, whose traditions seem irrelevant to him in this context. And he also enters the witch's manor where everything, according to Michelet, is done backwards and upside down.[70] Similarly, this hero's role is turned on its head in this Gothic-like setting where Felipe, who perceives himself to be in control of his domain, is really at the mercy of the magic that surrounds him. This bodily usurpation will be achieved through rituals, potions, and foods long associated with sorcery as imagined by Michelet but also with sacrificial ceremonies that implicitly restage Aztec ceremonies. Consuelo, who has placed an advertisement to lure a man into her house, has other treacherous plans for the victim.

Within the Gothic framework, Consuelo is the powerful villain who is split and has the power to conjure up doubles. She is a divided self who has lost her other half, General Llorente, but she can be made whole again by using magic to bring him back. Consuelo recalls many other witches in Gothic literature who have made a pact with the Devil in order to possess certain powers, such as Matilda in *The Monk*. Consuelo's magical power allows her to reincarnate her husband through Felipe's body. She, in effect, brings General Llorente back from the dead through Felipe's sacrifice, which recalls Jules Michelet's words describing the power that this bride of Satan can exercise: "She can heal, prophesy, predict, conjure up the spirits of the dead, can spell-bind you, turn you into a hare or a wolf, make you find a treasure, and most fatal gift of all, cast a love charm over you[,] there is no escaping! Awful attribute, more terrible than all the rest put together!"[71] Indeed, this is what Consuelo does—she casts a love charm through her supernatural powers and love potions and converts Felipe into a virtual prisoner.

Consuelo's interest in sorcery originates due to her inability to bear children when she was a young bride. In General Llorente's historical memoirs, he recalls how Consuelo becomes so obsessed with engendering a child that she evokes the powers found in herbs.[72] Through her experimentation with various mystical plants, she will finally be able to reproduce not a child but a younger image of herself: Aura, her doppelgänger. Of this birth she says, "Sí, sí, sí, he podido: la he encarnado; puedo convocarla, puedo darle vida, con mi vida"[73] (Yes, yes, yes, I've done it, I've re-created her! I can invoke her; I can give her life with my own life!).[74] In effect, she brings forth her double in the form of a young, beautiful woman, Aura.

While the image of the aged Consuelo is that of a typical ugly, aged, haggard, and repulsive type of witch, Aura represents the opposite: a young, beautiful, and seductive enchantress. Aura recalls other mythic witches like Circe and Medea from Greek mythology, enchantresses familiar with metamorphism and the power of potions. As previously mentioned, she also evokes Matilda, the emblematic Gothic witch, whose image causes such a great effect on Ambrosio in *The Monk*: "Her neck and arms were uncovered; in her hand she bore a golden wand; her hair was loose, and flowed wildly upon her shoulders; her eyes sparkled with terrific expression; and her whole demeanor was calculated to inspire the beholder with awe and admiration. 'Follow me!' she said to the monk in a low and solemn voice; 'all is ready!'"[75] In this same way, this younger witch, Aura, is a mesmerizing beauty that Felipe will gaze upon with delight, therefore further securing his compliance in the trap set for him. Her green eyes have an immediate hypnotic effect on Felipe. When her eyes meet his, his financial concerns are replaced with his bodily desire.[76] The historian who usually privileges reason now begins to succumb to his emotions. He is not only seduced through Aura's mesmerizing beauty; he is also given unusual foods and drinks that will convert him into a more willing sacrificial victim.

Gastronomical Seduction

Consuelo first dabbled in the dark arts when she was young, but it is apparent that, like Matilda, she has become a master of sorcery by the time she meets Felipe and therefore uses all her occult knowledge to seduce him, including serving him the same unusual dinner and drinks repeatedly. Each night he is served three specific foods: roasted tomatoes, kidneys, and a dense red wine. The meal is important in many cultures; according to Freud, sacrificial ceremonies usually involve the repetition of meals, which shows kinship and underscores the implicit agreement that a sacrifice will take place.[77] Serving a meal to a would-be victim appears in Gothic settings; Jonathan Harker shares a meal with Count Dracula before he is imprisoned and left to be consumed by Dracula's wives, which is frequently replicated in films based on Stoker's novel. Guillermo Grant in "El vampiro" also shared several lavish dinners before sacrificing the movie star and conjuring her double. Similarly, in Fuentes's *Vlad*, he, too, was served a revolting meal before the vampire finally fled with his wife and daughter. That is to say, the repetition of meals in Gothic literature can also presage imprisonment, death, and/or sacrifice.

Some of the concoctions and foods used in his meals are harvested from Aura's secret garden, described as overflowing with nightshade plants (*Solanaceae*) that have long been associated with both witchcraft and shamanistic astral traveling.[78] Consuelo combines both the American shamanic tradition with European pharmacopeia in order to transcend the usual malevolent hexes. Thus, the syncretic garden's mysterious and poisonous plants are not only psychotropic but are also used for casting spells and conjuring souls:

> Distingues las formas altas, ramosas, que proyectan sus sombras a la luz de cerilla que se consume, te quema los dedos, te obliga a encender uno nuevo para terminar de reconocer las flores, los frutos, los tallos que recuerdas mencionados en crónicas viejas: las hierbas olvidadas que crecen olorosas, adormiladas: las hojas anchas, largas, hendidas, vellosas de beleño: el tallo sarmentado de flores amarillas por fuera, rojas por dentro; las hojas acorazonadas y agudas de la dulcamara; la pelusa cenicienta del gordolobo, sus flores espigadas; el arbusto ramoso de evónimo y las flores blanquecinas; la belladona.[79]

> [You can make out the tall, leafy forms that cast their shadows on the walls in the light of a match. But it burns down, singeing your fingers, and you have to light another one to finish seeing the flowers, fruits, and plants you remember reading about in old chronicles, the forgotten herbs that are growing here so fragrantly and drowsily; the long broad downy leaves of the henbane; the twinning stems with flowers that are yellow outside, red inside; the pointed, heart-shaped leaves of the nightshade; the ash-colored down of the grape-mullein with its clustered flowers; the bushy gatheridge with its blossoms; the belladonna.][80]

Consuelo returns to ancient knowledge, drawing from the local and the foreign, in order to harness their power to cause harm and to generate life. Unsurprisingly, the foods and drinks that Felipe consumes affect him profoundly.

The tomato, a type of nightshade plant, was unknown to Europe and the rest of the world before the conquest of the Americas, and this fruit was initially met with suspicion. The tomato, cultivated by the Aztecs in Mexico, was commonly used in indigenous cooking and was deemed to increase sexual prowess.[81] Certainly the term "love apple" used by the French alludes to the popular notion that it contained aphrodisiacal properties. The term *lykos persica*, or wolf peach, refers to the popular myth that witches used these nightshade plants to transform men into wolves, suggesting that the plant's transformative properties will aid in transforming Felipe into something else.

The tomato plant's resemblance to the deadly nightshade (belladonna) led many in northern Europe to believe it was poisonous; therefore, its fruit was deemed unfit for consumption for many years. Belladonna was also believed to be an essential ingredient in witches' brews and also was supposedly used in the creation of a topical ointment used for flying. Most importantly: "There was even a folk belief that the herb could take on the form of a beautiful woman, which may offer another source for the plant's name."[82] That belladonna is explicitly described in *Aura* further solidifies the association with witches and pre-Columbian tradition.[83] Given the folkloric and superstitious myths pertaining to the tomato, it is not difficult to understand why the tomato formed part of Felipe's daily nourishment. This plant could serve as an aphrodisiac, and, because Felipe's virile body is needed to engender General Llorente, he was made to consume it.

Along with the roasted tomatoes, Felipe is served the unusual dish of pungent kidneys. Serving animal entrails to a guest and not a prime cut of meat would be, by most standards, an unacceptable way to honor a guest.[84] The kidney's function in the body is to produce urine and clean the body of other impurities. Since antiquity, medical writers have considered it an inferior meat given its "stinking" and "disgusting" smell; furthermore, the kidneys were deemed unfit for consumption because they were "bad juiced and fat juiced."[85] Athanasios Diamandopoulos, Andreas Skarpelos, and Georgios Tsiros in "The Use of the Kidneys in Secular and Ritual Practices according to Ancient Greek and Byzantine

Texts" argue that animal kidneys and surrounding fat were the favored part of sacrificial rituals in pagan and Jewish religions.[86] Furthermore, entrails are an esteemed form of offering to the gods according to certain Christian and Judaic traditions. More precisely in Leviticus 1:9, the King James Version of the Bible states the following about animal innards: "But its entrails and its legs shall he wash in water: and the priest shall burn all on the altar, to be a burnt sacrifice, an offering made by fire, of a sweet aroma unto the Lord."

In spite of this dietary condemnation, the kidneys and the perirenal fat were valued for their medicinal potency and were also responsible for the production of sexual desire; consequently, their consumption was believed to enhance virility, thus suggesting that Aura's cooking of the kidneys and its corresponding pungent smell was a way to honor Consuelo, represented as the metaphoric goddess. Given this context, it is not unusual that Aura consistently provided Felipe this meal because, by doing so, along with the tomatoes, she was also stimulating his desire. Further stimulation was induced with the inclusion of a mysterious red wine contained in an unmarked opaque green bottle. Presumably it has been altered in some way because this specific red wine is described as being dense: "Beben ese vino particularmente espeso"[87] (You drink that thick wine).[88] Adjectives such as rich, full-bodied, and sweet are usually used to describe wine—but certainly not dense. Perhaps it has been mixed with herbs taken from the hidden garden or some other metaphorically charged substance.

Dating from centuries back and even found in Wiccan spell books today, menstrual blood is a common ingredient in love potions. In popular folktales, men were warned against eating dark-colored food or drinks prepared by a woman for fear of blood contamination. Given the unusual description and the mystery surrounding the wine served to Felipe at his daily meals, and that he was affected immediately after drinking it, raises the possibility that this wine was indeed a love potion and was probably tainted with blood, along with the herbs allegedly associated with witchcraft, as mentioned earlier.

Blood is the universal life force full of power that forms part of many sacrificial rituals. The Aztecs performed human sacrifices, as they believed that blood was the source of life infused with incredible fertilizing power.[89]

In the Gothic tradition and folklore, blood is the vampire's primary sustenance. Witches seal their pact with the Devil through the use of blood, while in the Christian religion the blood of Christ is substantiated from wine when consumed in the celebration of the Eucharist. In other words, ritual wine is mystically transmuted to become the Savior's blood, which is then consumed. The Eucharist, Jesus's Last Supper, the ultimate divine sacrifice, allows for others' salvation. Similarly, Felipe's divine bodily offering will result in General Llorente's reembodiment. Thus, the suspicious beverage invokes rituals having to do with blood and wine. Yet, in spite of all the obvious clues, the overly rational Felipe fails to notice the multifaceted hexes put on him.

Engendering the Other Double

The supernatural seduction through the ritual meals and magical potions has but one purpose: to resurrect General Llorente; and like the wine at Eucharist he will be transubstantiated into the general. In order to resurrect the general's body, Felipe must also be made to participate in the witch's Black Mass, a sacrilegious imitation of the Catholic Mass used for magical purposes.[90] According to Michelet, during the Black Mass the witch "is priest, and altar, and consecrated host, whereof all the people communicate. In the last resort, is she not the very God of the Sacrifice as well?"[91] Aura, of course, fulfills these expectations when she makes love to Felipe and is described as the altar.[92] The presence of the black Christ and wafer that she breaks between her thighs further underscores the profane nature of this religious imitation and fetishization of Christian ritual, which will ultimately seal Felipe's fate. He will later realize that this ritual has indeed engendered his double: "Te llevas las manos a las sienes, tratando de calmar tus sentidos en desarreglo: esa tristeza vencida te insinúa, en voz baja, en el recuerdo inasible de la premonición, que buscas tu otra mitad, que la concepción estéril de la noche pasada engendró tu propio doble"[93] (You put your hands on your forehead, trying to calm your disordered senses: that dull melancholy is hinting to you in a low voice, the voice of memory and premonition, that you're seeking your other half, that the sterile conception last night engendered your own double).[94]

Consuelo engendered the first double, Aura, years ago, but now another double will emerge: General Llorente. Felipe, who has consistently misunderstood his real role and ignored all the warnings, still believes late in the game that he is the hero of the story. The reader is well aware that Felipe is doomed, but he, whether through witchcraft or perhaps due to his heroic imaginings, still misunderstands. He aims to finish his contract with Consuelo so that he can run away with Aura. Like many heroes in literature, he hopes to possess and save Aura, whom he believes is being kept in the mansion against her will by the tyrannical power of Consuelo. He asks Aura to see the danger she is in: "Trata de enterrarte en vida. Tienes que renacer, Aura"[95] (She's trying to bury you alive. You've got to be reborn, Aura).[96] Felipe understands the behavior of Gothic villains who bury women alive, yet he does not realize that, in fact, he is the damsel in distress, the one who is being interred, that General Llorente will be born of him, and that he will cease to exist as his former self. This is underscored when Aura literally tells Felipe that his death is necessary: "Hay que morir antes de renacer. . . . No. No entiendes. Olvida, Felipe; ténme confianza"[97] (You have to die before you can be reborn. . . . No, you don't understand. Forget about it Felipe, just have faith in me).[98] Her words also allude to both a Christ-like resurrection and cyclical birth as imagined in Aztec worldviews. Aura's words announce his imminent death, yet he interprets her words to mean something else. That is, he believes that Aura is the victim being buried alive, not realizing that he himself will be the sacrificial victim.

The novel not only inverts a predictable Gothic plot, whereby the victims, realizing their dire circumstances, attempt to flee; Felipe finally does not want to escape. When he is in the throes of passion with Aura, she transmogrifies into Consuelo. A beam of light enters the dark room and he sees her fleshless lips, toothless gums, and her naked body, which he now loves: "flojo, rasgado, pequeño y antiguo, temblando ligeramente porque tú lo tocas, tú lo amas, tú has regresado también"[99] (limp, spent, tiny, ancient, trembling because you touch her. You love her, you too have come back).[100] He is different from the usual Gothic victims, male and female, who might escape and kill the monster. Whether it is through witchcraft, potions, or his own desire, Felipe surrenders his body to Consuelo. Even when he momentarily realizes the complicated labyrinth in which he finds himself, he cooperatively succumbs to a deific death. This is perhaps the most contrasting difference between the Gothic and

Fuentes's work; the novel transcends the usual Gothic aim of eliciting fear. Instead of death being the most frightening event, Felipe behaves more like an Aztec sacrificial victim who is made worthy of divine sacrifice.

Fuentes's descriptions of Aura and Consuelo evoke contradictory sensations of awe and mystery as well as revulsion and gloom. Sacred sacrificial ceremonies are coupled with Gothic's negative aesthetics allowing for the creation of another formidable literary witch who surpasses the powers ascribed to her by Michelet and other witches found in Gothic literature. Witches in the Gothic often become evil and relish the arbitrary destruction of others; as a result, they ultimately meet a violent end and are condemned at the novel's conclusion. Consuelo, on the other hand, is not punished; she is able to fulfill her ultimate desire: to love General Llorente again and relive a blissful existence. She will not die like other doubles or Gothic villains, but she will be allowed to live beyond the normal boundaries of time. She metaphorically returns to the place of myth, to Omeyocán, which is known as the place of duality, where Ometecuhtli will be reunited with Omecíhuatl, gods representing both male and female forces. One couple replaces another, a case of metonymy, in which Consuelo and General Llorente stand for Aztec deities. By anchoring his literary creations in Mesoamerican and other worldviews, Fuentes transforms the predictable endings found in the Gothic and instead imagines doubles in terms of repetition, continuity, and transfiguration rather than a definitive rupture with previous entities.

Aura repeats many features found in the Gothic, yet this novel has many differentiating qualities. Fuentes restages pre-Columbian sacrifice, in which supernatural entities live beyond the boundaries of time through the host subject's divine bodily sacrifice. This appropriation of previous artistic works can be interpreted through Linda Hutcheon's theory of parody, a major formal and thematic mode of the twentieth century: "The pointing to a literariness of the text may be achieved by using parody: in the background will stand another text against which the creation is implicitly to be both measured and understood."[101] Given that *Aura* embodies the otherworldly, critics such as Jaime Miguel Alazraki, Ángel Náter, and Genaro Pérez have already underscored several affinities between *Aura* and the Gothic tradition. Náter sees *Aura* as the rewriting of the Gothic in relation to "the dead city to the abandoned town, in the perspective of the apocalyptic space understood as the parallel disintegration of the space, of the bodies and the minds."[102] On the other hand, Pérez analyzes how the Gothic form is inverted, where men are at the mercy of an enchantress, resulting in an ironic subversion of the male stereotype.[103]

Due to its recognizable Gothic form, *Aura* has been described as quasi-Gothic or even as an unsuccessful ghost story because it fails to instill fear in the reader, the usual aim of Gothic literature. Walter Langford in *The Mexican Novel Comes of Age* criticizes the novel for not meeting the genre's expectations: "The weakness in *Aura* is that the reader, any reader, sees from the beginning what is happening, and so the story is like a punctured balloon. Instead of tension and pressure all the way to the moment of revealing the secret, we have only a flaccid outer structure, which sags more and more as the pressure decreases. The story is well told and an atmosphere is created, which would have been highly effective if Fuentes had been able to keep his reader from distinguishing fantasy and reality at the very outset."[104]

The novel might disappoint because of the obvious and excessive repeating of certain words such as *Gothic* and the obvious references to familiar Gothic features. Botting states, "With genre, familiarity and repetition are necessary, but too much repetition breeds over-familiarity," and this over-familiarity could weaken its power to create horror or terror.[105] The text infringes upon the Gothic genre, but it does so to explore ideas associated with cyclical time and human sacrifice in the realm of the divine. *Aura* shares features that usually characterize Gothic texts, yet the author strategically transforms and subverts what is usually expected from formulaic plots. Fuentes syncretizes and alters the Gothic by infusing his stories with indigenous beliefs and colonial folktales, thereby creating an innovative version of a Gothic villain that undermine how these figures have previously been imagined. That is to say, inspired by elements of the Gothic, Fuentes does not follow the popular formulaic plot but rather evokes the Gothic to speak of something else, and this might explain why critics at times see the text as unsuccessful because it does not follow the conventions or plot one would expect from a Gothic tale. That is, Felipe is unlike the usual Gothic hero who tries to escape or kill the villain; instead, he joins Aura in the mythical space. Fuentes also complicates the work by describing events that are simultaneously revolting, macabre, and sacred.

The decrepit witch enthralls the protagonist, but he, in turn, willingly offers himself to her for a higher cause. In other words, Fuentes purposely suggests Gothic settings and features, but the literary text's ending is contrary to what one would expect from this genre of literature.

Although the Gothic's negative aesthetics inform *Aura*, this is not a Gothic novel but rather a borrowing and transfiguration of the genre whereby Fuentes revisits notions of eternal returns and pre-Columbian rituals.[106] Even though Fuentes plays with many Gothic conventions, fear is not necessarily provoked and order is not reestablished with the annihilation of the villain. In *Aura*, Felipe must die in order to maintain harmony and balance in Consuelo's supernatural world, which also corresponds to the way pre-Columbian death rituals have been imagined. Felipe metaphorically surrenders his heart and soul to Aura/Consuelo so that another entity can continue to live.

Text as Doppelgänger

Fuentes's pervasive and purposeful employment of the double and duplication is also a questioning of literary authenticity; just as characters are haunted and duplicated, texts are haunted by previous texts and films that, in turn, are haunted by their predecessors. Pedro García-Caro in "Aura y la teoría de Carlos Fuentes" proposes that *Aura* is a type of manifesto in which Fuentes formulates certain concepts and practices that will inform his subsequent texts, wherein the use of his doubles questions the notions of originality.[107] To continue with García-Caro's argument, another expression is that of describing the way in which the texts themselves function as monstrous doppelgängers.

Not only are the characters doubled, but *Aura* also demonstrates the way texts themselves function as doubles: they repeat, distort, and parody what has already been written. Doubled texts can also reinvent and reinvigorate old forms. Fuentes often unequivocally and openly mentions his sources in novels, short stories, articles, and interviews. In *Vlad* (2010), he explicitly mentions Vlad Tepes (and implicitly *Dracula*) as the model for his own vampiric creation. In *Aura* his epigraph plainly cites Jules Michelet's work on witchcraft, a model that inspires his nouvelle. In an article in which he describes his methods on writing, "On Reading and Writing Myself: How I Wrote 'Aura,'" he gives readers a road map to other works of art that are implicitly and explicitly reworked in his fiction. He not only models his texts on other novels, but he also duplicates previous filmic plots: *Aura* doubles aspects of *Sunset Boulevard*, while his novel *La muerte de Artemio Cruz* reflects many of the qualities of *Citizen Kane*.[108] John Brushwood addresses the criticism Fuentes has received because of his methods: "The objection may be to the author's unabashed and freely confessed adaptation of the styles of other novelists, most notably John Dos Passos."[109] Brushwood also explains that part of the reason Fuentes has drawn so much criticism is the flamboyance and excess of his fiction. Many can clearly identify the previous works that he parodies: Charles Dickens's *Great Expectations* (1861), Henry James's *The Aspern Papers* (1888), Billy Wilder's *Sunset Boulevard* (1950), and Kenji Mizoguchi's *Ugestu* (1953), to cite just a few.[110]

Fuentes's pervasive doubling of characters and texts implicitly undermines illusions of originality (often a parameter used to distinguish works of art, as T. S. Eliot noted), thus demonstrating how authors, like doubles, fight with past entities to create something new. Fuentes's texts emphasize that ancestors, both literary and historical, assert their presence vigorously with each new literary creation. Authors draw from the past, consciously or unconsciously, recycling and renewing what was already there, and these literary struggles echo characteristics bestowed on the double as well. Just as the more authentic self cannot annihilate the other, authors cannot erase former literary entities; hence, authors are both bound to and control previous artworks. Fuentes acknowledges "abashedly" recalling Brushwood's words, the former others, the literary ancestor, and willingly and openly pays tribute, surrendering to literary familial bloodlines and thus, in a certain sense, sacrificing illusions of authenticity. This, perhaps, is the reason he openly claims his predecessors and influences. *Aura* presents another way of imagining literary creations in which texts simultaneously represent continuity, transmutation, and metamorphoses rather than a definitive rupture with tradition, thus paying tribute to literary ancestors. Fuentes's approach to writing echoes notions of divine sacrifice paid to the gods in which his narratives signify continuity, transfiguration, and rebirth. The aforementioned texts also reveal cultural and aesthetic angsts that writers were grappling with and allegorizing through their literary doubles.

EPILOGUE
GLOBALIZED CURRENT MONSTERS

Over time Gothic monsters and vampires have become transatlantic, global, and ubiquitous, manifesting themselves vigorously across different media. As mentioned before, while vampire novels were not at the heart of literary production in Latin America, they have enjoyed a relatively prominent place in the region's film history. More specifically, compared to their literary companions, vampires took a protagonist's role in the Mexican film industry of the mid-twentieth century. These films illustrate how directors and screenwriters embraced, rivaled, and innovated vampiric imaginings that could also appeal to national sensibilities. This concluding chapter traces the vampire's filmic evolution using the Mexican film industry as an example, and then studies how the contemporary Mexican filmmaker Guillermo del Toro, whose creations are more transnational compared to his predecessors, has imagined new monstrous creatures. This epilogue also catalogs the vampire figure's presence in twenty-first-century Latin American literature and finally describes the new lurid entities emerging in literature, film, and other media, which apply an expression of monstrosity to a myriad of concerns throughout a more globalized world.

Mexican Vampire Films

After the success of Hollywood horror films in the 1930s and 1940s, including *Dracula* (and its Spanish-version companion, *Drácula*), the Mexican film industry also capitalized on the horror film boom by creating its own series of vampire films beginning in the 1950s. *El vampiro* (1957), directed by Fernando Méndez and written by Ramón Obón, was a sensational hit and led to the immediate production of its sequel, *El ataúd del vampiro* (1958) (The Vampire's Coffin), thus propelling the Mexican film industry's monster genre, whose film's popularity not only grew across the Latin American continent but also found admirers internationally.[1]

El vampiro follows a predictable plot commonly found in vampire films. In this rendition, two innocent characters, Marta and Enrique, travel to the rural and haunted Mexican town of Sicomoros. There they encounter the ominous and sinister Count Lavud, who has plans to illicitly acquire Marta's ancestral hacienda by slowly turning the family members into vampires. Marta's aunt Eloisa has already been converted into a vampire, while her other aunt, María Teresa, has been buried alive in the family crypt. Although María Teresa is presumed dead, she manages to awaken from her live burial and escapes into the hidden passageways of the home. From her place of hiding, she guards her niece from the vampires while simultaneously planning the demise of the monstrous usurpers. Ultimately, María Teresa, aided by Enrique, saves Marta, annihilates the vampires, and protects the family estate, promising a return to order.

Although the film on the surface might seem like a mere imitation of a Hollywood story, it is also celebrating national heroes and recalling previous invasions by foreign outsiders. Mexican critic Carlos Monsiváis argues that emerging Mexican film companies "nationalized" the Hollywood model in order to create their own popular domestic movies. He also argues that the Mexican film studios not only produced movies that would attract local filmgoers, but they also promoted cultural nationalism through the exaltation of enduring symbols that recalled important historical events, employed local humor, and celebrated national traditions and religion.[2] These signifiers of Mexican identity, or *mexicanidad*, are played out in very specific ways in *El vampiro*, as the villainous other and the heroes can best be understood within their national historical and cultural contexts. In the case of *El vampiro*, the film implicitly recalls the centennial of past Napoleonic incursions threatening state solidarity, remembering the sacrosanct heroes that guarded the nation and its citizens from foreign entities.[3] In this case, the vampiric count invades the home, a metaphor for the nation, and must be cast out. In the case of *El vampiro*, the enemy will be purged by María Teresa, who is represented as saintly: she is metonymically La Virgen de Guadalupe, the Mexican Madonna and emblematic protector of the people.

However, germane to this discussion is the way directors and screenwriters created innovative nonhuman entities and corresponding national heroes responsible for vanquishing them. Méndez innovates the vampire films by featuring one of the first female vampire killers on the silver screen. While female vampires are commonplace in Gothic literature and films, female vampire hunters do not usually form part of the earlier literary or filmic representations. In most vampire movies, the vampire killers are almost always male, such as Stoker's Van Helsing and Jonathan Harker. In *El vampiro*, María Teresa not only strangles her traitorous sister, a vampire, but also drives a stake through the vampire's heart, thus ending the vampire invasion. Her role brings to mind the Catholic iconography inspired by the Woman of the Apocalypse found in the book of Revelation in the Bible, in which the Virgin Mary defeats Satan, who is usually depicted as a serpent or dragon. Similar to the Holy Virgin, María Teresa annihilates the vampire—the metaphorical Devil—thus preventing the day of reckoning by saving the nation and humankind.

Having a female figure as vampire killer depicted in such aggressive terms in a film is unusual for the period and anticipates the way female roles in vampire annihilation narratives would change over time. Nowadays it is not shocking to feature these types of heroines in mass media; *Buffy the Vampire Slayer*, a popular television series that ran from 1992 to 2003, features a teenage heroine obsessed with vanquishing vampires. Anita Blake: Vampire Hunter, is the main protagonist in Laurell K. Hamilton's 1993 book *Guilty Pleasures*, who persecutes both vampires and zombies. The author has since added over twenty books to the series, and the character is also featured in Marvel Comics. In the 1998 film *Blade*, a female doctor fights alongside the movie's eponymous hero. In the more recent 2016 cable television series *Van Helsing*, Vanessa Helsing, a female vampire killer and a distant relative of Stoker's Abraham Van Helsing, possesses a special curing property within her that can transmute vampires into humans once again. The aforementioned US cultural products that began to emerge primarily in the 1990s represent modern examples of women playing active roles in destroying vampires and/or zombies. That is to say, female characters have transitioned from solely being cast as victims or female vampires themselves to agents of liberation and protection, which *El vampiro* already foreshadowed in 1957.

Méndez's film not only adds to film history by including a female heroine with agency; he also enhances the villain's fangs by making them more animalistic and aggressive compared to filmic predecessors and, as such, undertaking his demise makes the heroine all the more courageous. Count Lavud's fangs are different compared to those of the vampires featured in *Nosferatu* (1922) and *Dracula* (1931), for example. In these earlier films, the vampire's hypnotic and emphatic gaze are especially menacing compared to their actual teeth. The camera focuses on Nosferatu's phosphorescent eyes, his elongated face, his batlike pointy ears and razor-sharp nails. The film occasionally shows his narrow and uneven teeth resembling used nails that have pierced through a piece of wood, perhaps a coffin, yet the teeth are not presented as his most menacing quality. In Hollywood's 1931 version of *Dracula*, surprisingly, the vampire never reveals his fangs at all, and the camera almost exclusively focuses instead on Bela Lugosi's piercing gaze and his foreign accent, emphasizing his threatening otherness. The film critic Robert Cotter states in the audio commentary to *El vampiro* that the vampire's canine-like fangs were not usually part of the visual representation of vampires in films up to this point. By featuring sharper animal-like fangs, the villain becomes more frightening, thus elevating the danger that the heroes will have to overcome and conquer. Furthermore, devouring fangs have since become commonplace in contemporary films, in which the moment of the attack and the bite is almost always highly dramatized and, at times, gorier than in their precursors.

The Mexican film industry of the 1950s created vampires that speak to national identity, allegorizing its heroes and villains. While *El vampiro* and its sequel, *El ataúd del vampiro*, feature vampires as its stars, in subsequent films the monsters become secondary characters—specifically wrestlers, or *luchadores*, such as El Santo (The Saint)—displacing the monster's preeminence. El Santo, a national hero on and off the screen, began his career as a professional wrestler who frequently appeared on television and even in comic books. In comic books in particular, graphic artists portray him as a symbol of justice who protects the common folk, which is not at all surprising as his moniker already brands him with a saintlike status, suggesting that he is a venerated person who can intercede on behalf of others. In the film *El Santo contra las mujeres vampiro* (1962) (The Saint versus Female Vampires), the hero overtakes and defeats the demonic, vampiric women who plot to bring about the apocalypse by creating an army of monsters. In *Santo contra los zombis* (1961) (Santo versus Zombies) and in *Santo contra las lobas* (1972) (Santo versus the She-Wolves), as their titles indicate, the Mexican hero fights against she-wolves, vampires, and zombies.[4] At times El Santo fights alongside his rival the Blue Demon to defeat the monsters, such as in *Santo y Blue Demon contra Drácula y el hombre lobo* (1973) (Blue Demon and Santo versus Dracula and the Wolf-Man). These national and popular wrestling heroes were made even more heroic in films after being portrayed as casting out menacing monsters, which are so often symbols of threatening otherness. Robert Cotter's *The Mexican Masked Wrestler and Monster Filmography* provides a list of over one hundred films that feature mummies, vampires, wolf-men, zombies, wrestlers, and/or some other fantastic combination. The productions post-*El vampiro* can best be described as low-budget camp classics featuring over-the-top antics and humor, which in the end are not particularly frightening. Many would agree that the monster-wrestling films represent an artistic decline in the nation's film industry compared to the golden age of Mexican cinema (1930–1950s); however, these movies illustrate how studios took a formulaic and predictable genre and changed it into a financially lucrative and enticing product that appealed to the tastes of mass culture. These B-productions also reveal the way monsters—vampires in particular—contributed to a whole new and rare genre of monster-wrestling films that found many fans, both nationally and internationally.

Méndez, as well as other Mexican directors, celebrate mexicanidad in overt ways through heroic wrestlers that overcome menacing others, as embodied in the monsters. And the more numerous and menacing the monsters were, all the more heroic were their eradications. However, while earlier vampire films spoke to national sensibilities, many contemporary films and international collaborations no longer specifically address local culture. In particular, Guillermo del Toro, whose filmic representations are harder to ground in a specific national tradition, illustrates how vampires and vampire films have evolved in our global and interconnected world.

Guillermo del Toro is a director, screenwriter, film producer, and novelist who has become famous for producing dark fantasy films made domestically and internationally in Argentina, Spain, and the United States. Some of his most popular films include *Cronos* (1993), *El espinazo del diablo* (2001) (The Devil's Backbone), *Blade II* (2002), *El laberinto del Fauno* (2006) (Pan's Labyrinth), and *Crimson Peak* (2015). Del Toro's *Cronos* initiated his transnational filmmaking career, which underscores how films are now mostly financed and produced internationally in our growing global economy. Del Toro incorporates a Pan-American and bilingual cast in *Cronos*, including Ron Perlman (United States), Federico Luppi (Argentina), and Margarita Isabel (Mexico).[5] The characters at times speak both in English and Spanish in the film. For example, Perlman's character, Ángel de la Guardia, speaks to Luppi's character, Jesús Gris, in English, while Jesús in turn responds to him in Spanish. Ángel mostly speaks in English throughout the film, yet occasionally uses a few expletives or phrases in Spanish. The bilingual interaction is presented in a way that indicates that the characters completely understand each other, even though they are speaking two different languages—a type of conversation that could easily take place in a nonmonolingual home or social gathering. The international cast and the bilingual nature of the film indicate that the target audience is not solely Spanish-speaking but, rather, imagined as an international one.

Del Toro has also been successful in producing Hollywood films. In *Blade II*, starring Wesley Snipes, a black vampire hunter known as the "daywalker" is a hybrid creature with both human and vampiric qualities who uses modern medicine and age-old garlic elixirs to control his thirst for blood. Compared to the original *Blade* (1998), in the sequel del Toro incorporates a new and menacing strain of vampires that are more powerful, reproduce immediately, and demonstrate excessive blood lust, surpassing their predecessors' dreadfulness. These new vampires, aiming to devour both human and the older traditional vampire regimes, destabilize age-old human-vampire relations; therefore, the vampire elders call upon Blade to restore their former and arguably less monstrous order.

Similar to Méndez, del Toro too contributes to the evolution of the vampire's fangs, or, perhaps, de-evolution. These more infectious vampires do not display fangs in the traditional sense; rather, they have a developed suction system that both pierces and paralyzes their victims, thus presenting an even more terrorizing "bite." The vampire sting that del Toro employs in *Blade II* reemerges in his subsequent creations. However, these newer monsters travel freely and their infections spread quickly, while the ways to annihilate them become more elusive.

Del Toro not only directs films with vampires; along with Chuck Hogan, he co-wrote novels about them, including *The Strain* (2009), *The Fall* (2010), and *The Night Eternal* (2011). These novels have since been adapted for television under the title *The Strain*. Just as he approached the *Blade* characters, the creators simultaneously adopt features of older vampires while also imagining their monstrosity differently. *The Strain* presents viewers with different types of vampiric entities, which include gruesome child vampires that do not speak, make chirruping sounds, and scurry around like spiders with lightning speed, as well as the customary astute vampires, the leaders, who can telepathically control their minions. These vampiric minions travel collectively and behave like zombies that neither speak nor reason, viscerally and insatiably hunting humans. In order to feed, these vampires pierce through the victim's neck with a projectilelike tongue that simultaneously impales and sucks the blood of the victims. These vampires might also eat their victims' brains, which is reminiscent of zombie behavior. Unlike the *Twilight* saga, in which some of the vampires have been domesticated, del Toro creates a type of vampire that is more menacing, destructive, and infectious, whose virulence in a mere forty-one days infects the rest of the world. The mass multiplication of zombielike vampires brings the world to the end of days, in which there are only a few humans left to defeat them. The vampires hide in underground tunnels, then emerge en masse to hunt. They are also mysteriously interconnected, maintaining communication through a secret telepathic web that makes them even more unpredictable. Del Toro's new vampiric entities virtually dismantle national institutions such as the army and the police, who can no longer protect citizens from foreign infections; everyone is left to fight alone. Guillermo del Toro's texts not only present viewers with anxieties about contagion but also underscore how weakened institutions are unable to respond to or protect their citizens.

Newer Vampiric Entities and the Zombie Turn

Besides del Toro's filmic vampires, other new vampiric entities are emerging in twenty-first-century literature, film, and other media. In recent years, novels have appeared featuring vampires and have become the center of public attention. The Columbian author Carolina Andújar found success with her vampire series, which includes titles such as *Vampyr* (2009) and *Vajda: Príncipe Inmortal* (2012) (Vajda: Immortal Prince). The Mexican writer Ramón Obón (the son of *El vampiro*'s screenwriter) has published several terror novels, including a vampire trilogy: *El príncipe maldito* (2008) (The Cursed Prince), *Amantes de sangre* (2009) (Blood Lovers), and *La cofradía secreta* (2011) (The Secret Brotherhood). Similarly, the Mexican poet and novelist Adriana Díaz Enciso's book *La sed* (2001) (The Thirst) also features transgressive vampires. Danielle Borgia has already analyzed several of the aforementioned novels in her essay "Vampiros Mexicanos: Nonnormative Sexualities in Contemporary Vampire Novels of Mexico," in which she explores the ways the novels at times reaffirm or transgress normative heterosexual relationships. Puerto Rican writer Pedro Cabiya published *María V* (2011), which represents a revision of the Columbian writer Jorge Isaacs's celebrated romantic novel *María* (1837); however, he adds vampires into the mix.[6] Cabiya's novel literally becomes a monstrous double, in which he converts the classic nineteenth-century romantic novel into a Gothic one.

In addition to vampires, zombies are also making their way into Latin American cultural productions more vigorously. As previously discussed, del Toro bestows more zombielike features on some of his vampires: they are feeble-minded entities that travel collectively and move toward their victims with unprecedented speed. His vampiric entities are no longer the eloquent, seductive, cultured, and aristocratic vampires like Anne Rice's Lestat, but rather nonsentient creatures in sole search of human victims. Whereas the vampires present a threat to the civilized world, the zombies usually already inhabit an uncivilized one, in which humans are trying to survive at best. The aforementioned twenty-first-century fiction presents to readers a rich source material to further explore how authors might allegorize contemporary concerns.

Persephone Braham's discerning 2015 study *From Amazons to Zombies: Monsters in Latin America* describes how monstrosity had been used as a lens to understand and imagine the New World. The author analyzes the many representations of the monstrous as illustrated in Amazon women, cannibals, giants, mermaids, vampires, and zombies. Her insightful and detailed transatlantic study covers several centuries, spanning from antiquity to the present, in which she analyzes a variety of literary and filmic works. Persephone's book, mentioned above, also reveals that there is a growing interest in Latin American Gothic criticism in the twenty-first century. *Negrótico* (2015) by Nadina Olmedo and Osvaldo di Paolo examines the Gothic and its relation to crime fiction. In *Tropical Gothic in Literature and Culture: The Americas* (2016), edited by Justin Edwards and Sandra Guardini Vasconcelos, as the title suggests, examines the Gothic of the US South and the Caribbean, as well as transnational movements throughout the American continent. In the edited collection, *Latin American Gothic* (2018), the authors analyze contemporary literature under the guise of a "globalgothic," suggesting that the Gothic is no longer a singular European mode, but has become transnational and transcultural.

In particular, Braham dedicates a chapter entitled "The Caribbean Zombie Gothic" to address the way zombies "reveal the mechanisms of violence, racism, and misogyny inherent in monster-making."[7] Some of the fiction she mentions in relation to the zombie includes the Cuban writer Mayra Montero's *Tú, la oscuridad* (1995) (In the Palm of Darkness), and Pedro Cabiya's *Trance* (2007) and *Malas hierbas* (2010) (Wicked Weeds). Braham also discusses the successful Cuban zombie film *Juan of the Dead* (2011), directed by Alejandro Brugués, an obvious parody of *Shaun of the Dead* and its filmic predecessor, George Romero's cult classic *Night of the Living Dead* (1968). Braham posits that *Juan of the Dead* "satirizes the Cuban socialist state."[8] In the film, the zombies have overtaken the island, and a few less-than-heroic zombie killers set up an extermination business and try to vanquish them, but for a fee. Their victory seems unlikely, as they try to leave the island on makeshift *balsas*, a clear reference to the way some of Cuba's citizens have had to escape the island during economic and political hardships. The film turns the Cuban utopia on its head; what was promised by the revolution has become a nightmare version of an ideal, now overrun by flesh-eating monsters. Yet, the hero of the movie stays to conquer the zombies against all odds.

Zombie texts are also appearing outside the Caribbean. Argentinean filmmakers have produced their first-ever zombie film series, as illustrated by *Plaga Zombie* (1997–2013) (Zombie Plague), which has attracted an international cult following. The Chilean *Zombies en la moneda*, a comic series first published in 2009, depicts the apocalypse in Santiago, Chile, and represents another example of zombie figures emerging in other countries.[9] This zombie invasion unfolds in a world that is on the edge of annihilation or is already destroyed, in which a few ineffectual heroes still fight and whose success is doubtful.

In 2013, the Mexican writer Diego Velázquez Betacourt published a novel about a zombie apocalypse in Mexico, *La noche que asolaron Tokio* (The Night That Tokio Was Destroyed). In the novel, Andrés wakes up one day to find that all his friends and family have disappeared. The protagonist describes the end-times, an ecological disaster, in which the poles have melted and the water is undrinkable due to pollution. Ironically, Andrés before the crisis was collaborating on an absurd theatrical piece, a zombie musical, *La noche que los zombies asolaron Tokio*, which echoes the novel's name. Velázquez Betacourt's novel suggests that the commerce brought on by globalization has enslaved its citizens, destroying them and converting them into empty beings. In the novel, the zombies are in the background, emerging occasionally to have friendly interactions with Andrés and then going about their business. That is to say, the zombies are not actively attacking humans but are instead represented as decomposing bodies, aimlessly wandering about without purpose. In Velázquez Betancourt's rendition, the zombies are not as frightening as a world altered by climate change, pollution, and globalization. This turn toward zombies might suggest that vampires have lost their ability to embody the fears that threaten a society already in crisis. The societies in zombie fiction are already presented as being at the end of days, in which characters are trying to find meaning in a globalized and vacuous world. That is to say, the postapocalyptic settings address a fearful world in ruins with a few citizens left to find ways to exist. These pessimistic stories offer no viable return to order, presenting readers with an uncertain vision of a very dark future that tacitly addresses climate change, epidemics, exhausted resources, global fascism, overpopulation, and a host of other unsettling vicissitudes.

Monsters, including the newer versions of vampires and zombies, continue to embody multifaceted, intangible, and nameless fears, and evoking them is one way to allegorize these anxieties. With the new emerging monsters in literature, films, television series, and graphic novels, critics further explore the ways these new articulations reveal certain social crises that realist discourse insufficiently articulates. Or perhaps, as some have suggested, literary and filmic monsters are just monsters, and tell us nothing about our Gothic world.

Notes

Preface

1. Criticism is a modern form of autobiography. When you write about your readings you are really writing about your life. See Piglia, *Formas breves*, 141. All the translations in this book are mine, unless otherwise noted.

Introduction

1. Botting, *Gothic*, 2nd ed., 1.
2. Botting, *Gothic*, 6.
3. Here I use negative aesthetics as proposed in Botting's book *Gothic* and not Theodor Adorno's negative aesthetics as explored in *Aesthetic Theory*.
4. Mulvey-Roberts, introduction to *Handbook to Gothic Literature*, xvi.
5. Halberstam, *Skin Shows*, 16.
6. Contagion and blood contamination are also implied in the vampire figure, which spreads the vampire "disease" through its infectious bite. See Goddu, "Vampire Gothic," 125–41.
7. Julian Wolfreys, introduction to *Victorian Gothic*, xiv. For a more detailed study on how the movement of monstrous bodies from foreign lands to host countries also addressed fears about the other in terms of race, see Bienstock Anolik, and Howard, *Gothic Other*.
8. Kilgour, *Rise of the Gothic Novel*, 4–5.
9. Hogle, introduction to *Cambridge Companion*, 2.
10. Haggerty, *Queer Gothic*, 2.
11. Gothic terror has also been studied within notions of the sublime. Burke, *Philosophical Enquiry*; Morris, "Gothic Sublimity," 299–319.
12. Punter, *Literature of Terror*, 21.
13. Summers, *Gothic Quest*, 198.
14. Kilgour, *Rise of the Gothic Novel*, 30.
15. Hogle, introduction, 16; Botting, *Gothic* (1996), 2. Botting's 2014 introduction is significantly different from the one found in the 1996 edition.
16. For more information about *el modernismo*, see Pacheco, *Antología del Modernismo*, xi–li.
17. Skinner, *Gender*, 9. For more context, see Jrade, "Social-Political Concerns," 302–15.
18. Jrade, *Modernismo, Modernity*, 28.

19. See Jrade, *Rubén Darío*, where she explores occult and esoteric themes in the modernistas' works. According to Octavio Paz, the modernistas created another form of romanticism or, as he states, "su versión no fue una repetición, sino una metáfora: otro romanticismo" (Their version was not a repetition, but a metaphor: another romanticism). Paz, *Los hijos del limo*, 218.

20. Hayden White explains that because modern historians aspired to represent real events, limits had to be established as to the definition of what constituted a historical event, effectively excluding certain themes from the historical narrative: religious beliefs, rituals, miracles, magical occurrences, and godly events, for example. In other words, as White argues, the sublime was taken out of historical discourse. This meant that the supernatural and the magical, which had formed part of historical writing just a century before, were no longer admissible. See White, *Metahistory*.

21. Botting, *Gothic* (2014), 2.

22. Baldick and Mighall, "Gothic Criticism," 209.

23. Davidson, *History of the Gothic*, 3. Davidson also explains how there was a more "veiled" denunciation of the genre developed because of its association with women, who were primarily the ones producing and avidly reading the Gothic.

24. Breton, *Manifestoes*, 26.

25. Read, introduction to *Surrealism*, 23.

26. Breton, "Limits Not Frontiers," 106–07.

27. Breton, as quoted in "Radio Interviews with André Parinaud (1913–1952)," in *Conversations*, 63.

28. The vanguards' interest in pre-Columbian culture is especially evident in the *Dyn* circle in Mexico. *Dyn* is the name of a journal created by a group of writers and artists who left Europe and found refuge in Mexico City during World War II. Several artists had worked with Breton but broke away from him years later. See Leddy and Conwell, *Farewell to Surrealism*.

29. Some critics see the fantastic as an umbrella term that includes the Gothic, while others argue that the fantastic can find its roots in the Gothic. See Haggerty, *Queer Gothic*; Nieto, *Teoría general*; and Casares, prologue to *Antología*, where he acknowledges the Gothic as a precursor to literature of the fantastic.

30. Casares, prologue to *Antología*, 11, 17.

31. See Todorov, *Fantastic*.

32. Valdez Moses, "Magical Realism"; Bowers, *Magic(al) Realism*.

33. Bowers, *Magic(al) Realism*, 4.

34. Haggerty, *Gothic Fiction*, 81.

35. The question of whether cultural products emerging from mass culture,

such as film, could be considered art or a capitalist product for mass consumption and an instrument that converted citizens into passive consumers and apolitical actors has led to ongoing discussions addressing the question of what makes art art. Walter Benjamin saw the popular arena as one that could bring about social change, while Theodor Adorno saw its depoliticizing potential. See Adorno, *Complete Correspondence*.

36. For more information regarding Surrealism in Latin America, see Ades, Eder, and Speranza, *Surrealism in Latin America*. For a more detailed study on how the historical avant-garde aims (1920s–1930s) continued with artists that followed in the neo-avant-garde, see Bürger, Brandt, and Purdy, "Avant-Garde."

37. My translation from the original: "El modo en que toda una narrativa perteneciente a la cultura 'culta' utiliza, se apropia y transforma los códigos masivos." See Amar Sánchez, *Juegos de seducción*, 13.

38. Bennett, "Detective Fiction," 263.

39. See Lambert, "André Breton en México"; Lomnitz, *Death*, 24; Cruz Porchini and Ortega Orozco, "1940 International."

40. Eliot, "Tradition," 48–49.

41. Eliot, "Tradition," 49.

42. My translation. Pacheco, "Entre la plantación," 62.

43. Doniger, *Splitting the Difference*, 5.

44. Some editions have the title of the story as "Las vampiras."

45. Horacio Quiroga is neither a modernista nor a writer associated directly with the Surrealists; however, he was writing during a time when vanguard culture was at the forefront of literary production, and similar to them, he was also drawn to film. Cortázar did not belong to the vanguard movements per se, but his literature has been admired for its appropriation of certain surrealist themes. See Castro-Klaren, "Cortázar," 218–36. See also Garfield, "Exquisite Cadaver," 18–21; Alazraki, "Fantastic," 28–33.

46. See Aldana, *Spanish Gothic*, 42: "Overall, an estimated forty-five Gothic novels, mostly from British and French origin and almost exclusively translated from the French, entered Spain between the 1780s and the 1830s, and a significant number saw several editions over the course of those 50 years." More archival research would help establish when and how these texts might have reached Latin American readership.

47. Neoclassicism, a broad term, has no single definition; however, in general terms, artists follow Hellenic tradition and art that manifest certain ideals: decorum, beauty, and balance. M. H. Abrams states: "These authors exhibited a strong traditionalism, which was often joined to a distrust of radical innovation and was evidenced above all in their great respect for classical

writers—that is, the writers of ancient Greece and Rome—who were thought to have achieved excellence, and established the enduring models, in all the major literary genres. Hence the term "neoclassic." See Abrams, *Glossary*, 173–77.

Chapter 1

1. There are still other vampire stories yet to be identified. Juana Manuela Gorriti, an Argentinean writer associated with Romanticism and considered one of country's most influential writers of the nineteenth century, briefly mentions a ghostly vampire figure in her romantic novel *La Quena* (The Flute) (1845), published in the anthology *Sueños y realidades* (1865), which I do not analyze here. Yet it is the modernistas, in particular, who collectively evoke and feature vampiric entities in their literature. See Gorriti, *Sueños y realidades*.

2. Arellano-Sota, "Biology, Ecology," S615; Greenhall and Schmidt, *Natural History*, 1–15.

3. In Spanish, the word for bat is *murciéalgo*, which is derived from the Latin word *muris*, or rat, and *caecus*, or blind. See the Real Academia Española, http://dle.rae.es/?id=Q6me6bm. Díaz del Castillo, *Memoirs*, 217.

4. Cabeza de Vaca, *Comentarios*, 90–91; Varnum, *Álvar Núñez Cabeza de Vaca*.

5. Greenhall and Schmidt, *Natural History*, 234.

6. Darwin, *Voyage*, 32–33.

7. McNally and Florescu, *In Search of Dracula*, 125–26.

8. Stoker, *Dracula*, 150–51.

9. Kampen, "Classic Veracruz," 117.

10. The *Popul vuh* was transcribed from oral tradition to written text by the Dominican monk Francisco Ximénez in the seventeenth century.

11. J. E. S. Thompson, "Maya Hieroglyphs," 180–81.

12. Thompson, "Maya Hieroglyphs," 176.

13. The Toba are an indigenous community from the Chaco region of northern Argentina. Caribbean Taíno and Columbian artifacts also feature bat imagery, suggesting that they were important to their culture. Wilson, "Taíno Social"; Benson, "Bats in South American Iconography," 165–90; Benson "BATS in South American Folklore."

14. Romero Sandoval, *Zotz*, 11.

15. Romero Sandoval, *Zotz*, 41, 34.

16. José Emilio Pacheco's introduction to *Antología del modernismo* (1884–1921) provides an insightful and thorough discussion of el modernismo and argues, like Max Enriquez Ureña, that there were several stages of the movement. The first texts were more refined and artificial, while in later

years the poems were inspired by autochthonous culture and regional history, as illustrated by Turcios's novel. See also Auladell Pérez, "Caupolicán a Rubén Darío."

17. Johnston, "Darío's Acquaintance," 271.
18. Olivio Jiménez, *Verónica*, 6.
19. The Argentinean Juana Manuela Gorriti published *Sueños y realidades* in 1865, which critics have also described as a precursor to the fantastic literature. See Regazzoni, "Exótico."
20. Gwen Kirkpatrick and Adriana Gordillo have also explored vampiric qualities in Agustini's work. See Kirkpatrick, "Limits of Modernismo." See also Gordillo, "Transformaciones."
21. Baudelaire and other French poets were great admirers of Edgar Allan Poe's works. This was also the case for many Latin American writers, who often allude to or directly cite Poe's works in their own writings. See Culler, "Baudelaire and Poe."
22. Halberstam, *Skin Shows*, 89.
23. Hughes, "Fictional Vampires," 147.
24. Margarita Vargas, email correspondence, August 10, 2017.
25. Skinner, *Gender*, 75.
26. Dijkstra, *Evil Sisters*, 5, 3–4.
27. Lugones, "La vampira," 79.
28. See Plato, "Myth Told by Aristophanes"; Batra, "After Androgyny," 54.
29. Mora, "Decadencia," 193.
30. Ruiz Pérez, "Contra-Escrituras," 187–88.
31. Translations mine unless otherwise noted. Vincenzi *Froylán Turcios*.
32. Turcios, *El vampiro*, 39.
33. Turcios, *El vampiro*, 168.
34. Turcios, *El vampiro*, 30.
35. Turcios, *El vampiro*, 66.
36. Turcios, *El vampiro*, 67–68.
37. Poe, "Ligeia," 334.
38. Cortázar, "El hijo del vampiro," 34.
39. See Bautista, "Cortázar"; Fleming, introduction to *Horacio Quiroga*; Kelman, "Afterlife"; and Stavans, *Mutual Impressions*.
40. Bautista, "Cortázar," 11.
41. Lloyd-Smith, "Nineteenth-Century American Gothic," 113–14.

Chapter 2

1. Even though plenty of evidence shows that German Expressionist films reached Latin America, this fact is rarely mentioned in film criticism; if it is

mentioned, the information is sparse. Most books about film culture and society in Latin American cities deal primarily with two topics: US film presence in Latin America and/or national film development.

2. Film critic Tom Gunning claims that it is unlikely this dramatic exit ever occurred given that thrill-seeking spectators were quite accustomed to these new inventions. See Gunning, "Aesthetic."
3. Gunning, "Aesthetic," 822–23.
4. Quoted in Reyes de la Maza, *Salón rojo*, 15–16.
5. Translations are mine unless otherwise noted.
6. "Foreign Market Possibilities."
7. There were similar motion-picture devices such as the Kinetoscope and the Vitascope, which arrived in Latin America before 1896; however, they did not provoke the same public response as the Lumière Cinematographe. See Reyes de la Masa, *Salón rojo*, 7.
8. Reyes de la Masa, *Salón rojo*, 19.
9. Glücksmann was Austrian born and emigrated to Argentina in 1890, becoming a powerful film and music industry mogul.
10. King, *Magical Reels*, 11.
11. For example, Glücksmann brought the Spanish version of Universal's *Dracula* (1931's *Drácula*) to his theaters in South America.
12. Kaye, "Gothic Film," 180.
13. K. Thompson, "Dr. Caligari," 124–25.
14. Thompson, "Dr. Caligari," 154.
15. Roussel quoted in Thompson, "Dr. Caligari," 151.
16. Audiences in 2008 were reminded of this film's transatlantic journey when the long-lost original version of *Metropolis* was found in the archives of Museo del Cine in Buenos Aires. According to the *New York Times*, shortly after the film premiered in Berlin, the picture was edited to appeal to more audiences. It was believed that the original film footage was forever lost; however, Adolfo Wilson, an Argentinean film distributor who was in Berlin when the original film premiered in 1927, purchased the movie rights and returned to Buenos Aires with the film reels in his luggage. Thanks to this Argentinean film distributor's transoceanic business dealings and voyage, audiences can now see—as they did in 1927 in Buenos Aires—the original version of *Metropolis*. See Rohter, "Footage Restored."
17. Barlow, *German Expressionist Film*, 7.
18. Kracauer, "From Caligari to Hitler," 189.
19. Barlow, *German Expressionist*, 39–40.
20. See González de León, "Buñuel, Poe," 49. Also see IMDB.com, where he is credited for writing the screenplay for the film *The Monk* (1972).

21. See Fine, "From Berlin to Hollywood," 282.
22. Kaye, "Gothic Film," 181. The most commonly given release date is 1920 (Germany) and 1921 (Argentina, Mexico, US); however, some books state 1919, which corresponds to the production year.
23. See Flynn, *Cinematic Vampires*, 39; Phillips, *Projected Fears*, 13.
24. Abbott, *Celluloid Vampires*, 61; Skal, *Hollywood Gothic*.
25. For a detailed description of Spanish-language filmmaking and filmmaking in other languages, see Vicendeau, "Hollywood Babel"; Jarvinen, *Rise of Spanish-Language Filmmaking*.
26. See Pinto, "Hollywood's Spanish-Language Films," 474.
27. Skal, "Spanish Dracula," 41.
28. Flynn, *Cinematic Vampires*, 41.
29. Some of the Spanish-version films were of inferior quality and hastily shot. They also featured little-known actors and not the emerging Hollywood stars that they had been accustomed to viewing. Audiences wanted to enjoy the same feature films coming out of the studios that US spectators saw and not diminished copies.
30. The US film dominance in the Spanish-speaking countries also suppressed national filmmaking, making it difficult for industries to develop early on. See Borge, *Latin American Writers*, 235–37. He summarizes how Hollywood films were commercial products and a propaganda force that strove to conquer and maintain their financial stronghold in foreign markets, including Latin America.
31. Castro Leal, *Novela de la Revolución*, 925.
32. Duffey, *De la pantalla*, 16.
33. Duffey, "Pancho Villa," 42.
34. González Casanova, *El cine*, 376–83.
35. Quiroga, *Cine y literatura*, 13–14.
36. Quiroga, *Cine y literatura*, 21.
37. This information about Bombal is from a personal interview with Guerra-Cunningham by the author on March 12, 2008.
38. See Acosta-Lugo, "De la pantalla grande," 78; Speratti-Piñero, "Horacio Quiroga," 1247; Gómez-Sicre, "La escritora," 49–51.
39. Quiroga, "Miss Dorothy Phillips," 145.
40. De Costa, *Vicente Huidobro*, 121.
41. Quoted in De Costa, *Vicente Huidobro*, 130.
42. De Costa, *Vicente Huidobro*, 128; Morelli, introduction to *Cagliostro*, 31–32.
43. Morelli, introduction to *Cagliostro*, 12. Both de Costa and Morelli discuss the history of this novel in detail. The editors of the 1934 edition of

Cagliostro, published by Zig-Zag, state in "Nota de la edición original" that various fragments of the novels were published in vanguard novels in 1921–1922. The editors also mention how a French company started filming *Cagliostro*; however, they went bankrupt before it was ever released. Subsequently, the Spanish text was translated into English as a novela-film. See Huidobro, *Mirror of a Mage*.

44. See Twitchell, *Living Dead*.

45. Merriam-Webster Online, s.v. "spectator," Merriam-Webster.com, http://www.merriam-webster.com/dictionary/spectator; "specter," http://www.merriam-webster.com/dictionary/specter.

46. See Mulvey, "Visual Pleasure"; Metz, *Imaginary Signifier*.

47. De Costa, *Vicente Huidobro*, 42.

48. In spite of their contentious relationship, Huidobro was close to Buñuel and had seen and admired his films. As kindred spirits, both men shared similar sensibilities, and while Huidobro expressed his ideas in words, Buñuel did so through cinema. See Morelli, "Contra el Surrealismo," 129–40.

49. See de Costa, "Huidobro y el Surrealismo," 74–80.

50. *Caligramas* are texts that create images with words that have an association with the theme of the work itself.

51. Quoted in Morelli, "Contra el Surrealismo," 131.

52. This is a text that he worked on and revised from 1920 to 1934. It was finally published as a novela-film. He was concerned with aesthetics and defining his own legacy within the vanguards, which he fiercely defended as illustrated in the many letters he wrote to his friends and foes.

53. De Costa, *Vicente Huidobro*, 130.

54. Quoted in Morelli, *Cagliostro*, 58.

55. Huidobro, *Cagliostro*, 65.

56. Huidobro, *Cagliostro*, 65.

57. The same ineffectual hero who appears in the novel *Dracula* (Jonathan Harker) turns up in the films *Nosferatu*, *Vampyr*, and *Dracula*, but he is given a different name in each: Hutter, Allan Gray (sometimes spelled Grey), and John Harker, respectively.

58. Huidobro, *Cagliostro*, 67.

59. Huidobro, *Cagliostro*, 84.

60. Huidobro, *Cagliostro*, 142.

61. Huidobro, *Cagliostro*, 115.

62. Paz Soldán, "Avant-Garde," 67.

63. De Costa, *Vicente Huidobro*, 136.

64. Huidobro and Quiroga's texts compliment what cultural theorists and avant-garde filmmakers would continue to explore. Some imagined spectators

completely dominated by films' illusion, while others saw cinema as a vehicle for social change, as illustrated in the films and essays of Hugo Münsterberg, Rudolf Arnheim, Béla Balázs, Sergei Eisenstein, Louis Delluc, Germaine Dulac, Jean Epstein, Siegfried Kracauer, Walter Benjamin, Erwin Panofsky, John Grierson, and Paul Rotha, who explored films' multifaceted possibilities. See Hagener, *Emergence of Film Culture*.

65. The continuous interruptions by the narrator in which he makes his presence known recalls Dziga Vertov's experimentation with film shots in his famous silent documentary film, *Man with a Movie Camera* (1929). Among the many images that he captures of the nascent Soviet regime, he also includes images of the camera in which he himself appears filming, thus reminding spectators that indeed the film is an illusion. Showing disdain for the mimetic, he states: "Until now, we have violated the movie camera and forced it to copy the work of our eye. And the better the copy, the better the shooting was thought to be. Starting today we are liberating the camera and making it work in the opposite direction—away from copying." He was also critical of fiction films that hid their technique and appreciated how documentaries in particular could be used for social transformation. See Vertov, *Kino-eye*, 16. Huidobro's text also foreshadows what Bertolt Brecht explores in "Alienation Effects in Chinese Acting" (1936). The alienation effect is a technique used in theater (and film) that limits the audience's ability to become completely immersed in the text, thus limiting their ability to fully empathize with the characters. See Brecht, *Brecht on Theatre*.

66. Huidobro, *Cagliostro*, 61.

67. Huidobro, *Cagliostro*, 66.

68. Huidobro's approach to his literature is also reminiscent of Victor Shklovsky's concept of defamiliarization or "estrangement" found in his essay "Art as Device." Shklovsky argues that when we see objects over and over again our perception becomes automatic, thus affecting our ability to really "see." He suggests that automation devours things, habits, furniture, women, and even the fear of war: "If we start to examine the general laws of perception, we see that as perception becomes habitual, it also becomes automatic" and life fades into nothingness. Art, therefore, can help us see things for the first time. In a certain sense, Huidobro, through his metafictional text, turns habitual reading into an innovative activity in which he provokes readers to see the fiction as fiction. Shklovsky, *Theory of Prose*, 4–6.

Chapter 3

1. Live burials as punishment have been documented throughout time and around the world. See Bondeson, *Buried Alive*, and Cruz Porchini and Ortega

Orozco, "1940 International." See "St. Vitalis"; also see "Burying Alive" in *Encyclopaedia Britannica; or A Dictionary of Arts, Sciences, and Miscellaneous Literature* (Edinburgh: Printed for Archibald Constable, 1823), 24, http://books.google.com/books?id=FMcnAAAAMAAJ.

2. Meyers, *Femicidal Fears*, ix.
3. Furneaux, "Gendered Cover-Ups."
4. Galt, "Buried Alive," 330.
5. Hewitt, *John Galt*, 270.
6. Mangham, "Buried Alive," 13.
7. Poe satirizes *Blackwood's* format in his essay "How to Write a Blackwood Article."
8. Stoker, *Dracula*, 30.
9. In contemporary films, female live burials have become a common feature to express female entrapment under the force of a villainous character. In Quentin Tarantino's *Kill Bill: Volume 2* (2004), Uma Thurman's character Bride/Black Mambo is buried alive in a coffin. In *Double Jeopardy* (1999), Ashley Judd's character is buried alive in a crypt in a New Orleans cemetery.
10. Sedgwick, *Coherence*, 3.
11. Carpentier, prologue to *El reino*, 2.
12. Carpentier, "On the Marvelous Real," 85.
13. The ability for zombies to awaken from the living-dead state after consuming salt is documented by Alfred Métraux: "Their docility is total provided you never give them salt. If imprudently they are given a plate containing even a grain of salt the fog which cloaks their minds instantly clears away and they become conscious of their terrible servitude." See Métraux, *Voodoo in Haiti*, 283.
14. Carpentier, *El reino*, 36.
15. Carpentier, *Kingdom*, 27.
16. Haitian zombie folklore informed William Seabrook's *The Magic Island* (1929), a travelogue sensationalizing Haitian Vodou religious practices that describes how sorcerers resurrect dead men forcing them to work in cane fields. Seabrook's text inspired early zombie films, including the 1932 Hollywood B movie *White Zombie* as well as *I Walked with a Zombie* (1943).
17. Carpentier, *El reino*, 108.
18. Carpentier, *Kingdom*, 103.
19. See A. Gordon, *Ghostly Matters*.
20. Carpentier, *Kingdom*, 124.
21. Huidobro, *Cagliostro*, 111.
22. See Pacheco, "Batalla del surrealismo," 49.
23. Leal, "Torres Bodet," 292.

24. Soon after the war ended in 1920, the government incited authors to write about the civil war in a way that would unify and consolidate a meaning for the revolution and serve their purposes. See Rutherford, *Mexican Society*. The official patronage, coupled with the public's interest in the topic, led to a marked increase in the production and publication of historical novels that addressed the Mexican Revolution and culminated in the republication in 1925 of Mariano Azuela's *Los de abajo* (1915) (*The Underdogs*), heralded as the most important novel that addressed this civil war. These historically based novels, which reached peak production between the 1920s and 1940s, recounted battles and celebrated its heroes while trying to give meaning to the nation's chaotic and violent past. Lanin Gyurko further emphasizes the significance of these texts when he states, "*La mexicanidad* in literature finds much of its inspiration as the result of the cataclysmic Revolution, a movement that gave Mexico a sense of its own identity and produced a creative explosion in literature, painting, and film" (243). See Gyurko, "Twentieth-Century Fiction," 243–303.

25. García Gutiérrez, "Dama de corazones," 262.

26. García Gutiérrez, "Dama de corazones," 277. See also Lomnitz, *Death*. Lomnitz carefully studies the way in which death is central to Mexican identity. He analyzes the history of the Day of the Dead and explores the death theme as a national totem.

27. Villaurrutia, "Dama de corazones," 585.

28. Villaurrutia, "Dama de corazones," 586.

29. Villaurrutia, "Dama de corazones," 586.

30. Mexico's pre-Columbian history was influential for Surrealists' and other modernists' imaginings, who at times fetishized and appropriated Mexican traditions and cosmography for their own aims. André Breton appreciated Mexico's dark humor and Guadalupe Posada's prints, known for creating humorous skeletal figures as political commentary. See Lomnitz, *Death*, 24. See also Barajas Durán, *Posada Mito*, 400. Mexican artists, although first drawn to Surrealism, later distanced themselves from Breton and others, creating their own distinct vanguard styles that could speak to national sensibilities.

31. He is one of Mexico's most esteemed poets and a Nobel Prize winner whose early works were inspired by Surrealism. He left for Paris and joined Breton and the Surrealists but later broke away from this group. See Pacheco, "Batalla del surrealismo," 49.

32. Ariès, *Hour of Our Death*, 473. See also Bronfen, *Over Her Dead Body*. Her provocative study explores the overrepresentations of the female dead body and considers the many ways in which the language of desire often

accompanies descriptions of the dead, deathbed scenes, and the revenant, which is exactly what Huidobro does in *Cagliostro* and Rulfo does in *Pedro Páramo*.

33. Rulfo, *Páramo y el llano*, 101.
34. Rulfo, *Pedro Páramo*, 123.
35. Poe, "Philosophy of Composition," 816.
36. Rulfo, *Pedro Páramo*, 91.
37. Rulfo, *Pedro Páramo*, 79.
38. Rulfo, *Pedro Páramo*, 96.
39. Rulfo, *Páramo y el llano*, 66–67.
40. Rulfo, *Páramo y el llano*, 63.
41. Rulfo, *Pedro Páramo*, 76.
42. Rulfo, *Páramo, y el llano*, 52.
43. Rulfo, *Pedro Páramo*, 61.
44. Bronfen, in *Over Her Dead Body*, explores this distinction between male and female authors, arguing that women writers deploy the representation of female death differently. Bronfen discusses "how women writers install, comply with, critique and rewrite the cultural image repertoire that links the feminine subject position to a speaking through and out of death" (xiii).
45. Wallace, "Haunting Idea," 26.
46. See Wallace and Smith, introduction to *Female Gothic*, for a more thorough analysis.
47. Fleenor, *Female Gothic*, 10–13.
48. Horner, "Heroine," 116.
49. Bombal, *Última niebla*, 12.
50. The work was later translated to English under the title *The House of Mist*. However, the author made significant changes and additions to this version that don't always correspond to the original text; therefore, some excerpts are my translations of the original Spanish-language novel.
51. Bombal, *Última niebla*, 12–13.
52. Guerra-Cunningham, *Narrativa*, 51.
53. Mangham, "Buried Alive," 10.
54. Bombal, *Amortajada*, 112.
55. Bombal, *Amortajada*, 98.
56. Bombal, *Amortajada*, 99.
57. Bombal, *Amortajada*, 143.
58. Bombal, *Shrouded Woman*, 226.
59. Guerra-Cunningham, *Narrativa*, 29.
60. Bombal, *Amortajada*, 144.
61. Bombal, *Shrouded Woman*, 227. Bombal translated *La amortajada*

herself; however, her English translation does not always correspond to the words she uses in Spanish.

62. Bombal, *Amortajada*, 143.
63. Bombal, *Shrouded Woman*, 226.
64. Bombal, *Amortajada*, 96.
65. Bombal, *Amortajada*, 95–96.
66. Bombal, *Amortajada*, 150.
67. Bombal, *Shrouded Woman*, 248.
68. See Guerra-Cunningham's analysis in *Narrativa* of death as a union with the cosmos (99).
69. LeFanu, "Carmilla," 136.
70. LeFanu, "Carmilla," 118.
71. LeFanu, "Carmilla," 118.
72. LeFanu, "Carmilla," 114.
73. LeFanu, "Carmilla," 110.
74. Bombal, *Amortajada*, 163
75. Bombal, *Shrouded Woman*, 259.
76. Bombal, *Amortajada*, 163.
77. Bombal, *Shrouded Woman*, 259.
78. Guerra-Cunningham, *Narrativa*, 105.

Chapter 4

1. Satirical coins depicting Napoleon III as a vampire appeared after he surrendered to Prussia. In some coins he is wearing a Prussian helmet while the reverse side of the coin reads "Vampire Français" or "Vampire de la France." Some of these coins were re-engraved from original issues, while others were made from original dies. See *Numismatist*. Napoleon Bonaparte appears as a character in Paul Feval's 1865 *La vampire*; however, the text has also been understood as a coded condemnation of Napoleon III's Second Empire (1852–1870), which coincides with the novel's publication. See Gibson, *Fantastic*. Victor Hugo's political pamphlet, *Napoléon le Petit* (1852) criticizes Napoleon III's regime, underscoring his despotic qualities and his penchant for bloodshed. See Hugo, *Napoleon the Little*.
2. Gordon and Hollinger, introduction to *Blood Read*, 3.
3. See Carlos Fuentes's book review, "A Despot, Now and Forever," in which he mentions how Roa Bastos, under Stroessner, was one of three citizens expressly forbidden to return.
4. McNally and Florescu, *Essential Dracula*, 12.
5. Hogle, introduction to *Cambridge Companion*, 16.
6. Albright, "No Time," 50.

7. Roa Bastos, "Interview with Beatriz," 25.
8. Stoker, *Dracula*, 5.
9. Ezquerro, introduction to *Yo el supremo*, 44.
10. Roa Bastos, *Yo el supremo*, 22.
11. Roa Bastos, *I, the Supreme*, 11.
12. Roa Bastos, *Yo el supremo*, 165.
13. Roa Bastos, *I, the Supreme*, 133.
14. Doniger, *Splitting the Difference*, 223.
15. Roa Bastos, *Yo el supremo*, 505.
16. Roa Bastos, *I, the Supreme*, 424.
17. Roa Bastos, *Yo el supremo*, 39.
18. Roa Bastos, *I, the Supreme*, 25.
19. Roa Bastos, *Yo el supremo*, 40.
20. Roa Bastos, *I, the Supreme*, 26.
21. Stoker, *Dracula*, 22.
22. Roa Bastos, *Yo el supremo*, 40.
23. Roa Bastos, *Yo el supremo*, 40–41.
24. Roa Bastos, *I, the Supreme*, 26–27.
25. Roa Bastos, *Yo el supremo*, 41.
26. Roa Bastos, *I, the Supreme*, 27.
27. Roa Bastos, *Yo el supremo*, 41.
28. Roa Bastos, *I, the Supreme*, 27.
29. Roa Bastos, *Yo el supremo*, 169.
30. Roa Bastos, *I, the Supreme*, 136.
31. Roa Basto, *Yo el supremo*, 175–76.
32. Roa Bastos, *I, the Supreme*, 141.
33. Stoker, *Dracula*, 276.
34. See McNally and Florescu, *In Search of Dracula*, 12–13, 178–81.
35. McNally and Florescu, *In Search of Dracula*, 5.
36. McNally and Florescu, *In Search of Dracula*, 27.
37. Roa Bastos, *Yo el supremo*, 56.
38. Roa Bastos, *I, the Supreme*, 40.
39. McNally and Florescu, *Essential Dracula*, 23–24.
40. McNally and Florescu, *In Search of Dracula*, 122.
41. Roa Bastos, *Yo el supremo*, 23–24.
42. Roa Bastos, *I, the supreme*, 12.
43. Roa Bastos, *Yo el supremo*, 114–15.
44. Roa Bastos, *I, the Supreme*, 89–90.
45. He is referring to Napoleon Bonaparte (1769–1821).
46. Holley, "Bloodthirsty Bonaparte," 8.

47. Roa Bastos, *Yo el supremo*, 117.
48. Roa Bastos, *I, the Supreme*, 91.
49. Roa Bastos, *I, the Supreme*, 90.
50. Roa Bastos, *Yo el supremo*, 512.
51. Roa Bastos, *I, the Supreme*, 429.
52. Roa Bastos, *Yo el supremo*, 513.
53. Roa Bastos, *I, the Supreme*, 430.
54. Stoker, *Dracula*, 212.
55. Fuentes's appropriation and play with Gothic features and its vampires is not all that surprising because his other novels already demonstrate his predilection for this type of literature, as exemplified in his *Aura* (1962).
56. Fuentes, *Vlad*, 27.
57. Fuentes, *Vlad*, trans. Bumas and Branger, 28.
58. Count Radu could refer to Vlad Tepes's brother, or Fuentes could be referring to the well-known Dracula expert Radu Florescu, who co-wrote *The Essential Dracula*.
59. Hughes, "Fictional Vampires," 147.
60. Socolow, *Women*, 6–8.
61. Fuentes, *Vlad*, 104.
62. Fuentes, *Vlad*, trans. Bumas and Branger, 113.
63. Quoted in Poole, *Our Lady of Guadalupe*, 5.
64. Asunción fits into the female dichotomy in which female figures are bestowed with qualities associated both with La Virgen de Guadalupe and Mexico's allegorical figure of betrayal, La Malinche. María Teresa Martínez-Ortiz argues in "We Are All Malinche: The Collapse of the National Mexican Mother and Its Representations in Literature and Film" that the Guadalupe-Malinche paradigm has been continually reconfigured with each national project. She also argues that more contemporary writers—female intellectuals especially—have contested and transgressed this well-known literary feature, creating other female models in their artistic works to speak of the nation. However, Fuentes is not one of these writers; instead, he returns to the traditional national mother paradigm, in which women are framed within this Guadalupe-Malinche dichotomy. Asunción is portrayed as both a suffering mother and a duplicitous figure who has made an unsavory arrangement with an invading power. If Asunción—as an allegory for the nation—is the reincarnation of La Malinche, then she is aiding a foreigner, and Vlad has taken the place of Cortés in this latest literary articulation of subjugation. Martínez-Ortiz, "We Are All Malinche," 111.
65. Leal, "Malinche-Llorona Dichotomy," 134.
66. Leal, "Malinche-Llorona Dichotomy," 135.

67. Leal, "Malinche-Llorona Dichotomy," 138.
68. Paz, "Los hijos de la Malinche," 98.
69. Paz, *Labyrinth of Solitude*, 75.
70. Since the 1990s Ciudad Juarez has seen a pervasive increase of femicides in which thousands of women have been abducted and tortured, but those responsible are rarely brought to justice. The slaughtering of young women throughout Mexico has also been made more acute due to increasing and ongoing drug violence. See González Rodríguez, *Huesos*; Wright, "Necropolitics," 707–31.
71. See R. Romero, "Foundational Motherhood," 28–43.
72. See Porter, "Globalization."
73. Fuentes, *Vlad*, 95.
74. Fuentes, *Vlad*, trans. Bumas and Branger, 104.
75. For a detailed report on the drug trade in Mexico, see the *CRS Report for Congress*.
76. Stoker, *Dracula*, 212.

Chapter 5

1. The image of the double is also a central feature in stories associated with *la literatura fantástica*, which has been widely studied in a Latin American context; Jorge Luis Borges's "Borges y yo" and Julio Cortázar's "Lejana" being just two singular examples. However, the aim of this chapter is to analyze those stories that feature portentous doubles that demonstrate more Gothic characteristics and aesthetics.
2. Some of the novels and short stories most often mentioned in relation to doubles include Jean Paul's (Johann Paul Friedrich Richter's) *Siebenkäs* (1796), Matthew Lewis's *The Monk* (1796), E. T. A. Hoffmann's "The Devil's Elixir" (1815), Mary Shelley's *Frankenstein* (1818), Edgar Allan Poe's "William Wilson" (1839), Fyodor Dostoyevsky's *The Double* (1846), Guy de Maupassant's *Le Horla* (1887), and Oscar Wilde's *The Picture of Dorian Gray* (1890), to name just a few.
3. The Taínos were a group of indigenous people that inhabited the Caribbean and were nearly annihilated soon after the conquest of the Americas.
4. Freud, *Uncanny*, 142–43.
5. Girard, *Violence and the Sacred*, 165.
6. Poe's emblematic story of the double is often cited in criticism, which is also discussed in Freud's *Uncanny*.
7. See Robisch, *Wolves*.
8. Webber, *Doppelgänger*, 3.
9. Webber, *Doppelgänger*, 5.

10. Webber, *Doppelgänger*, 8.
11. This chapter uses *nahual*, although *nagual* is often used as well.
12. See Genesis 3:1; Revelation 20:2.
13. For a more detailed description of werewolf literature and its relationship to the Gothic, see Hughes, Punter, and Smith, *Encyclopedia of the Gothic*.
14. Middleton, *Magic, Witchcraft, and Curing*, 70–71; Correa, "El espíritu del mal," 77.
15. López Agustín, "La fauna maravillosa," 56.
16. Middleton, *Magic, Witchcraft, and Curing*, 70–71.
17. Manly, "Regeneration."
18. Quiñones Keber, "Xolotl," 234.
19. Cortázar, "Axolotl," in *Cuentos Completos*, 521.
20. Cortázar, "Axolotl," in *End of Games*, 8.
21. See Kauffmann, "Narrating the Other," 135–55.
22. Carpentier, *El reino*, 7.
23. Carpentier, "On the Marvelous Real in America," 87–88.
24. Carpentier, *El reino*, 5.
25. Carpentier, "On the Marvelous," 86–87.
26. See Atsma, *Theoi Greek Mythology*.
27. For more information regarding wolf folklore, see Kropfelder, *Esoteric Codex*; Steiger, *Werewolf Book*.
28. See Merriam-Webster.com, s.v. "Lycanthropy," http://www.merriam-webster.com/dictionary/lycanthropy.
29. Kropfelder, *Esoteric Codex*, 10.
30. Carpentier, *El reino*, 1.
31. Zamora and Ferris do not include the epigraph. I have taken the translation found at http://pocolitandanticolonialactivism.qwriting.qc.cuny.edu/files/2014/08/carpentier-marvelous.pdf.
32. The title to Cervantes's text has appeared as both "Segismunda" and "Sigismunda"; however, according to *La real academia de Española* (www.rae.es), Sigismunda is the correct spelling.
33. See Kingsley *West African Studies*, 200. She describes the bush-soul as "the soul that lives in an animal away wild in the bush." Malcolm, "Short Notes," 219–22.
34. Carpentier, *El reino*, 37.
35. Carpentier, *Kingdom*, 28.
36. These beliefs were brought to the island by slaves from Africa, mostly from Yoruba and Kongo.
37. Wilson, "Taíno Social," 52.

38. See Barreda-Tomás, "Alejo Carpentier," 34–44.
39. Carpentier, *El reino*, 45.
40. Carpentier, *Kingdom*, 35–36.
41. Carpentier, *El reino*, 45.
42. Carpentier, *Kingdom*, 36.
43. Carpentier, *El reino*, 148.
44. Translation mine. This fragment is missing from the English translation. The omission of the Cervantes epigraph from the English translation and the exclusion of the word *lycanthropy* in this citation significantly alters the reading.
45. Carpentier, *El reino*, 146.
46. Carpentier, *Kingdom*, 150.
47. Carpentier, *Kingdom*, 149.
48. León-Portilla, "Those Made Worthy," 41.
49. Miller and Taube, *Gods and Symbols*, 30.
50. The statue's name can be written *chacmool* or *chac-mool*; however, Fuentes uses *Chac Mool* in the story.
51. Miller and Taube, *Gods and Symbols*, 59–60.
52. This situation is reminiscent of the creature found in Guy Maupassant's *Horla*; the Chac Mool will suck the life force out of Feliberto, making their relationship an implicitly vampiric one. See Campa Marcé, "Carlos Fuentes."
53. Herrera-Ávila, "De lo mítico," 150.
54. Herrera-Ávila, "De lo mítico," 155.
55. "Chac Mool," in *Cuentos completos*, 35.
56. "Chac Mool," in *Burnt Water*, 14.
57. See Gyurko, "Self, Double," 363–84.
58. See Durán, *Archetypes*. Durán describes the recurring theme of human sacrifice in Fuentes's texts.
59. Albán de Viqueira, "Estudio de las fuentes," and Rojas, "El torno," have already underscored the many similarities Fuentes's witch has with Michelet's sympathetic depiction of this female enchantress, as found in his historical book *La sorcière*. See also Titiev, "Witchcraft," 395–405.
60. Hell, "Angel's Enigmatic Eyes," 373.
61. Hell, "Angel's Enigmatic Eyes," 372.
62. For more information on Michelet's place in history see Hooper, "Changing Perceptions."
63. See Fuentes, "On Reading." He openly refers to these characters as models in his creation of Consuelo and General Llorente.
64. Fuentes, *Aura*, 8, 38.
65. Fuentes, *Aura*, 36, 42.

66. Miller and Taube, *Gods and Symbols*, 30–31.
67. Miller and Taube, *Gods and Symbols*, 127–28.
68. Fuentes, *Aura*, 16.
69. Fuentes, *Aura*, 64.
70. Michelet, *Satanism and Witchcraft*, chapter 9.
71. Michelet, *Satanism and Witchcraft*, chapter 10.
72. Fuentes, *Aura*, 131–32.
73. Fuentes, *Aura*, 132.
74. Fuentes, *Aura*, 133.
75. Lewis, *Monk*, 257.
76. See Durán, *Magia y las brujas*. Durán also describes the significance of Aura's green eyes in relation to the image of the witch.
77. Freud, "Totem and Taboo," 498.
78. See Carruthers, "Lines of Flight," 119–32. In this article, Carruthers explains the use of nightshade in shamanistic practices as described in Carlos Castañedas' well-known work, *The Teachings of Don Juan: A Yaqui Way of Knowledge* (1968). The book was the first in a series of books that describe Yaqui Indian shamanism in northern Mexico.
79. Fuentes, *Aura*, 100, 102.
80. Fuentes, *Aura*, 101, 103.
81. McNamee, *Movable Feasts*, 168.
82. Davidson, "Nightshade," 830.
83. For a more detailed description of the plants that have often been associated with witchcraft, see Cull, "On Reading Fuentes," 18–27.
84. The word *riñones*, which means kidneys, appears as "liver" in the English translation. Although both are innards, *kidneys*' subtle meaning in connection with sacrificial rituals is important but loses its meaning in the English version. See Fuentes, *Aura*, 38–39.
85. Diamandopoulos, Skarpelos, and Tsiros, "Use of the Kidneys," 401.
86. Diamandopoulos, Skarpelos, and Tsiros, "Use of the Kidneys," 399.
87. Fuentes, *Aura*, 40.
88. Fuentes, *Aura*, 41.
89. Clendinnen, *Aztecs*, 37.
90. Monter, "Black Mass," 125.
91. Michelet, *Satanism and Witchcraft*, chapter 11.
92. Fuentes, *Aura*, 108.
93. Fuentes, *Aura*, 116.
94. Fuentes, *Aura*, 117.
95. Fuentes, *Aura*, 122.
96. Fuentes, *Aura*, 123.

97. Fuentes, *Aura*, 122.
98. Fuentes, *Aura*, 123.
99. Fuentes, *Aura*, 144.
100. Fuentes, *Aura*, 145. In the Spanish original the narrator states that he loves the body, which is withered and old, whereas in the English translation states that he loves her.
101. Hutcheon, *Theory of Parody*, 31.
102. Náter, "Imaginación enfermiza," 73.
103. Pérez, "Configuración de elementos góticos," 9.
104. Langford, *Mexican Novel*, 140.
105. Botting, *Gothic* (2014), 15.
106. See Leal, "History and Myth," 8–25. Leal describes the mythic themes Fuentes often invokes in his fiction.
107. García-Caro, "Aura y la teoría narrativa," 143.
108. The author himself acknowledges Orson Welles's influence. Lanin Gyurko and Patrick Duffey, among others, have analyzed *Artemio Cruz* in relation to *Citizen Kane*.
109. Brushwood, *Spanish American Novel*, 213.
110. See Kadir, "Another Sense."

Epilogue

1. See Serrano, "Revamping Dracula," which more thoroughly analyzes the way the film addresses national notions of belonging.
2. Monsiváis, "Función corrida," 265.
3. Hughes, "Fictional Vampires," 147.
4. These are just three examples; for a complete list, see Cotter, *Mexican Masked Wrestler*.
5. See Stock, "Migrancy," 19–30.
6. See Braham, *Amazons to Zombies*, in which she analyzes these works more thoroughly.
7. Braham, *Amazons to Zombies*, 18.
8. Braham, *Amazons to Zombies*, 175.
9. See Mella Vilches, *Zombies en la Moneda*.

Bibliography

Abbott, Stacey. *Celluloid Vampires: Life after Death in the Modern World*. Austin: University of Texas Press, 2007.

———. "Spectral Vampires: *Nosferatu* in the Light of New Technology." In *Horror Film: Creating and Marketing Fear*, edited by Steffen Hantke, 3–20. Jackson: University Press of Mississippi, 2004.

Abrams, M. H. *Glossary of Literary Terms*. Boston: Heinle and Heinle, 1999.

Acosta-Lugo, Maribel. "De la pantalla grande al papel: Los elementos del séptimo arte en *la amortajada* de María Luisa Bombal." *Focus* 2 (2003): 73–80.

Ades, Dawn, Rita Eder, and Graciela Speranza, eds. *Surrealism in Latin America: Vivísimo Muerto*. Los Angeles: Getty Research Institute, 2012.

Adorno, Theodor. *Aesthetic Theory*. Edited by Gretal Adorno and Rolf Tiedemann. Translated by Robert Hullot-Kentor. Minneapolis: University of Minnesota Press, 1997.

Theodor Adorno: The Complete Correspondence, 1928–1940. Edited by Nicholas Walker and Walter Henri Lonitz. Cambridge, MA: Harvard University Press, 2001.

Agustini, Delmira. *Cantos de la mañana*. 1910. Montevideo: Antítesis Editorial, 2014.

———. "El vampiro." Madrid: Central virtual Cervantes, 1997–2016. http://cvc.cervantes.es/literatura/escritores/agustini/antologia/vampiro.htm. Accessed December 15, 2016.

Alazraki, Jaime. "The Fantastic of Surrealist Metaphors." *Dada/Surrealism* 5 (1975): 28–33.

———. "Theme and System in Carlos Fuentes' *Aura*." In *Carlos Fuentes: A Critical View*, edited by Robert Brody and Charles Rossman, 119–31. Austin: University of Texas, 1982.

Albán de Viqueira, Ana María. "Estudios de las fuentes de *Aura* de Carlos Fuentes." *Comunidad* 2 (1967): 396–402.

Albright, Richard S. "No Time Like the Present: *The Mysteries of Udolpho*." *Journal for Early Modern Cultural Studies* 5, no. 1 (2005): 49–75. https://muse.jhu.edu/article/182703. Accessed March 10, 2017.

Aldana Reyes, Xavier. *Spanish Gothic: National Identity, Collaboration and Cultural Adaptation*. London: Palgrave Macmillan, 2017. ProQuest

Ebook Central, https://ebookcentral.proquest.com/lib/albanyedu-ebooks/detail.action?docID=4825697.
Amar Sánchez, Ana María. *Juegos de seducción y traición: Literatura y cultura de masas*. Rosario, Argentina: B. Viterbo Editora, 2000.
Andújar, Carolina. *Vajda: Príncipe Inmortal*. Bogotá: Grupo Editorial Norma, 2012.
———. *Vampyr*. Bogotá: Grupo Editorial Norma, 2009.
El ángel exterminador. 1962. Directed by Luis Buñuel. New York: Criterion Collection, 2009. DVD.
Arellano-Sota, Carlos. "Biology, Ecology and Control of the Vampire Bat." *Reviews of Infectious Diseases* 10, no. 4 (1988): S615–S619.
Ariès, Philippe. *The Hour of Our Death: The Classic History of Western Attitudes toward Death over the Last One Thousand Years*. New York: Vintage Books, 1982.
The Arrival of a Train at La Ciotat Station: L'arrivée d'un train en gare de La Ciotat. 1896. Directed by Auguste Lumière and Louis Lumière. Kino Lorber Films, 2002. DVD.
El ataúd del vampiro. 1958. Directed by Fernando Méndez. San Francisco: CasaNegra Entertainment, 2006. DVD.
Atsma, Aaron. *Theoi Greek Mythology: Exploring Mythology in Classical Literature and Art*. New Zealand: Aaron Atsma, 2000. http://www.theoi.com/Heros/Lykaon.html. Accessed January 10, 2017.
Auladell Pérez, Miguel Ángel. "De Caupolicán a Rubén Darío." *América Sin Nombre*, no. 5–6 (December 2004). Alicante: Biblioteca Virtual Miguel de Cervantes. http://www.cervantesvirtual.com/nd/ark:/59851/bmctx3q0. Accessed June 10, 2017.
Austen, Jane. *Northanger Abbey*. 1818. London: Penguin Books, 2003.
Azuela, Mariano. *Los de abajo: La novela de la Revolución Mexicana*. 1925. New York: Penguin Books, 1997.
———. *The Underdogs*. Edited by Seymour Menton. Pittsburgh: University of Pittsburgh Press, 1992.
Baldick, Chris, and Robert Mighall. "Gothic Criticism." In *A Companion to the Gothic*, edited by David Punter, 209–28. Oxford: Blackwell, 2000.
Barajas Durán, Rafael. *Posada Mito y Mitote: La caricatura política de José Guadalupe Posada y Manuel Alfonso Manilla*. Mexico: D. F. Fondo de Cultura Económica, 2009.
Bareiro Saguier, Rubén. "Estratos de la lengua guaraní en la escritura de Augusto Roa Bastos." *Revista de Critica Literaria Latinoamericana* 10, no. 19 (1984): 35–45.
Barlow, John D. *German Expressionist Film*. Boston: Twayne, 1982.

Barreda-Tomás, Pedro M. "Alejo Carpentier: Dos visiones del negro, dos conceptos de la novela." *Hispania* 55, no. 1 (1972): 34–44.
Barthes, Roland. *S/Z*. New York: Macmillan, 1974.
Batra, Nandita. "After Androgyny: The Dialectics of Gender." *Atenea* 14, no. 1 (1994): 53–63.
Baudelaire, Charles. *The Flowers of Evil* (English and French ed.). Translated by James McGowan. Oxford: Oxford University Press, 1993.
Bautista, Daniel. "Cortázar: Translator of Poe." *Romance Review* 11 (2001): 11–19. ejournals.bc.edu/ojs/index.php/romance/article/download/ 9201/8272. Accessed June 10, 2017.
Beal, Timothy. "Our Monsters, Ourselves." *Chronicle of Higher Education*, November 9, 2001. LexisNexis Academic. http://chronicle.com/weekly/ v48/i11/11b01801.htm. Accessed June 10, 2017.
Benedetti, Mario. "El otro yo." *La muerte y otras sorpresas*. Barcelona: Penguin Random House Grupo Editorial España, 1968. Kindle edition.
Bennett, Maurice J. "The Detective Fiction of Poe and Borges." *Comparative Literature* 35, no. 3 (1983): 262–75.
Benson, Elizabeth P. "BATS in South American Folklore and Ancient Art." *Bats Magazine* 9, no. 1 (Spring 1991): n.p. http://www.batcon.org/ resources/media-education/bats-magazine/bat_article/466. Accessed June 15, 2017.
———. "Bats in South American Iconography." *Andean Past* 1 (1987): 165–90.
Bienstock Anolik, Ruth, and Douglas L. Howard. *The Gothic Other: Racial and Social Constructions in the Literary Imagination*. Jefferson, NC: McFarland, 2004.
Blade. 1998. Directed by Stephen Norrington. Los Angeles: New Line Home Video, 2006. DVD.
Blade II. 2002. Directed by Guillermo del Toro. Los Angeles: New Line Home Video, 2005. DVD.
Bombal, María Luisa. *House of Mist; The Shrouded Woman*. Translated by María Luisa Bombal. Austin: University of Texas Press, 1995.
———. *La última niebla; La amortajada*. 1935, 1938. Barcelona: Seix Barral, 1988.
Bondeson, Jan. *Buried Alive: The Terrifying History of Our Most Primal Fear*. New York: Barnes and Noble, 2006.
Borge, Jason. *Avances de Hollywood: Crítica cinematográfica en Latinoamérica, 1915–1945*. Rosario, Argentina: Beatriz Viterbo Editora, 2005.
———. *Latin American Writers and the Rise of Hollywood Cinema*. New York: Routledge, 2010.

Borges, Jorge Luis. "Borges y yo." *Obras Completas 1923–1972*, 808. Buenos Aires: Emecé Editores, 1974.

Borges, Jorge L., Adolfo Bioy Casares, and Silvina Ocampo, eds. 1940. *Antología de la literatura fantástica*. Barcelona: Edhasa, 2008.

———. *The Book of Fantasy*. New York: Viking, 1988.

Borgia, Danielle. "Vampiros Mexicanos: Nonnormative Sexualities in Contemporary Vampire Novels of Mexico." In *Vampires and Zombies: Transcultural Migrations and Transnational Interpretations*, edited by Dorothea Fischer-Hornung and Monika Mueller, 110–29. Jackson: University Press of Mississippi, 2016.

Botting, Fred. *Gothic*. London: Routledge, 1996.

———. *Gothic*. 2nd ed. London: Routledge, 2014.

Bowers, Maggie Ann. *Magic(al) Realism*. London: Routledge, 2010.

Braham, Persephone. *From Amazons to Zombies: Monsters in Latin America*. Lewisburg, PA: Bucknell University Press, 2015.

Brecht, Bertolt. *Brecht on Theatre: The Development of an Aesthetic*. New York: Hill and Wang, 1996.

Breton, André. *Conversations: The Autobiography of Surrealism*. Translated by Mark Polizzotti. New York: Paragon House English, 1993.

———. "Limits Not Frontiers of Surrealism." 1936. In *Surrealism*, edited by Herbert Read, 93–116. London: Faber and Faber, 1971.

———. *Manifestoes of Surrealism*. Ann Arbor: University of Michigan Press, 2012.

Bronfen, Elisabeth. *Over Her Dead Body: Death, Femininity, and the Aesthetic*. Manchester, UK: Manchester University Press, 1992.

Brontë, Charlotte. *Jane Eyre*. 1847. Philadelphia: Blakiston, 1944.

Brontë, Emily. *Wuthering Heights*. 1847. New York: Random House, 1943.

Brushwood, John. *The Spanish American Novel: A Twentieth-Century Survey*. Austin: University of Texas Press, 1975.

Budd, Mike. *The Cabinet of Dr. Caligari: Texts, Contexts, Histories*. New Brunswick, NJ: Rutgers University Press, 1990.

Buñuel, Luis. *Luis Buñuel: El ojo de la libertad: [Exposición] febrero–mayo 2000*. Madrid: Publicaciones de la Residencia de Estudiantes, 2000.

Bürger, Peter. *Theory of the Avant-Garde*. Minneapolis: University of Minnesota Press, 1984.

Bürger, Peter, Bettina Brandt, and Daniel Purdy. "Avant-Garde and Neo-Avant-Garde: An Attempt to Answer Certain Critics of 'Theory of the Avant-Garde.'" *New Literary History* 41, no. 4 (2010): 695–715. http://www.jstor.org/stable/23012702. Accessed June 20, 2017.

Burke, Edmund. *A Philosophical Enquiry into the Origin of Our Ideas of the Sublime and Beautiful*. 1757. Edited by James T. Boulton. London: Routledge, 1958.

Cabeza de Vaca, Alva Núnez. *Los comentarios de Alvar Núñez Alvar Núñez Cabeza de Vaca: Adelantado y gobernador del Río de Plata*. Asunción: Talleres de H. Kraus, 1902. Google Books. https://books.google.com/books?id=BLhkAAAAMAAJ. Accessed July 17, 2017.

The Cabinet of Dr. Caligari: Das Cabinet des Dr. Caligari. 1920. Directed by Robert Wiene. Kino Lorber, 2014. DVD.

Cabiya, Pedro. *Malas Hierbas*. New York: Zemí Book, 2011.

———. *Trance*. Santo Domingo, Dominican Republic: Grupo Editorial Norma, 2008.

———. *Wicked Weeds: A Novel*. Simsbury, CT: Mandel Vilar Press, 2016.

Cabiya, Pedro, and Jorge Isaacs. *Maria V*. New York: Zemí Book, 2011.

Campa Marcé, Carlos. "Carlos Fuentes entre Maupassant y Cortázar (pasando por Borges): 'Chac Mool' y el relato como montaje." *Espéculo: Revista de Estudios Literarios* 43 (2009). http://www.ucm.es/info/especulo/numero43/chacmool.html. Accessed December 15, 2016.

Campobello, Nellie. *Cartucho: Relatos de la lucha en el norte de México*. 1931. Edited by Fernando Tola de Habich. Mexico City: Factoría Ediciones, 2003.

Carmen. 1915. Directed by Cecil B. DeMille. Chatsworth, CA: Image Entertainment, 2001. DVD.

Carpentier, Alejo. *The Kingdom of This World*. Translated by Harriet de Onís. New York: Penguin Books, 1980.

———. "On the Marvelous Real in America." 1949. In *Magical Realism: Theory, History, Community*, edited by Lois P. Zamora and Wendy B. Faris, 75–88. Durham, NC: Duke University Press, 1995.

———. *El reino de este mundo*. 1949. New York: Rayo Planeta, 2009.

Carruthers, David M. J. "Lines of Flight of the Deadly Nightshade: An Enquiry into the Properties of the Magical Plant, Its Literature and History." *Mosaic: A Journal for the Interdisciplinary Study of Literature* 48, no. 2 (2015): 119–32.

Casanova-Vizcaíno, Sandra, and Inés Ordiz, eds. *Latin American Gothic in Literature and Culture*. New York: Routledge, 2018.

Casares, Adolfo Bioy. Prologue to *Antología de la literatura fantástica*, edited by Jorge Luis Borges, Adolfo Bioy Casares, and Silvina Ocampo, 11–22. Barcelona: Edhasa, 2008.

Castañeda, Carlos. *The Teachings of Don Juan: A Yaqui Way of Knowledge*. Berkeley: University of California Press, 1968.

Castro Leal, Antonio. *La novela de la Revolución Mexicana*. Vol. 1. Mexico City: M. Aguilar Editor S.A., 1969.

Castro-Klaren, Sara. "Cortázar, Surrealism, and 'Pataphysics.'" *Comparative Literature* 27, no. 3 (1975): 218–36. Accessed July 28, 2017. doi:10.2307/1769547.

Cervantes, Saavedra Miguel. *Los trabajos de Persiles y Sigismunda*. Barcelona: www.Linkgua.com, 2011. http://www.cervantesvirtual.com/nd/ark:/59851/bmcpv6go. Accessed December 10, 2016.

Cháves, Julio César. *El supremo dictador: Biografía de José Gaspar de Francia*. Madrid: Ediciones Atlas, 1964.

Un chien andalou; Un perro andaluz. Zaragoza: Heraldo de Aragón, 2012. DVD.

La chute du la maison Usher; The Fall of the House of Usher. 1928. Directed by Jean Epstein and Luis Buñuel. Alexandria, VA: All Day Entertainment, 2001. DVD.

Citizen Kane. 1941. Directed by Orson Welles. Burbank: Warner Home Video, 2016. DVD.

Clendinnen, Inga. *Aztecs: An Interpretation*. Cambridge: Cambridge University Press, 1995.

Cohen, Jeffrey Jerome. "Monster Culture (Seven Theses)." In *Monster Theory: Reading Culture*, edited by Jeffrey Jerome Cohen, 3–25. Minneapolis: University of Minnesota Press, 1996.

Correa, Gustavo. "El espíritu del mal en Guatemala." In *Nativism and Syncretism*, edited by Munro S. Edmonson and William Madsen, 41–102. New Orleans: Middle American Research Institute, Tulane University, 1960.

Cortázar, Julio. "Axolotl." In *Cuentos completos*, 1:517–22. Mexico City: Punto de Lectura, 2015.

———. "Axolotl." In *End of Games, and Other Stories*, 3–9. New York: Pantheon Books, 1967.

———. *Final del Juego*. Mexico City: Los Presentes, 1956.

———. "El hijo del vampiro." In *Julio Cortázar: Cuentos completos*, 1:31–35. Mexico City: Punto de Lectura, 2015.

———. "Lejana." In *Julio Cortázar: Cuentos Completos*, 1:147–55. Buenos Aires: Punto de Lectura, 2015.

———. "La noche boca arriba." In *Julio Cortázar: Cuentos completos*, 1:523–31. Mexico City: Punto de Lectura, 2015.

———. *La otra orilla*. Madrid: Punto de Lectura, 2008.

de Costa, René. "Huidobro y el surrealismo." In *Surrealismo/surrealismos: Latinoamérica y España*, edited by Peter G. Earle and Germán Gullón, 74–80. Philadelphia: Department of Romance Languages, University of Pennsylvania, 1977.

———. *Vicente Huidobro: The Careers of a Poet*. Oxford: Clarendon Press/Oxford University Press, 1984.

Cotter, Robert. Audio commentary on *El vampiro*. San Francisco: CasaNegra Entertainment, 2006. DVD.

———. *The Mexican Masked Wrestler and Monster Filmography*. Jefferson, NC: McFarland, 2005.
Crimson Peak. 2015. Directed by Guillermo del Toro. Universal City: Universal, 2016. DVD.
Cronos. 1993. Directed by Guillermo del Toro. In *Trilogía de Guillermo del Toro*. New York: Criterion Collection, 2016. DVD.
CRS Report for Congress: Mexico's Drug Cartels. Order code RL3 4215. Prepared by Colleen W. Cook. https://www.fas.org/sgp/crs/row/RL34215.pdf. Accessed November 15, 2016.
Cruz Porchini, Dafne, and Adriana Ortega Orozco. "The 1940 International Exhibition of Surrealism: A Cosmopolitan Art Dialogue in Mexico City." *Dada/Surrealism* 21 (2017). http://ir.uiowa.edu/cgi/viewcontent.cgi?article=1329&context=dadasur. Accessed June 15, 2017.
———. "St. Vitalis." In *The Catholic Encyclopedia*. New York: Robert Appleton. http://www.newadvent.org./cathen/15486a.htm. Accessed December 1, 2016.
Cull, John T. "On Reading Fuentes: Plant Lore, Sex, and Death in 'Aura.'" *Chasqui* 18, no. 2 (1989): 18–27.
Culler, Jonathan. "Baudelaire and Poe." In *Critical Insights: The Poetry of Edgar Allan Poe*, edited by Steven Frye, 188–209. Pasadena, CA: Salem Press, 2011.
Darío, Rubén. "Edgar Poe y los sueños." In *El mundo de los sueños*, edited by Angel Rama, 180–95. Puerto Rico: Editorial Universitaria, University of Puerto Rico, 1973.
———. *Poesía*. Madrid: Alianza Editorial, 1997.
———. *Los raros*. Chicago: Linkgua, 2014.
———. "Thanatopia" (1893). In *Verónica y otros cuentos fantásticos*, edited by José Olivio Jiménez, 8–14. Madrid: Alianza Editorial, 1995.
Darwin, Charles. *Voyage of the Beagle*. 1839. New York: P. F. Collier, 1909.
Davidson, Carol Margaret. *History of the Gothic: Gothic Literature, 1764–1824*. Cardiff, UK: University of Wales Press, 2009.
Davidson, Jane P. "Nightshade." In *Encyclopedia of Witchcraft: The Western Tradition*, edited by Richard M. Golden, 830. Santa Barbara: ABC-CLIO, 2006.
Diamandopoulos, Athanasios, Andreas Skarpelos, and Georgios Tsiros. "The Use of the Kidneys in Secular and Ritual Practices according to the Ancient Greek and Byzantine Texts." *Kidney International* 68, no. 1 (2005): 399–404.
Díaz del Castillo, Bernal. *The Memoirs of the Conquistador Bernal Díaz del Castillo: Containing a True and Full Account of the Discovery and*

Conquest of Mexico and New Spain. Vol. 2. Translated by John I. Lockhart. London: J. Hatchard and Son, 1844. Hathi Trust Digital Library. https://hdl.handle.net/2027/hvd.32044014362628. Accessed June 10, 2018.

Díaz, Enciso A. *La sed*. Mexico City: Secretaría de Cultura Puebla, 2001.

Dickens, Charles. *Great Expectations*. 1861. New York: Alfred A. Knopf, 1992.

Dijkstra, Bram. *Evil Sisters: The Threat of Female Sexuality and the Cult of Manhood*. New York: Alfred A. Knopf, 1996.

Doniger, Wendy. *Splitting the Difference: Gender and Myth in Ancient Greece and India*. Chicago: University of Chicago Press, 1999.

Dostoyevsky, Fyodor. *The Double: Two Versions*. Ann Arbor: Ardis, 1985.

Double Jeopardy. 1999. Directed by Bruce Beresford. Burbank: Warner Brothers, 2000.

Dr. Jekyll and Mr. Hyde. 1931. Directed by Rouben Mamoulian. Burbank: Warner Home Video, 2004. DVD.

Dracula. 1931. Directed by Tod Browning. Universal City: Universal Studios Home Entertainment, 2004. DVD.

Drácula. 1931. Directed by George Melford. Universal City: Universal Studios Home Entertainment, 2004. DVD.

Duffey, J. Patrick. *De la pantalla al texto: La influencia del cine en la narrativa mexicana del siglo veinte*. Mexico City: UNAM, 1996.

———. "Pancho Villa at the Movies: Cinematic Techniques in the Works of Guzmán and Muñoz." In *Latin American Literature and Mass Media*, edited by Edmundo Paz Soldán and Debra Castillo, 41–56. New York: Garland, 2001.

Duncan, Cynthia. *Unraveling the Real: The Fantastic in Spanish-American Ficciones*. Philadelphia: Temple University Press, 2010.

Durán, Gloria. *The Archetypes of Carlos Fuentes: From Witch to Androgyne*. Hamden, CT: Archon Book, 1980.

———. *La magia y las brujas en la obra de Carlos Fuentes*. Mexico City: UNAM, 1976.

Earle, Peter G., and Germán Gullón. *Surrealismo/surrealismos: Latinoamerica y España*. Philadelphia: Department of Romance Languages, University of Pennsylvania, 1977.

Ebert, Roger. "Film Review: *The Fall of the House of Usher*." RogerEbert.com. March 3, 2002. http://www.rogerebert.com/reviews/great-movie-the-fall-of-the-house-of-usher-1928. Accessed November 15, 2016.

Edwards, Justin, and Sandra Guardini Vasconcelos, eds. *Tropical Gothic in Literature and Culture: The Americas*. London: Routledge, 2016.

Eliot, T. S. "Tradition and the Individual Talent." 1919. In *The Sacred Wood: Essays on Poetry and Criticism*, 47–59. London: Methuen, 1960.
El espinazo del diablo. 2001. Directed by Guillermo del Toro. In *Trilogía de Guillermo del Toro*. New York: Criterion Collection, 2016. DVD.
Ezquerro, Milagros, ed. Introduction to *Yo el supremo*, by Augusto Roa Bastos, 7–76. Madrid: Cátedra, 1983.
The Fall of the House of Usher. 1928. Directed by J. S. Watson Jr. and Melville Webber. Youtube.com. https://www.youtube.com/watch?v=MUvckfi_frE. Accessed July 15, 2016.
Fantomas. Directed by Louis Feuillade. 1913–1914. New York: Kino, 2010. DVD.
Faust. 1926. Directed by F. W. Murnau. Kino Lorber, 2009. DVD.
Féval, Paul. *Vampire City*. 1865. Translated by Brian M. Stableford. Encino, CA: Black Coat Press, 2003.
Fine, David. "From Berlin to Hollywood: Echoes of Expressionism in Fritz Lang's *The Woman in the Window* and *Scarlet Street*." *Literature/Film Quarterly* 35, no. 4 (2007): 282–93.
Fischer, Sibylle M. "El sujeto y su discurso: La construccíon de la voz indígena en *Yo el Supremo*." *Revista Hispanica Moderna* 44, no. 1 (1991): 93–107.
Fischer-Hornung, Dorothea, and Monika Mueller, eds. *Vampires and Zombies: Transcultural Migrations and Transnational Interpretations*. Jackson: University Press of Mississippi, 2016.
Fleenor, Juliann E. *The Female Gothic*. Montreal: Eden Press, 1983.
Fleming, Leonor, ed. Introduction to *Horacio Quiroga: Cuentos*, by Horacio Quiroga, 9–109. Madrid: Cátedra, 1994.
Flores, Angel. "Magical Realism in Spanish American Fiction." *Hispania* 38, no. 2 (1955): 187–92.
Flynn, John L. *Cinematic Vampires: The Living Dead on Film and Television, from "The Devil's Castle" (1896) to Bram Stoker's "Dracula" (1992)*. Jefferson, NC: McFarland, 1992.
"Foreign Market Possibilities." *Variety*, November 6, 1934, sec. Foreign Film, n.p.
Frankenstein. 1931. Directed by James Whale. Universal City, CA: Universal Studios Home Entertainment, 1999. DVD.
Freud, Sigmund. "Totem and Taboo." In *The Freud Reader*, edited by Peter Gray, 481–513. New York: W. W. Norton, 1989.
———. *The Uncanny*. New York: Penguin Books, 2003.
Fuentes, Carlos. *Aura*. 1962. New York: Noonday Press, 1986.
———. "Chac Mool." In *Burnt Water*, translated by Margaret Sayers Peden, 3–14. New York: Farrar, Straus and Giroux, 1980.

———. "Chac mool." 1954. In *Cuentos completos*, 27–35. Mexico City: Fondo de Cultura Económica, 2013.

———. *The Death of Artemio Cruz*. Translated by Alfred MacAdam. New York: Macmillan, 2013.

———. "A Despot, Now and Forever." *New York Times*, April 6, 1986. http://www.nytimes.com/books/00/09/24/nnp/supreme.html. Accessed June 18, 2017.

———. *Los días enmascarados*. 1954. Barcelona: Círculo de Lectores, 1996.

———. *Inquieta Compañía*. Mexico City: Alfaguara, 2004.

———. "Malintzin de las maquilas." In *La frontera de cristal: Una novela en nueve cuentos*, 129–60. Mexico City: Alfaguara, 2007.

———. *La muerte de Artemio Cruz*. 1962. Madrid: Suma de Letras, 2001.

———. "On Reading and Writing Myself: How I Wrote *Aura*." *World Literature Today* 57, no. 4 (1983). 531–39.

———. *Vlad*. 2004. Mexico City: Alfaguara, 2010.

———. *Vlad*. Translated by Ethan Shaskan Bumas and Alejandro Branger. Champaign, IL: Dalkey Archive Press, 2012.

Furneaux, Holly. "Gendered Cover-Ups: Live Burial, Social Death, and Coverture in Mary Braddon's Fiction." *Philological Quarterly* 84, no. 4 (2005): 425–49.

Galt, John. "The Buried Alive." 1821. *The Steamboat*, 329–35. Edinburgh: William Blackwood, 1822. https://play.google.com/books/reader?id=ItYtsZwivjEC&printsec=frontcover&output=reader&hl=en&pg=GBS.PA169. Accessed July 10, 2016.

García Canclini, Nestor. *Culturas híbridas: Estrategias para entrar y salir de la modernidad*. Buenos Aires: Paidós, 2001.

———. *Hybrid Cultures: Strategies for Entering and Leaving Modernity*. Minneapolis: University of Minnesota Press, 1995.

García-Caro, Pedro. "Aura y la teoría narrativa de Carlos Fuentes." In *En breve: La novela corta en México*, edited by Cecilia Eudave and Anadeli Bencomo. Guadalajara: Universidad de Guadalajara, 2014.

García Gutiérrez, Rosa. "Dama de corazones de Xavier Villaurrutia en la génesis de los Nocturno." *Anales de Literatura Hispanoamericana* 26, no. 2 (1997): 259–77.

Garfield, Evelyn P. "'The Exquisite Cadaver of Surrealism.'" *Review* (1972): 18–21.

Garro, Elena. "Un hogar sólido." *Un hogar sólido y otras piezas en un acto*, 9–34. Xalapa, Mexico: Universidad Veracruzana, 1958.

Gibson, Matthew. *The Fantastic and European Gothic: History, Literature and the French Revolution*. Cardiff: University of Wales Press, 2013.

Girard, René. *Violence and the Sacred*. Translated by Patrick Gregory. Baltimore: Johns Hopkins University Press, 1977.

Goddu, Teresa A. "Vampire Gothic." *American Literary History* 11, no. 1 (1999): 125–41. http://www.jstor.org/stable/490080. Accessed October 1, 2017.

The Golem: Der Golem. 1915. Directed by Henrik Galeen and Paul Wegener. New York: Kino Lorber, 2004. DVD.

Gómez-Sicre, José. "La escritora en la niebla." *Américas* 33, no. 2 (1981): 49–51.

González Casanova, Manuel. *El cine que vió fósforo: Alfonso Reyes y Martín Luis Guzmán*. Mexico City: Fondo de Cultura Económica, 2003.

González de León, Fernando. "Buñuel, Poe and Gothic Cinema." *Edgar Allan Poe Review* 8, no. 2 (2007): 49–64.

González Rodríguez, Sergio. *The Femicide Machine*. Los Angeles: Semiotext(e), 2012.

———. *Huesos en el desierto*. Mexico: Editorial Anagrama, 2006.

Gordillo, Adriana. "Transformaciones del vampiro en la literatura hispanoamericana: Aproximaciones al 'género' en Darío, Agustini y Cortázar." *Polifonía* 2, no. 2 (2012): 88–105. https://www.apsu.edu/sites/apsu.edu/files/polifonia/e6.pdf. Accessed July 1, 2016.

Gordon, Avery. *Ghostly Matters: Haunting and the Sociological Imagination*. Minneapolis: University of Minnesota Press, 1997.

Gordon, Joan, and Veronica Hollinger, eds. *Blood Read: The Vampire as Metaphor in Contemporary Culture*. Philadelphia: University of Pennsylvania Press, 1997.

Gorriti, Juana Manuela. *Sueños y realidades*. Vol. 1. Edited by Vicente Gregoria Quesada. Buenos Aires: Imprenta de Mayo de C. Casavalle, 1865. Google Play. https://books.google.com/books?id=DBqfgbR3keEC. Accessed July 17, 2017.

Greenhall, Arthur M., and Uwe Schmidt. *Natural History of Vampire Bats*. Boca Raton, FL: CRC Press, 1988.

Guerra-Cunningham, Lucía. *La narrativa de María Luisa Bombal: Una visión de la existencia femenina*. Madrid: Playor, 1980.

———. Personal interview with Guerra-Cunningham by the author on March 12, 2008.

Gunning, Tom. "An Aesthetic of Astonishment: Early Film and the (In)Credulous Spectator." In *Film Theory and Criticism*, 5th ed., edited by Leo Braudy and Marshall Cohen, 818–32. New York: Oxford University Press, 1999.

Guzmán, Martín L. *El águila y la serpiente*. 1928. In *La novela de la*

Revolución Mexicana, vol. 1, edited by Antonio Castro Leal, 207–424. Mexico City: M. Aguilar Editor S.A., 1969.

———. *The Eagle and the Serpent*. Translated by Harriet de Onis. Garden City, NY: Dolphin Books, 1969.

Gyurko, Lanin A. "Borges and the Theme of the Double." *Ibero-Amerikanisches Archiv* 2, no. 3 (1976): 193–226.

———. "*La muerte de Artemio Cruz* and *Citizen Kane*: A Comparative Analysis." In *Carlos Fuentes: A Critical View*, edited by Robert Brody and Charles Rossman, 8–25. Austin: University of Texas Press, 1982.

———. "Myth and Mythification in Fuentes' *Aura* and Wilder's *Sunset Boulevard*." *Hispanic Journal* 7, no. 1 (1985): 91–113.

———. "Self, Double, and Mask in Fuentes's *La Muerte de Artemio Cruz*." Texas Studies in Language and Literature, no. 16 (1974): 363–84.

———. "Twentieth-Century Fiction." In *Mexican Literature: A History*, edited by David William Foster, 243–303. Austin: University of Texas Press, 2012.

Hagener, Malte, ed. *The Emergence of Film Culture: Knowledge Production, Institution Building, and the Fate of the Avant-Garde in Europe, 1919–1945*. New York: Berghahn Books, 2014.

Haggerty, George E. *Gothic Fiction/Gothic Form*. University Park: Pennsylvania State University Press, 1989.

———. *Queer Gothic*. Urbana: University of Illinois Press, 2006.

Halberstam, Judith. *Skin Shows: Gothic Horror and the Technology of Monsters*. Durham, NC: Duke University Press, 1995.

Hamilton, Laurell K. *Guilty Pleasures*. New York: Berkley Books, 2002.

Hamilton, Laurell K., Jonathon Green, and Wellinton Alves. *Anita Blake, Vampire Hunter*. New York: Marvel, 2008.

Hanich, Julian. *Cinematic Emotion in Horror Films and Thrillers: The Aesthetic Paradox of Pleasurable Fear*. New York: Routledge, 2011.

Hansen, Miriam. *Cinema and Experience: Siegfried Kracauer, Walter Benjamin, and Theodor W. Adorno*. Berkeley: University of California Press, 2012.

Haraway, Donna J. *Simians, Cyborgs, and Women: The Reinvention of Nature*. New York: Routledge, 1991.

Hell, Julia. "The Angel's Enigmatic Eyes, or The Gothic Beauty of Catastrophic History in W. G. Sebald's 'Air War and Literature.'" *Criticism* 46, no. 3 (2004): 361–92.

Herrera-Ávila, Tatiana. "De lo mítico a lo profano: Chac Mool como monstruo." *Revista de Filología y Lingüística de la Universidad de Costa Rica* 42 (2016). http://revistas.ucr.ac.cr/index.php/filyling/article/view/26471/26702. Accessed November 1, 2016.

Girard, René. *Violence and the Sacred*. Translated by Patrick Gregory. Baltimore: Johns Hopkins University Press, 1977.
Goddu, Teresa A. "Vampire Gothic." *American Literary History* 11, no. 1 (1999): 125–41. http://www.jstor.org/stable/490080. Accessed October 1, 2017.
The Golem: Der Golem. 1915. Directed by Henrik Galeen and Paul Wegener. New York: Kino Lorber, 2004. DVD.
Gómez-Sicre, José. "La escritora en la niebla." *Américas* 33, no. 2 (1981): 49–51.
González Casanova, Manuel. *El cine que vió fósforo: Alfonso Reyes y Martín Luis Guzmán*. Mexico City: Fondo de Cultura Económica, 2003.
González de León, Fernando. "Buñuel, Poe and Gothic Cinema." *Edgar Allan Poe Review* 8, no. 2 (2007): 49–64.
González Rodríguez, Sergio. *The Femicide Machine*. Los Angeles: Semiotext(e), 2012.
———. *Huesos en el desierto*. Mexico: Editorial Anagrama, 2006.
Gordillo, Adriana. "Transformaciones del vampiro en la literatura hispanoamericana: Aproximaciones al 'género' en Darío, Agustini y Cortázar." *Polifonía* 2, no. 2 (2012): 88–105. https://www.apsu.edu/sites/apsu.edu/files/polifonia/e6.pdf. Accessed July 1, 2016.
Gordon, Avery. *Ghostly Matters: Haunting and the Sociological Imagination*. Minneapolis: University of Minnesota Press, 1997.
Gordon, Joan, and Veronica Hollinger, eds. *Blood Read: The Vampire as Metaphor in Contemporary Culture*. Philadelphia: University of Pennsylvania Press, 1997.
Gorriti, Juana Manuela. *Sueños y realidades*. Vol. 1. Edited by Vicente Gregoria Quesada. Buenos Aires: Imprenta de Mayo de C. Casavalle, 1865. Google Play. https://books.google.com/books?id=DBqfgbR3keEC. Accessed July 17, 2017.
Greenhall, Arthur M., and Uwe Schmidt. *Natural History of Vampire Bats*. Boca Raton, FL: CRC Press, 1988.
Guerra-Cunningham, Lucía. *La narrativa de María Luisa Bombal: Una visión de la existencia femenina*. Madrid: Playor, 1980.
———. Personal interview with Guerra-Cunningham by the author on March 12, 2008.
Gunning, Tom. "An Aesthetic of Astonishment: Early Film and the (In)Credulous Spectator." In *Film Theory and Criticism*, 5th ed., edited by Leo Braudy and Marshall Cohen, 818–32. New York: Oxford University Press, 1999.
Guzmán, Martín L. *El águila y la serpiente*. 1928. In *La novela de la*

Revolución Mexicana, vol. 1, edited by Antonio Castro Leal, 207–424. Mexico City: M. Aguilar Editor S.A., 1969.

———. *The Eagle and the Serpent*. Translated by Harriet de Onis. Garden City, NY: Dolphin Books, 1969.

Gyurko, Lanin A. "Borges and the Theme of the Double." *Ibero-Amerikanisches Archiv* 2, no. 3 (1976): 193–226.

———. "*La muerte de Artemio Cruz* and *Citizen Kane*: A Comparative Analysis." In *Carlos Fuentes: A Critical View*, edited by Robert Brody and Charles Rossman, 8–25. Austin: University of Texas Press, 1982.

———. "Myth and Mythification in Fuentes' *Aura* and Wilder's *Sunset Boulevard*." *Hispanic Journal* 7, no. 1 (1985): 91–113.

———. "Self, Double, and Mask in Fuentes's *La Muerte de Artemio Cruz*." *Texas Studies in Language and Literature*, no. 16 (1974): 363–84.

———. "Twentieth-Century Fiction." In *Mexican Literature: A History*, edited by David William Foster, 243–303. Austin: University of Texas Press, 2012.

Hagener, Malte, ed. *The Emergence of Film Culture: Knowledge Production, Institution Building, and the Fate of the Avant-Garde in Europe, 1919–1945*. New York: Berghahn Books, 2014.

Haggerty, George E. *Gothic Fiction/Gothic Form*. University Park: Pennsylvania State University Press, 1989.

———. *Queer Gothic*. Urbana: University of Illinois Press, 2006.

Halberstam, Judith. *Skin Shows: Gothic Horror and the Technology of Monsters*. Durham, NC: Duke University Press, 1995.

Hamilton, Laurell K. *Guilty Pleasures*. New York: Berkley Books, 2002.

Hamilton, Laurell K., Jonathon Green, and Wellinton Alves. *Anita Blake, Vampire Hunter*. New York: Marvel, 2008.

Hanich, Julian. *Cinematic Emotion in Horror Films and Thrillers: The Aesthetic Paradox of Pleasurable Fear*. New York: Routledge, 2011.

Hansen, Miriam. *Cinema and Experience: Siegfried Kracauer, Walter Benjamin, and Theodor W. Adorno*. Berkeley: University of California Press, 2012.

Haraway, Donna J. *Simians, Cyborgs, and Women: The Reinvention of Nature*. New York: Routledge, 1991.

Hell, Julia. "The Angel's Enigmatic Eyes, or The Gothic Beauty of Catastrophic History in W. G. Sebald's 'Air War and Literature.'" *Criticism* 46, no. 3 (2004): 361–92.

Herrera-Ávila, Tatiana. "De lo mítico a lo profano: Chac Mool como monstruo." *Revista de Filología y Lingüística de la Universidad de Costa Rica* 42 (2016). http://revistas.ucr.ac.cr/index.php/filyling/article/view/26471/26702. Accessed November 1, 2016.

Hewitt, Regina. *John Galt: Observations and Conjectures on Literature, History, and Society.* Lewisburg, PA: Bucknell University Press, 2012.

Higson, Andrew, and Richard Maltby, eds. *"Film Europe" and "Film America": Cinema, Commerce and Cultural Exchange, 1920–1939.* Exeter, UK: University of Exeter Press, 1999.

Hoffmann, E. T. A. *The Devil's Elixir.* 1824. Edinburgh: W. Blackwood. Google Play. http://books.google.com/books?id=gEoHAAAAQAAJ&oe=UTF-8. Accessed November 1, 2016.

Hogle, Jerrold E., ed. Introduction to *The Cambridge Companion to Gothic Fiction*, 1–20. Cambridge: Cambridge University Press, 2002.

Holley, William Bradley. "A Bloodthirsty Bonaparte: Redefining Historical Figures through the Historical Novel and the Fantastic Tale in Paul Féval's *La vampire.*" *Erudit Franco-Espagnol: An Electronic Journal of French and Hispanic Literatures* 3 (2013): 2–10.

Hooper John. "Changing Perceptions of Jules Michelet as Historian: History between Literature and Science, 1831–1874." *Journal of European Studies* 23, no. 3 (2016): 283–98.

Horner, Avril. "Heroine." In *The Handbook to Gothic Literature*, edited by Marie Mulvey-Roberts, 115–19. New York: New York University Press, 1998.

The House of the Devil: Le du diable. 1896. Directed by Georges Méliès. Flicker Alley, 2008. DVD.

Hughes, William. "Fictional Vampires in the Nineteenth and Twentieth Centuries." In *A Companion to the Gothic*, edited by David Punter, 143–54. Oxford: Blackwell, 2000.

Hughes, William, David Punter, and Andrew Smith, eds. *The Encyclopedia of the Gothic.* Malden, MA: Blackwell, 2013. Kindle edition.

Hugo, Victor. *Napoleon the Little.* 1885. New York: Wallachia, 2015.

Huidobro, Vicente. *Cagliostro.* 1934. Edited by Gabriele Morelli. Madrid: Cátedra, 2011.

———. *Mirror of a Mage.* Translated by Warren Bradley Wells. Boston: Houghton Mifflin, 1931.

The Hunchback of Notre Dame; Notre-Dame de Paris. 1911. Directed by Albert Capellani. Sunrise Silents, 2008. DVD.

Hutcheon, Linda. *A Theory of Parody: The Teachings of Twentieth-Century Art Forms.* New York: Methuen, 1985.

I Walked with a Zombie. 1943. Directed by Jacques Tourneur. Burbank: Warner Bros. Entertainment, 2013. DVD.

Issacs, Jorge. *María.* 1837. Barcelona: Planeta, 1984.

Jackson, Rosemary. *Fantasy: The Literature of Subversion.* London: Routledge, 1998.

James, Henry, and Adrian Poole. *The Aspen Papers.* Oxford: Oxford University Press, 2013.

———. *The Turn of the Screw: An Authoritative Text, Backgrounds and Sources, Essays in Criticism.* Edited by Robert Kimbrough. New York: W. W. Norton, 1966.

Jameson, Fredric. "No Magic, No Metaphor." *London Review of Books* 39, no. 12 (2017): 21–32. https://www.lrb.co.uk/v39/n12/fredric-jameson/no-magic-no-metaphor. Accessed May 27, 2018.

Jarvinen, Lisa. *The Rise of Spanish-Language Filmmaking: Out from Hollywood's Shadow, 1929–1939.* New Brunswick, NJ: Rutgers University Press, 2012. Kindle edition.

The Jazz Singer. 1927. Directed by Alan Crosland. Burbank: Warner Home Video, 2007. DVD.

Johnston, Marjorie C. "Rubén Darío's Acquaintance with Poe." *Hispania* 17, no. 3 (1934): 271–78.

Jrade, Cathy L. *Delmira Agustini, Sexual Seduction, and Vampiric Conquest.* New Haven, CT: Yale University Press, 2012.

———. *Modernismo, Modernity, and the Development of Spanish American Literature.* Austin: University of Texas Press, 1998.

———. *Rubén Darío and the Romantic Search for Unity: The Modernist Recourse to Esoteric Tradition.* Austin: University of Texas Press, 1983.

———. "Social-Political Concerns in the Poetry of Rubén Darío." In *From Romanticism to Modernismo in Latin America*, edited by David William Foster and Daniel Altamiranda, 302–15. New York: Garland, 1997.

Juan de los Muertos; Juan of the Dead. 2011. Directed by Alejandro Brugués. Port Washington, NY: Entertainment One, 2012. DVD.

Kadir, Djelal. "Another Sense of the Past: Henry James' 'The Aspern Papers' and Carlos Fuentes' 'Aura.'" *Revue de Littérature Comparée* 50, no. 4 (1976): 448–54.

Kampen, M. E. "Classic Veracruz Grotesques and Sacrificial Iconography." *Man,* n.s. 13, no. 1 (1978): 116–26.

Kauffmann, Robert L. "Narrating the Other: Julio Cortázar's 'Axolotl' as Ethnographic Allegory." In *Primitivism and Identity in Latin America: Essays on Art, Literature, and Culture*, edited by Erik Camayd-Freixas and José E. González, 135–55. Tucson: University of Arizona Press, 2000.

Kaye, Heidi. "Gothic Film." In *A Companion to the Gothic*, edited by David Punter, 180–92. Oxford: Blackwell, 2000.

Kelman, David. "The Afterlife of Storytelling: Julio Cortázar's Reading of Walter Benjamin and Edgar Allan Poe." *Comparative Literature* 60, no. 3 (2008): 244–60. http://www.jstor.org/stable/40279415. Accessed August 5, 2016.

Kilgour, Maggie. *The Rise of the Gothic Novel*. London: Routledge, 1995.

Kill Bill: Volume 2. 2004. Directed by Quentin Tarantino. Miramax Home Entertainment, 2012. DVD

King, John. *Magical Reels: A History of Cinemas in Latin America*. London: Verso, 1990.

Kingsley, Mary. *West African Studies*. Hoboken: Taylor and Francis, 2013.

Kirkpatrick, Gwen. "The Limits of Modernismo: Delmira Agustini and Julio Herrera y Reissig." *Romance Quarterly* 36, no. 3 (1989): 307–24. http://www.cervantesvirtual.com/nd/ark:/59851/bmc4x5s5. Accessed November 1, 2016.

Kostova, Elizabeth. *The Historian: A Novel*. New York: Little, Brown, 2005.

Kracauer, Siegfried. "From 'From Caligari to Hitler.'" In *Film Theory and Criticism*, 5th ed., edited by Leo Braudy and Marshall Cohen, 183–94. New York: Oxford University Press, 1999.

Kristeva, Julia. *Desire in Language: A Semiotic Approach to Literature and Art*. New York: Columbia University Press, 1980.

Kropfelder, Normand. *The Esoteric Codex: Werewolves*. Morrisville, NC: Lulu Books, 2015.

El laberinto del Fauno. 2006. Directed by Guillermo del Toro. In *Trilogía de Guillermo del Toro*. New York: Criterion Collection, 2016. DVD.

Lambert, Jean Clarence. "André Breton en México" *Vuelta* 148, no. 13 (1989): 9–16.

Langford, Walter M. *The Mexican Novel Comes of Age*. Notre Dame, IN: University of Notre Dame Press, 1971.

Leal, Luis. "History and Myth in the Narrative of Carlos Fuentes." In *Carlos Fuentes: A Critical View*, edited by Robert Brody and Charles Rossman, 8–25. Austin: University of Texas Press, 1982.

———. "The *Malinche-Llorona* Dichotomy: The Evolution of a Myth." In *Feminism, Nation and Myth: La Malinche*, edited by Amanda N. Harris and Rolando Romero, 28–43. Houston: Arte Público Press, 2005.

———. "Torres Bodet y los 'Contemporáneos.'" *Hispania* 40, no. 3 (1957): 290–96.

Leddy, Annette, and Donna Conwell. *Farewell to Surrealism: The Dyn Circle in Mexico*. 2013. http://news.getty.edu/images/9036/farewell_surrealism_extended.pdf. Accessed June 18, 2017.

LeFanu, Sheridan. "Carmilla." 1872. In *Three Vampire Tales*, edited by Anne Williams, 86–148. Boston: Wadsworth, 2003.

León-Portilla, Miguel. "Those Made Worthy by Divine Sacrifice: The Faith of

Ancient Mexico." In *South and Meso-American Native Spirituality: From the Cult of the Feathered Serpent to the Theology of Liberation*, edited by Gary H. Gossen and Miguel León-Portilla, 41–64. New York: Crossroad, 1993.

Levack, Brian P. *The Oxford Handbook of Witchcraft in Early Modern Europe and Colonial America*. Oxford: Oxford University Press, 2013. Kindle edition.

Lewis, Matthew G. *The Monk: A Romance*. 1796. London: Penguin Books, 1998.

Lloyd-Smith, Allan. "Nineteenth-Century American Gothic." In *A Companion to the Gothic*, edited by David Punter, 109–21. Oxford: Blackwell, 2000.

Lomnitz, Claudio. *Death and the Idea of Mexico*. Brooklyn: Zone Books, 2005.

López Agustín, Alfredo. "La fauna maravillosa de Mesoamérica." In *Fauna fantástica de Mesoamérica y los Andes*, edited by Luis Millones and Alfredo López Agustín. Mexico City: UNAM, 2013.

Lugones, Leopoldo. "La vampira." 1897. *Las primeras letras de Leopoldo Lugones: Reproducción facsimilar de sus primeros trabajos literarios escritos entre sus dieciocho y veinticinco años*, 79–80. Buenos Aires: Ediciones Centurión, 1963.

Malcolm, L. W. G. "Short Notes on Soul-Trapping in Southern Nigeria." *Journal of American Folklore* 35, no. 137 (1922): 219–22.

Mangham, Andrew. "Buried Alive: The Gothic Awakening of Taphephobia." *Journal of Literature and Science* 3, no. 1 (2010): 10–22. http://www.literatureandscience.org/issues/JLS_3_1/JLS_vol_3_no_1_Mangham.pdf. Accessed July 1, 2016.

Manly, David. "Regeneration: The Axolotl Story." *Scientific American*, April 13, 2011. http://blogs.scientificamerican.com/guest-blog/regeneration-the-axolotl-story. Accessed November 1, 2016.

Marchiselli, Antonella. "Un análisis comparativo: Los personajes femeninos de *La última niebla* y *La amortajada* de María Luisa Bombal y Susana San Juan de Juan Rulfo." *Espéculo: Revista de Estudios Literarios* 39 (2008).

Martínez-Ortiz, María Teresa. "We Are All Malinche: The Collapse of the National Mexican Mother and Its Representations in Literature and Film." In *(M)othering the Nation: Constructing and Resisting National Allegories through the Maternal Body*, edited by Lisa Bernstein, 111–23. Newcastle: Cambridge Scholars, 2008.

Maturin, Charles R. *Melmoth the Wanderer: A Tale*. 1820. Lincoln: University of Nebraska Press, 1961.

Maupassant, Guy de. "The Horla." In *Selected Tales of Guy de Maupassant*, 27–42. New York: Random House, 1950.
McNally, Raymond T., and Radu Florescu. *The Essential Dracula*. New York: Mayflower Books, 1979.
———. *In Search of Dracula: The History of Dracula and Vampires*. Boston: Houghton Mifflin, 1994.
McNamee, Gregory. *Movable Feasts: The History, Science, and Lore of Food*. Westport, CT: Praeger, 2007.
Méliès, Georges. *Georges Méliès: First Wizard of Cinema (1896–1913)*. Blackhawk Films Collection, 2008. DVD.
Mella Vilches, Manuel, ed. *Zombies en La Moneda: Saga Santiago*. Santiago: Mythica Ediciones, 2011.
Metropolis. 1927. Directed by Fritz Lang, Alfred Abel, and Friedrich W. Murnau. New York: Kino Lorber, 2010. DVD.
Métraux, Alfred. *Voodoo in Haiti*. Translated by Hugo Charteris. Oxford: Oxford University Press, 1959.
Metz, Christian. *The Imaginary Signifier: Psychoanalysis and the Cinema*. Bloomington: Indiana University Press, 1981.
Meyers, Helene. *Femicidal Fears: Narratives of the Female Gothic Experience*. Albany: SUNY Press, 2001.
Michelet, Jules. *Satanism and Witchcraft: A Study in Medieval Superstition*. Translated by Alfred Richard Allinson. New York: Citadel Press, 1939. Kindle edition.
———. *La sorcière*. Paris: Flammarion, 1966.
Middleton, John. *Magic, Witchcraft, and Curing*. Garden City, NY: Published for the American Museum of Natural History of New York by the Natural History Press, 1967.
Miller, Mary E., and Karl A. Taube. *The Gods and Symbols of Ancient Mexico and the Maya: An Illustrated Dictionary of Mesoamerican Religion*. New York: Thames and Hudson, 1993.
Moers, Ellen. "Female Gothic." *Gothic: Critical Concepts in Literary and Cultural Studies* 1 (2004): 123–44.
Monsiváis, Carlos. "Función corrida (El cine mexicano y la cultura popular urbana)." In *Los estudios culturales en México*, edited by José Manuel Valenzuela Arce, 261–95. Mexico City: Fondo de Cultura Económica, 2003.
Monter, William. "Black Mass." In *Encyclopedia of Witchcraft*, edited by Richard M. Golden. Santa Barbara: ABC-CLIO, 2006.
Montero, Mayra. *In the Palm of Darkness: A Novel*. New York: Harper Collins, 1997.

———. *Tu, la oscuridad*. Barcelona: Tusquets, 1995.

Mora, Gabriela. "Decadencia y vampirismo en el modernismo hispanoamericano: Un cuento de Clemente Palma." *Revista de Crítica Literaria Latinoamericana* 23, no. 46 (1997): 191–98. http://www.jstor.org/stable/4530934. Accessed November 2, 2016.

Morelli, Gabriele. "Contra el Surrealismo: Cartas inéditas de Vicente Huidobro a Luis Buñuel." In *Surrealismo y literatura en España*, edited by Jaume Pont, 129–40. Lleida, Spain: Ediciones de la Universitat de Lleida, 2001.

Morelli, Gabriele, ed. Introduction to *Cagliostro* by Vicente Huidobro, 9–49. Madrid: Cátedra, 2011.

Morris, David B. "Gothic Sublimity." *New Literary History* 16, no. 2 (1985): 299–319.

Mulvey, Laura. "Visual Pleasure and Narrative Cinema." In *Film Theory and Criticism*, 5th ed., edited by Leo Braudy and Marshall Cohen, 833–44. New York: Oxford University Press, 1999.

Mulvey-Roberts, Marie, ed. Introduction to *The Handbook to Gothic Literature*, xv–xviii. New York: New York University Press, 1998.

Náter, Miguel Ángel. "La imaginación enfermiza: La ciudad muerta y el gótico en *Aura* de Carlos Fuentes." *Revista Chilena de Literatura* 64 (2004): 73–89.

Negroni, María. *Galería fantástica*. Mexico City: Siglo XXI, 2009.

Nieto, Omar. *Teoría general de lo fantástico: Del fantástico clásico al posmoderno*. Mexico City: UACM, 2015.

Night of the Living Dead. 1968. Directed by George Romero. New York: Elite Entertainment, 2002. DVD

Nosferatu. 1922. Directed by Friedrich W. Murnau. New York: Kino Lorber Films, 2013. DVD.

The Numismatist. Vol. 27. Federalsburg, MD: Stowell Press, 1914.

Obón, Ramón. *Amantes de sangre*. Mexico City: Ediciones B, 2009.

———. *La cofradía secreta*. Mexico City: Ediciones B, 2010.

———. *Príncipe maldito*. Barcelona: Ediciones B, 2008.

Olivio Jiménez, José, ed. *Verónica y otros cuentos fantásticos*. Madrid: Alianza Editorial, 1995.

Olmedo, Nadina, and Osvaldo Di Paolo. *Negrótico*. Madrid: Ediciones Pliegos, 2015.

Los olvidados: The Young and the Damned. 1950. Directed by Luis Buñuel. Mexico City: Televisa S. A. de C. V., 2004. DVD.

Pacheco, José Emilio. *Antología del modernismo (1884–1921)*. Mexico: UNAM, 1970.

———. "La batalla del Surrealismo." In *Surrealismo/Surrealismos: Latinoamérica y España*, edited by Peter G. Earle and Germán Gullón, 49–54. Philadelphia: Department of Romance Languages, University of Pennsylvania, 1977.

———. "Entre la plantación y el matadero." *Proceso 1406*, October 12, 2003, 62. http://www.proceso.com.mx/190385/entre-la-plantacion-y-el-matadero. Accessed November 2, 2016.

Palma, Clemente. "Vampiras." 1906. *Cuentos malévolos*, 207–27. Paris: Librería P. Ollendorff, 1912. Hathi Trust. https://babel.hathitrust.org/cgi/pt?id=yale.39002029844587;view=1up;seq=251. Accessed July 15, 2017.

———. "Las vampiras." 1906. *Cuentos malévolos*, 130–41. Lexington, KY: CreateSpace, 2016.

———. "Vampiras." 1906. *Cuentos malévolos*, 2nd. ed., 1913. Lima: Editorial Nuevos Rumbos, 1959.

The Passion of Joan of Arc: Le passion de Jeanne d'Arc. 1928. Directed by Carl Theodor Dreyer. New York: Criterion Collection, 1999. DVD.

Paz, Octavio. "Los hijos de la Malinche." 1950. In *El laberinto de la soledad*, 88–113. New York: Penguin Books, 1997.

———. *Los hijos del limo: Del romanticismo a la vanguardia*. 1972. Barcelona: Seix Barral, 1993.

———. *El laberinto de la soledad*. 1950. New York: Penguin Books, 1997.

———. *The Labyrinth of Solitude: Life and Thought in Mexico*. Translated by Lysander Kemp, Yara Milos, and Rachel Phillips Belash, 65–88. New York: Grove Press, 1985.

———. "Todos santos, día de los muertos." 1950. In *El laberinto de la soledad*, 68–87. New York: Penguin Books, 1997.

Paz Soldán, Edmundo. "The Avant-Garde and Cinematic Imaginary: Huidobro's Novela-Film." In *Latin American Literature and Mass Media*, edited by Edmundo Paz Soldán and Debra Castillo, 57–70. New York: Garland, 2001.

Pérez, Genaro. "La configuración de elementos góticos en 'Constancia,' *Aura* y 'Tlactocatzine, del jardín de Flandes' de Carlos Fuentes." *Hispania* 80, no. 1 (1997): 9–20.

Phillips, Kendall R. *Projected Fears: Horror Films and American Culture*. Westport, CT: Praeger, 2005.

Piglia, Ricardo. *Formas breves*. Barcelona: Editorial Anagrama, 2000.

Pinto, Alfonso. "Hollywood's Spanish-Language Films: A Neglected Chapter of the American Cinema, 1930–1935." *Films in Review* 24 (1973): 474–87.

Plaga zombie, zona mutante. Directed by Pablo Parés and Hernán Sáez. Media Blasters, 2005. DVD.

Plato. "The Myth Told by Aristophanes." In *The Myths of Plato*. London: Macmillan, 1905. Hathi Trust. https://babel.hathitrust.org/cgi/pt?id=uc2.ark:/13960/t8rb76730;view=1up;seq=9. Accessed June 3, 2017.

Poe, Edgar A. "Anabel Lee." *Works*, 12–13.

———. "Berenice." 1835. *Works*, 313–19.

———. "The Cask of Amontillado." 1846. *Works*, 205–9.

———. "The Fall of the House of Usher." 1839. *Works*, 273–86.

———. "How to Write a Blackwood Article." 1838. Raleigh, NC: Alex Catalogue. http://search.ebscohost.com.libproxy.albany.edu/login.aspx?direct=true&scope=site&db=nlebk&db=nlabk&AN=1085990. Accessed May 22, 2016.

———. "Ligeia." 1838. *Works*, 324–34.

———. "Morella." 1835. *Works*, 335–39.

———. "The Oval Portrait." 1842. *Works*, 311–13.

———. "The Philosophy of Composition." *Works*, 812–20.

———. "The Premature Burial." 1844. Raleigh, NC: Alex Catalogue, n.d. eBook Collection.

———. "Ulalume." 1847. *Works*, 8–10.

———. "William Wilson." 1839. *Works*, 224–38.

———. *The Works of Edgar Allan Poe*. Edited by Hervey Allen. New York: Walter J. Black, 1927.

Polidori, John William. "The Vampyre: A Tale." 1819. In *Three Vampire Tales*, edited by Anne Williams, 68–85. Boston: Wadsworth, 2003.

Pont, Jaume. *Surrealismo y literatura en España*. Spain: Edicions de la Universitat de Lleida, 2013.

Poole, Stafford. *Our Lady of Guadalupe: The Origins and Sources of a Mexican National Symbol, 1531–1797*. Tucson: University of Arizona Press, 1995.

Popul vuh, libro común de los quiches. Edited by Adrián Recinos. Havana: Casa de las Américas, 1969.

Porter, Eduardo. "Globalization and the Narcotics Trade." *New York Times*, August 2, 2007. http://www.nytimes.com/2007/08/02/opinion/02iht-edporter.1.6957148.html?_r=0. Accessed November 2, 2016.

Potter, Sara Anne. "Disturbing Muses: Gender, Technology and Resistance in Mexican Avant-Garde Cultures." Ph.D. diss., Washington University in St. Louis, 2013. https://openscholarship.wustl.edu/etd/1154.

Punter, David. *The Literature of Terror: A History of Gothic Fictions from 1765 to the Present Day*. London: Longmans, 1980.

Quiñones Keber, Eloise. "Xolotl: Dogs, Death, and Deities in Aztec Myth." *Latin American Indian Literatures Journal: A Review of American Indian Texts and Studies* 7, no. 2 (Fall 1991): 229–39.
Quiroga, Horacio. "El almohadón de pluma." *Horacio Quiroga: Cuentos*, 34–37. Caracas: Biblioteca Ayacucho, 1981.
———. *Anaconda*. 1921. Buenos Aires: Losada, 1963.
———. *Cine y literatura*. Buenos Aires: Losada, 2007.
———. *Cuentos de amor, de locura y de muerte*. 1917. New York: Penguin Books, 1997.
———. "Decálogo del perfecto cuentista." 1927. *Horacio Quiroga: Cuentos*, 307–10. Caracas: Biblioteca Ayacucho, 1981.
———. "A la deriva." 1917. *Horacio Quiroga: Cuentos*, 78–80. Caracas: Biblioteca Ayacucho, 1981.
———. "El espectro." 1921. *Horacio Quiroga: Cuentos*, 4:75–89. Montevideo: Claudio García y Cía, 1937.
———. "El hombre muerto." *Horacio Quiroga: Cuentos*, 190–93. Caracas: Biblioteca Ayacucho, 1981.
———. *Más allá*. 1934. Buenos Aires: Losada, 1954.
———. "Miss Dorothy Phillips, mi esposa." 1919. *Horacio Quiroga: Cuentos*, 144–74. Caracas: Biblioteca Ayacucho, 1981.
———. "El puritano." 1926. *Más Allá*, 161–75. Montevideo: Ediciones de la Sociedad Amigos del Libro Rioplatense, 1935.
———. "El vampiro." 1927. *Horacio Quiroga: Cuentos*, 277–93. Caracas: Biblioteca Ayacucho, 1981.
Radcliffe, Ann W. *The Italian; or, The Confessional of the Black Penitents, a Romance*. 1797. Oxford: Oxford University Press, 1981.
———. *The Mysteries of Udolpho*. 1794. Edited by Terry Castle. Oxford: Oxford University Press, 1998.
Rank, Otto. *The Double: A Psychoanalytic Study*. Chapel Hill: University of North Carolina Press, 1971.
Read, Herbert. Introduction to *Surrealism*, edited by Herbert Read, 17–91. London: Faber and Faber, 1971.
Regazzoni, Susanna. "Lo exótico en la literatura hispanoamericana: Juana Manuela Gorriti." In *Actas del XIV Congreso de la Asociación Internacional de Hispanistas, IV: Literatura hispanoamericana*, 565–74. Newark, DE: Cuesta, 2004.
Rengger, Johann Rudolph, and Marcelin Longchamp. *The Reign of Doctor Joseph Gaspard Roderick de Francia in Paraguay: Being an Account of Six Years' Residence in That Republic, from July, 1819, to May, 1825*. London: T. Hurst E. Chance, 1827.

Reyes de la Maza, Luis. *Salón rojo: Programas y crónicas del cine mudo en México*. Mexico City: UNAM, 1968.
Ribas-Casasayas, Alberto, and Amanda L. Petersen. *Espectros: Ghostly Hauntings in Contemporary Transhispanic Narratives*. Lewisburg, PA: Bucknell University Press, 2016.
Rice, Anne. *Interview with the Vampire*. New York: Ballantine Books, 1997.
Richter, Johann Paul Friedrich (Jean Paul). *Flower, Fruit and Thorn Pieces: Or, the Married Life, Death, and Wedding of the Advocate of the Poor, Firmian Stanislaus Siebenkäs*. Boston: Ticknor and Fields, 1863.
———. *Siebenkäs*. 1796. Munich: Ed. Text + Kritik, 1991.
Roa Bastos, Augusto. *El fiscal*. Madrid: Alfaguara, 1994.
———. *I, the Supreme*. Translated by Helen Lane. New York: Knopf, 1986.
———. Interview with Beatriz Rodríguez Alcalá de González Oddone, *Commentarios sobre "Yo el Supremo."* Asunción: Ediciones Club del Libro, 1975.
———. "Interview with Silvia Lemus." Princeton, NJ: Films for the Humanities and Sciences, 1998. Video.
———. *Yo el supremo*. 1974. Edited by Milagros Ezquerro. Madrid: Cátedra, 2003.
———. *Yo el supremo*. Madrid: Ediciones Alfaguara, 1985.
Robertson, John Parish, and William Parish Robertson. *Francia's Reign of Terror: Being a Sequel to "Letters on Paraguay."* Philadelphia: E. L. Carey and A. Hart, 1839.
———. *Letters on Paraguay: Comprising an Account of a Four Years' Residence in That Republic, under the Government of the Dictator Francia*. 1838. New York: AMS Press, 1970.
Robisch, S. K. *Wolves and the Wolf Myth in American Literature*. Reno: University of Nevada Press, 2009. Kindle edition.
Rodenas, Adriana. "Narcissus in Bloom: The Desiring Subject in Modern Latin American Narrative—María Luisa Bombal and Juan Rulfo." In *Latin American Women's Writing: Feminist Readings in Theory and Crisis*, edited by Anny Brooksbank Jones and Catherine Davies, 104–25. Oxford: Clarendon Press, 1996.
Rohter, Larry. "Footage Restored to Fritz Lang's 'Metropolis.'" *New York Times*, May 4, 2010. http://www.nytimes.com/2010/05/05/movies/05metropolis.html. Accessed July 10, 2016.
Rojas, Lourdes. "El torno al epígrafe de Michelet en *Aura*." In *La obra de Carlos Fuentes: Una vision múltiple*, edited by Ana María Hernández de López, 69–86. Madrid: Editorial Pliegos, 1988.
Romero, Rolando. "Foundational Motherhood: Malinche/Guadalupe in

Contemporary Mexican and Chicano/Chicana Culture." In *Feminism, Nation and Myth: La Malinche*, edited by Amanda N. Harris and Rolando Romero, 28–43. Houston: Arte Público Press, 2005.

Romero Sandoval, Roberto. *Zotz: El murciélago en la cultura maya*. Mexico City: UNAM, 2013.

Ruiz Pérez, Ignacio. "Contra-Escrituras: Delmira Agustini, Alfonsina Storni y la subversión del modernismo." *Revista Hispánica Moderna* 61, no. 2 (2008): 183–96. http://www.jstor.org/stable/40647488. Accessed August 1, 2016.

Rulfo, Juan. *Pedro Páramo*. Translated by Margaret S. Peden. New York: Grove Press, 1994.

———. *Pedro Páramo y el llano en llamas*. 1955. Barcelona: Planeta, S.A., 2000.

Rutherford, John. *Mexican Society during the Revolution: A Literary Approach*. Oxford: Clarendon, 1971.

Santo contra las lobas. 1972. Directed by Jiménez Pons. Mexico City: Televisa Home Entertainment, 2008. DVD.

El Santo contra las mujeres vampiro. 1962. Directed by Alfonso Corona Blake. Santa Monica, CA: Veranda Entertainment, 2000. Amazon Video.

Santo contra los zombis. 1961. Directed by Benito Alazraki. Mexico City: Cinematográfica Rodríguez, 2000. DVD.

Santo y Blue Demon vs. Drácula y el hombre lobo. 1973. Directed by Miguel M. Delgado. Tulsa: VCI Entertainment, 2014. DVD.

Satanás: Satana. 1912. Directed by Luigi Maggi. Società Anonima Ambrosio.

Seabrook, William. *The Magic Island*. 1929. New York: Dover, 2016.

Sedgwick, Eve K. *The Coherence of Gothic Conventions*. New York: Arno Press, 1980.

Serrano, Carmen. "El vampiro en el espejo: Elementos góticos en *Yo el supremo*." *Revista Iberoamericana* 76, no. 232–33 (2010): 899–912.

———. "Revamping Dracula on the Mexican Silver Screen: Fernando Méndez's *El vampiro*." In *Vampires and Zombies: Transcultural Migrations and Transnational Interpretations*, edited by Dorothea Fischer-Hornung and Monika Mueller, 149–67. Jackson: University Press of Mississippi, 2016.

Shaun of the Dead. Directed by Edgar Wright. Universal City, CA: Universal, 2004.

Shelley, Mary Wollstonecraft. *Frankenstein*. 1818. London: Penguin, 2012.

Shklovsky, Viktor. *Theory of Prose*. Normal, IL: Dalkey Archive Press, 1990.

Skal, David J. *Hollywood Gothic: The Tangled Web of Dracula from Novel to Stage to Screen*. New York: Norton, 1990.

———. "The Spanish Dracula: Production of the Spanish Film Version of *Dracula*." *American Film* 15, no. 12 (1990): 38–41.

Skinner, Lee. *Gender and the Rhetoric of Modernity in Spanish America, 1850–1910*. Gainesville: University Press of Florida, 2016.

Socolow, Susan M. *The Women of Colonial Latin America*. Cambridge: Cambridge University Press, 2000.

Speratti-Piñero, Emma Susana. "Horacio Quiroga: Precursor de la relación cine-literatura en la América Hispánica." *Nueva Revista de Filología Hispánica* 36, no. 2 (1988): 1239–49.

Stavans, Ilan. *Mutual Impressions: Writers from the Americas Reading One Another*. Durham, NC: Duke University Press, 1999.

Steiger, Brad. *The Werewolf Book: The Encyclopedia of Shape-Shifting Beings*. Detroit: Visible Ink Press, 1999.

Stevenson, Robert Louis. *The Strange Case of Dr. Jekyll and Mr. Hyde, and Other Famous Tales*. 1886. New York: Dodd, Mead, 1961.

Stock, Ann Marie. "Migrancy and the Latin American Cinemascape: Towards a Post-National Critical Praxis." *Revista Canadiense de Estudios Hispánicos* 20, no. 1 (1995): 19–30.

Stoker, Bram. *Dracula*. 1897. New York: Barnes and Noble, 1996.

The Student of Prague. 1913. Directed by Paul Wegener, Stellan Ryem, and Hanns Heinz Ewers. Alpha Home Entertainment, 2004. DVD.

The Student of Prague. 1926. Directed by Henrik Galeen. Alpha Video, 2004. DVD.

Summers, Montague. *The Gothic Quest: A History of the Gothic Novel*. 1938. New York: Russell and Russell. 1964.

Sunset Boulevard. 1950. Directed by Billy Wilder. Burbank: Warner Bros, 2008. DVD.

Tebb, William. *Premature Burial and How It May Be Prevented*. 1896. London: Swan Sonnenschein, 2015. http://www.gutenberg.org/files/50460/50460-h/50460-h.htm. Accessed October 13, 2017.

Thompson, J. Eric S. "Maya Hieroglyphs of the Bat as Metaphorgrams." *Man*, n.s. 1, no. 2 (1966): 176–84.

Thompson, Kristin. "Dr. Caligari at the Folies-Bergere, or, The Successes of an Early Avant-Garde Film." In *The Cabinet of Dr. Caligari: Texts, Contexts, Histories*, edited by Mike Budd, 121–70. New Brunswick, NJ: Rutgers University Press, 1990.

Titiev, Janice Geasler. "Witchcraft in Carlos Fuentes' *Aura*." *Revista de Estudios Hispánicos* 15, no. 3 (1981): 395–405.

Todorov, Tzvetan. *The Fantastic: A Structural Approach to a Literary Genre*. Ithaca, NY: Cornell University Press, 1975.

del Toro, Guillermo, and Chuck Hogan. *The Fall*. New York: William Morrow, 2010.
———. *Night Eternal*. New York: William Morrow, 2011.
———. *The Strain*. New York: William Morrow, 2009.
A Trip to the Moon: Le voyage dans la lune. 1902. Directed by Georges Méliès. Flicker Alley, 2008. DVD.
Turcios, Froylán. *El vampiro*. 1910. Brimfield, MA: Casasola, 2013.
Twitchell, James B. *The Living Dead: A Study of the Vampire in Romantic Literature*. Durham, NC: Duke University Press, 1981. Kindle edition.
Ugestu. 1954. Directed by Kenji Mizoguchi. New York: Criterion Collection, 2004.
Valdez Moses, Michael. "Magical Realism at World's End." *Literary Imagination* 3, no. 1 (2001): 105–33.
El vampiro. 1957. Directed by Fernando Méndez. San Francisco: CasaNegra Entertainment, 2006. DVD.
Vampyr. 1932. Directed by Carl Theodor Dreyer. New York: Criterion Collection, 2008. DVD.
Van Helsing. Syfy cable television series. Nomadic Pictures, 2016.
Varnum, Robin. *Álvar Núñez Cabeza de Vaca: American Trailblazer*. Norman: University of Oklahoma Press, 2014.
Velázquez Betacourt, Diego. *La noche que asolaron Tokio*. Mexico City: Ediciones del Ermitaño, Conaculta, 2013.
Vertov, Dziga. *Kino-eye: The Writings of Dziga Vertov*, edited by Annette Michelson. Berkeley: University of California Press, 1984.
Vicendeau, Ginnette. "Hollywood Babel: The Coming of Sound and the Multiple-Language Version." In *"Film Europe" and "Film America": Cinema, Commerce and Cultural Exchange, 1920–1939*, edited by Andrew Higson and Richard Maltby, 207–24. Exeter, UK: University of Exeter Press, 1999.
Villaurrutia, Xavier, "Dama de corazones." 1928. In *Obras: Poesía, teatro, prosas varias, críticas*, edited by Alí Chumacero, Miguel Capistrán, and Luis M. Schneider, 571–96. Mexico City: Fondo de Cultura Económica, 1966.
———. "Nostalgia de la muerte." In *Obras: Poesía, teatro, prosas varias, críticas*, edited by Alí Chumacero, Miguel Capistrán, and Luis M. Schneider, 44–73. Mexico City: Fondo de Cultura Económica, 1938.
Vincenzi, Moisés. *Froylán Turcios: Su vida y sus obras*. San José, C. R.: Imprenta María v. de Lines, 1921. Hathi Trust. babel.hathitrust.org/cgi/pt?id=wu.89099404915;view=1up;seq=. Accessed December 2, 2016.
Viridiana. 1961. Directed by Luis Buñuel. New York: Criterion Collection, 2006. DVD.

Volek, Emil. "Realismo mágico entre la modernidad y la postmodernidad: Hacia una remodelización cultural y discursiva de la nueva narrativa hispanoamericana." *INTI* 1, no. 31 (1990): 3–20.

Wagnleitner, Reinhold. *Coca-Colonization and the Cold War: The Cultural Mission of the United States in Austria after the Second World War*. Chapel Hill: University of North Carolina Press, 2003.

Wallace, Diana. "'The Haunting Idea': Female Gothic Metaphors and Feminist Theory." In *The Female Gothic: New Directions*, edited by Diana Wallace and Andrew Smith, 26–41. New York: Palgrave Macmillan, 2009.

Wallace, Diana, and Andrew Smith, eds. *The Female Gothic: New Directions*. New York: Palgrave Macmillan, 2009.

Walpole, Horace. *The Castle of Otranto*. 1764. London: Penguin Classics, 2001.

Webber, Andrew J. *The Doppelgänger: Double Visions in German Literature*. Oxford: Clarendon Press, 1996.

White, Hayden V. *Metahistory: The Historical Imagination in Nineteenth-Century Europe*. Baltimore: Johns Hopkins University Press, 1973.

White Zombie. 1932. Directed by Victor Halperin. New York: Kino Classics, 2013. DVD.

Wilde, Oscar. *The Picture of Dorian Gray*. 1890. London: Penguin, 2012.

Wilson, Samuel M. "The Taíno Social and Political Order." In *Taíno: Pre-Columbian Art and Culture from the Caribbean*, edited by Ricardo E. Alegria and Jose Arrom, 46–55. New York: La Monacelli Press, 1997.

Wolfreys, Julian. Introduction to *Victorian Gothic: Literary and Cultural Manifestations in the Nineteenth Century*, edited by Ruth Robbins and Julian Wolfreys, xi–xx. Houndmills, England: Palgrave, 2000.

Wright, Melissa W. "Necropolitics, Narcopolitics, and Femicide: Gendered Violence on the Mexico-U.S. Border." *Signs* 36, no. 3 (2011): 707–31.

Zamora, Lois Parkinson, and Wendy B. Faris. *Magical Realism: Theory, History, Community*. Durham, NC: Duke University Press, 2006.

Index

Abel, Alfred, 59
Abrams, M. H., 189n47
Acosta-Lugo, Maribel, 65–66
aesthetics, 35; concern for literary, 91; cultural anxieties and, 22–24; evoking, 87; experimentation with, 67–68; hauntings described using, 142; negative, 13, 20, 81, 162, 173, 187n3; Orientalist, 32; traditional view of, 17
afterlife, 98; freedom in, 22; pleasure in, 104; as space for self-realization, 81
El águila y la serpiente (The Eagle and the Serpent) (Guzmán), 53, 63–64
Agustini, Delmira, 32, 34, 41–42, 191n20
Alazraki, Jaime Miguel, 171
Albright, Richard, 112
alienation effect, 195n65
Amar Sánchez, Ana María, x, 17
ambiance, 2–3, 75
La amortajada (The Shrouded Woman) (Bombal), 22, 65–66, 81, 98–107
anachronistic historical fiction, 111–21
Anaconda (Quiroga), 51
androgyny, 38–39
Andújar, Carolina, 182
animal-doubles, 23, 141–42, 145–55
Antología de la literatura fantástica (The Book of Fantasy) (Borges, Casares, and Ocampo), 12–13
anxieties. *See* cultural anxieties
Apollinaire, Guillaume, 72
architecture, xi
Argentina, cinema houses in, 56
Ariès, Philippe, 93
The Arrival of a Train at La Ciotat Station (*L'arrivée d'untrain en gare de La Ciotat*), 54, 56
art, 195n68; antimimetic, 24; film as, 49; ideals manifested in, 189n47; as influenced by previous works, 19; reevaluation of, 16–17; social change through, 189n35; Surrealists evaluating world of, 10–11; visual, 16
artifacts, from mass culture, 16
The Aspern Papers (James), 174
El ataúd del vampiro (The Vampire's Coffin), 175–76, 178
atavism, romantic, 8, 11, 43
Aura (Fuentes), 23, 141–42, 156–74, 201n55, 205n76
Austen, Jane, 82
authenticity, 5, 24, 114, 158–59, 173–74
authoritarianism, xi, 2, 81, 123, 149
automatism, 72
Avances de Hollywood: Crítica cinematográfica en Latinoamérica, 1915–1945 (Borge), 64
avant-garde, 10–11, 63, 67, 72, 91, 189n36

233

"Axolotl," 51, 141, 147–48
Azuela, Mariano, 53, 63–64, 197n24

Baldick, Chris, 9
Bareiro Saguier, Rubén, 121–22
Barlow, John, 60
Barthes, Roland, 17–18
bats, 5; anthropomorphic, 28, 30–31; characteristics of, 20; *Dracula* association with, 21–23; evil association with, 30, 119; indigenous names for, 29; influence of, on imaginings of vampires, 21; in Mexico, 31; as supernatural, 120; symbolism of, 132; types of, 28; vampire, 28–31, 44–47
Baudelaire, Charles, 10, 32, 34, 46, 191n21
beauty, 5; death and, 93; of female corpse, 103–4; seduction through, 165
belief, perception and, 8
Benedetti, Mario, 144–45
"Berenice," 51, 83
bestializando, 121
Beyond (*Más allá*) (Quiroga), 48
Blade and *Blade II*, 177, 180
Bombal, María Luisa, ix, 14, 18, 53; *The House of Mist*, 100–101; *The Shrouded Woman*, 22, 65–66, 81, 98–107
Bonaparte, Napoleon, 126, 199n1
The Book of Fantasy (*Antología de la literatura fantástica*) (Borges, Casares, and Ocampo), 12–13
Borge, Jason, 64
Borges, Jorge Luis, 12, 14, 17, 65, 202n1
"Borges y yo," 202n1

Borgia, Danielle, 182
Botting, Fred, 2, 6, 9, 172, 187n3
bourgeoisie, 49, 129
Bowers, Maggie, 15
Braham, Persephone, 182–83
Breton, André, 10, 18, 19, 72, 188n28, 197n30
Brontë, Emily, ix, 5, 99
Browning, Tod, 58
Bruce-Novoa, Juan, x–xi
Brushwood, John, 174
Buffy the Vampire Slayer, 177
Buñuel, Luis, 18, 60–61, 72, 194n48
burials, live, 2, 6, 22, 74, 130, 195n1, 196n9; Carpentier describing, 85–88; describing of, 81–90, 96–98, 142; female experience of, 101–7
"The Buried Alive," 82–83, 90

Cabeza de Vaca, Álvar Núñez, 28, 30
The Cabinet of Dr. Caligari, 21, 57–59, 61, 67, 73, 84–85
Cabiya, Pedro, 182
Cagliostro, 22, 53, 67–77, 89–90, 193n43
Caligari, 60
Campobello, Nellie, 63–64
Cantos de la mañana (Agustini), 34
"Carmilla," 27, 65, 105, 162
Carpentier, Alejo, ix, 18, 81, 149–55; animal doubles and, 23, 141–42; live burials described by, 85–88
Cartucho (Campobello), 63–64
Casares, Adolfo Bioy, 12–14
"The Cask of Amontillado," 83
The Castle of Otranto (Walpole), 3, 5, 10, 13
Castle, Terry, 112
Catholic Church, 3, 131

Cervantes, Miguel de, 151, 155, 203n32
"Chac Mool," 23, 141–42, 156–58, 204n52
characters: ability to empathize with, 195n65; emotions felt by, 20; as evil, 111–12; mental instability of, 59; as mysterious, 2; names of, 51; plagiarization felt by, 24; predetermined types of, 74
Chaves, Julio César, 116
Chekhov, Anton, 50
Un chien Andalou, 60
chronology, undermining, 113, 116
La chute dula maison Usher, 60, 84
cinema houses, 56
cinematic voyeurism, 71
El cine que vió fósforo: Alfonso Reyes y Martín Luis Guzmán (González Casanova), 64
Cine y literatura (Quiroga), 64
Citizen Kane, 174, 206n108
The Coherence of Gothic Conventions (Sedgwick), 85
colonization, xi, 2
color, in film, 62–63
Contemporaneos, 91
Cortázar, Julio, ix, 12–14, 21, 27, 202n1; short stories by, 49–50, 51, 141, 146–49; Surrealism and, 189n45
Cortés, Hernán, 28, 133–34
de Costa, René, 73, 193n43
Cotter, Robert, 178–79
Creationism (*Creacionismo*), 18, 72
Cuentos de amor, de locura y de muerte (Stories of Love, Madness, and Death) (Quiroga), 48
cultural anxieties, 99, 149; aesthetics and, 22–24; articulation of, 69; about contagion, 182; contemporary, 137; about social crises, 185
Culturas híbridas: Estrategias para entrar y salir de la modernidad (Hybrid Cultures: Strategies for Entering and Leaving Modernity) (García Canclini), 18
cultures: artifacts from mass, 16; fear of contemporary, 23; interchange between media and, 20; magic found in, 18; negotiation between, 18; politics and, 8

Dalí, Salvador, 18, 60
Dame of Hearts (*Dama de corazones*) (Villaurrutia), 90–92
Darío, Rubén, 8, 21, 27, 43; poetry by, 32–33; *Verónica y otros cuentos fantásticos*, 33–36
Darwin, Charles, 29–30
Davidson, Carol Margaret, 9
Day of the Dead (Mexico), 18–19, 92, 197n26
death: beauty and, 93; eroticism in, 104–5; freedom found in, 106–7; as safe haven, 97–98; themes of, 33; as ultimate ailment, 119
Decalogue of the Perfect Short Story Writer (*Decálogo del perfecto cuentista*) (Quiroga), 50–51
De la pantalla al texto: La influencia del cine en la narrativa mexicana del siglo veinte (From Screen to Text: The Influence of Cinema in Mexican Narratives of the Twentieth Century) (Duffey), 63
Delmira Agustini, Sexual Seduction, and Vampiric Conquest (Jrade), 41–42

De lo mítico a lo profano: Chac Mool como monstruo (From the Mythic to the Profane: Chac Mool as Monster) (Herrera Ávila), 157–58
Devil, 5, 143, 164, 169, 177
Díaz, Porfirio, 136
Díaz del Castillo, Bernal, 30
Díaz Enciso, Adriana, 182
Dickens, Charles, 83, 174
dictatorships, 111–17
Dijkstra, Bram, 37–40
domestication, of women, 41
domesticity, 41
Doniger, Wendy, 19–20, 117
doppelgänger, 2, 5, 23, 117; in "El espectro," 70; literary world of, 143–45; Romanticism and, 141; in "El vampiro," 68
The Doppelgänger: Double Visions in German Literature (Webber, Andrew J.), 144
doubles, 2, 5–6, 9, 39, 143–44; animal, 23, 141–42, 145–55; Cortázar portrayal of, 147–49; Fuentes pervasive use of, 24, 155–61; power to conjure, 164; representations of, 20, 23; in terms of transfiguration, 171
doubling, 76–77, 117
Dracula, 21, 57–58, 61–62, 85
Drácula (Spanish), 62, 192n11
Dracula (Stoker), 4, 13, 58, 85, 111–19, 138–39, 178; association with bats, 21–23; negative aesthetics and, 162; vampires portrayed in, 27–30
dreadfulness, 5
dreams, 24; reimagining, 15
dreamscapes, 10

Dreyer, Carl Theodor, 58, 65–66, 77, 85, 99
Dr. Jekyll and Mr. Hyde, 61
drug trade, violence from, 137–38, 202n70
duality, 117, 122–24, 141, 171
Duchamp, Marcel, 16
Duffey, Patrick, 63–64
Duncan, Cynthia, 12

The Eagle and the Serpent (*El águila y la serpiente*) (Guzmán), 53, 63–64
Ebert, Roger, 60
economy: agrarian, 8; industrialized, 8
Edwards, Justin, 183
"El almohadón de pluma" ("The Feather Pillow"), 48
Eliot, T. S., 19
emotions: dangers of, 48; expression of, 39; as extreme and negative, 2; instability of, 60; provoking of, 89
Enlightenment, 5
Epstein, Jean, 60, 84
eroticism, 37, 94–95, 102; in death, 104–5
erotic language, 81
"El espectro," 22, 53, 67, 69–71
The Essential Dracula (McNally and Florescu), 124, 201n58
estrangement, 195n68
evil: bats association with, 30, 119; characters as, 111–12
Evil Sisters: The Threat of Female Sexuality and the Cult of Manhood (Dijkstra), 37–38

"The Fall of the House of Usher," 5, 12, 58, 83–84

The Fall of the House of Usher, 60
family dynamics, 37–38, 131
fantastic, 1, 11–16, 188n29
The Fantastic: A Structural Approach to a Literary Genre (Todorov), 12
fantastic literature (literatura fantástica), 21, 52, 191n19, 202n1; early examples of, 33; emergence of, 12–13; vampires deployed in, 27–28
Faust, 58
fear, 13, 20; ambiance instilling, 2–3; of contemporary culture, 23; as cornerstone emotion, 6; element of, 74, 89; employing of, 6; as power, 121
"The Feather Pillow" ("El almohadón de pluma"), 48
female corpse, 22, 35, 45, 93–94, 197n32; beauty of, 103–4; description of, 98; images of, 100
female deities, in Mexico, 132–35, 201n64
female Gothic, 99
"Female Vampires" ("Vampiras"), 21, 40, 47
Femicidal Fears (Meyers), 82
femicide, 202n70
feminism, 71
feminist theory, 99
feudalism, 2
Fevál, Paul, 126, 199n1
film: adaptations of literature, 16; advanced technology influencing, 55–56; as art, 49; artistic reaction to foreign, 63–67; classic Surrealist, 60; color in, 62–63; evolution of vampires in, 175; history of, 21; inferior quality of, 193n29; invention of, 10; Quiroga drawn to, 189n45; reaching Latin America, 53–57; reaction to, 54–55; realism in, 65; Spanish-language, 62; as vehicle for social change, 195n64. *See also* German Expressionist films
Fischer, Sibylle, 121–22
Les fleurs du mal (Baudelaire), 34
Flores, Angel, 14
Florescu, Radu, 111, 122, 124, 201n58
Fountain (Duchamp), 16
Frankenstein, 58, 61
Frankenstein (Shelley), 4, 58, 76
freedom: in afterlife, 22; found in death, 106–7
French Revolution, 76
Freud, Sigmund, 10, 11, 143, 202n6
From Amazons to Zombies: Monsters in Latin America (Braham), 182–83
From Screen to Text: The Influence of Cinema in Mexican Narratives of the Twentieth Century (*De la pantalla al texto: La influencia del cine en la narrativa mexicana del siglo veinte*) (Duffey), 63
From the Mythic to the Profane: Chac Mool as Monster (*De lo mítico a lo profano: Chac Mool como monstruo*) (Herrera Ávila), 157–58
Froylán Turcios: His Life and Works (*Froylán Turcios: Su vida y sus obras*) (Vincenzi), 43
Fuentes, Carlos, ix, 12, 14; *Aura*, 23, 141–42, 156–74, 201n55, 205n76; *La muerte de*

Fuentes, Carlos (*continued*)
    Artemio Cruz, 158–59, 174, 206n108; pervasive use of double by, 24, 155–61; short stories by, 23, 141–42, 156–58, 204n52; *Vlad*, 23, 89, 109, 129–39

Galeen, Henrik, 59
Galt, John, 82–83, 90, 97
Games of Seduction and Betrayal: Mass Literature and Culture (*Juegos de seducción y traición: Literatura y cultura de masas*) (Amar Sánchez), 17
García Canclini, Nestor, 18
García Gutiérrez, Rosa, 91
García Márquez, Gabriel, ix
Garro, Elena, ix
Gender and the Rhetoric of Modernity in Spanish America, 1850–1910 (Skinner), 8, 37
gender roles: modernization altering, 37; reaffirming of, 47–48; shift in, 36. See also women
General Theory of the Fantastic: From the Classic to the Postmodern Fantastic (*Teoría general de lo fantástico: Del fantástico clásico al posmoderno*) (Nieto), 12
German Expressionist films, 58–63, 72–77, 191n1
ghosts, 5, 92–93
Girard, René, 143
globalization, 37, 138, 184
Glücksmann, Max, 57, 192nn9–11
González Casanova, Manuel, 64
González de León, Fernando, 60

Gothic (Botting), 2
The Gothic Quest (Summers), 6
Great Expectations (Dickens), 174
grotesque, 33
Guaraní, 120–22
Guerra-Cunningham, Lucía, 65, 100–103, 107
Guzmán, Martín Luis, 53, 63–64

Haggerty, George, 15–16
Halberstam, Judith, 4, 36
hauntings, 33, 44, 57, 87, 135, 142
Hawthorne, Nathaniel, 83
hegemonic movements, 24
Hell, Julia, 160
Herrera Ávila, Tatiana, 157–58
"El hijo del vampiro" ("The Son of the Vampire"), 49–50, 146
historical truth, 115
History of the Gothic: Gothic Literature, 1764–1824 (Davidson), 9
Hoffman, E. T. A., 12
Hogle, Jerrold, 6, 112
Hollywood, 59, 61, 69, 193n30
Hollywood Gothic, 61–62
houngáns (Vodou priests), 87, 152
The Hour of Our Death (Ariès), 93
The House of Mist (*La última niebla*) (Bombal), 100–101
Hughes, William, 36, 130
Hugo, Victor, 10
Huidobro, Vicente, 18, 22, 53, 67, 72–78, 89–90; Buñuel relationship with, 194n48; cinematic techniques of, 63
Hutcheon, Linda, 17–18, 171
Hybrid Cultures: Strategies for Entering and Leaving Modernity (*Culturas híbridas: Estrategias para entrar y salir*

de la modernidad) (García Canclini), 18
hybridization, 18, 145
hypnotism, 27

I, the Supreme (*Yo el supremo*) (Roa Bastos), x, 23, 88–89, 109–29, 135
identity: gender, 38; Mexican, 131–33, 176; national, 32, 145, 178; poetry and, 18
immortality, 27; securing of, 23, 142, 143; of vampires, 23, 113; of villains, 23
indigenous beliefs, 2, 122, 149
indigenous worldviews, 23
industrialization, 37
intertextuality, 17–18
Interview with the Vampire (Rice), 113
Isaacs, Jorge, 182
The Italian (Radcliffe), 3, 10

James, Henry, 12, 174
The Jazz Singer, 62, 67
Joan of Arc (*Le passion de Jeanne d'Arc*), 65–66
Joyce, James, 13
Jrade, Cathy, 8, 33, 41–42
Juegos de seducción y traición: Literatura y cultura de masas (Games of Seduction and Betrayal: Mass Literature and Culture) (Amar Sánchez), 17
jungle, power of, 51

Kafka, Franz, 12–13
Kampen, M. E., 31
Kaye, Heidi, 58, 61
Kilgour, Maggie, 6

Kinetoscope, 192n7
King, John, 57
The Kingdom of This World (*El reino de esto mundo*) (Carpentier), 23, 81, 85–88, 141, 149–55
Kipling, Rudyard, 50
Kristeva, Julia, 17–18

Lang, Fritz, 59, 61
Langford, Walter, 172
Latin American Gothic, xii, 183
Leal, Luis, 134, 206n106
Leclerc, Georges-Louis, 29
LeFanu, Sheridan, 13, 27, 65, 105
"Lejana," 202n1
Leni, Paul, 61
Lewis, Mathew, 3, 10, 42, 61, 162–65
Lichtenstein, Roy, 16
"Ligeia," 42, 45–47, 51
Linder, Max, 56
literatura fantástica. *See* fantastic literature
locked-in syndrome, 82
Los de abajo (The Underdogs) (Azuela), 53, 63–64, 197n24
luchadores (wrestlers), 178–79
Lugones, Leopoldo, 8, 34, 38–40, 43; as modernista, 145; as poet, 27, 32
Lumière Cinematographe, 53–55, 192n7
lycanthropy, 23, 144, 146, 150–51, 204n44

madness, 38, 47, 68–72, 94
Magic, Witchcraft, and Curing (Middleton), 146
magical realism, 1, 14–15

INDEX

Magical Reels: A History of Cinema in Latin America, 57
magicians, 5, 76
makeup, 59–60
Mallarmé, Stéphane, 32
Man with a Movie Camera, 195n65
María (Isaacs), 182
Más allá (Beyond) (Quiroga), 48
masculinity, 36–41
mass media, 18, 20, 177
matricide, 5
Maturin, Charles, 10
de Maupassant, Guy, 12–13, 50
McNally, Raymond, 111, 122, 124, 201n58
melancholy (*melancolía*), 104
Melford, George, 62
Méliès, Georges, 54–55
Melmoth the Wanderer (Maturin), 10
The Memoirs of the Conquistador Bernal Díaz del Castillo, 28
Méndez, Fernando, 175–77, 179
Mercado, Walter, ix
Metamorphosis (Kafka), 12
Metropolis, 57, 59, 192n16
mexicanidad, 176, 179, 197n24
The Mexican Masked Wrestler and Monster Filmography (Cotter), 179
The Mexican Novel Comes of Age (Langford), 172
Mexican Revolution, 63, 136, 197n24
Mexico, 18–19, 91–92; bats presence in, 31; bourgeoisie in, 129; cinema houses in, 56; drug trade in, 137–38; female deities in, 132–35, 201n64; identity in, 131–33, 176; invasions in, 136; social reality in, 63

Meyers, Helene, 82
Michelet, Jules, 159–61, 164, 169–71, 173, 204n59
Middleton, John, 146
Mighall, Robert, 9
mirrors, vampires relationship with, 124–26
Mizoguchi, Kenji, 174
modernism (*modernismo*), 190n16; aspects defining, 43; attraction to, 32; material world undermined by, 15
modernistas, 7, 8, 190n1; anxieties expressed by, 42; drawn to Romanticism, 21; drawn to vampires, 33; inspiration of, 32; women imagined by, 36
modernity, 8; acceleration of, 11, 20; impact of, 21; loathing for, 43; newness of, 73
modernization, xi, 2; gender roles altered by, 37; results of, 18
Moers, Ellen, 99
The Monk (Lewis), 3, 10, 42, 61, 162–65
monsters: as demonstrative, 109; employing of, 6; global influence of, 175; migration of, 4; as residing in human soul, 110; as ruling, 14; women becoming, 38–39. *See also* lycanthropy; vampires; zombies
Moore, Thomas, 10
"Morella," 51
Morelli, Gabriele, 73, 193n43
Moro, César, 19
La muerte de Artemio Cruz (Fuentes), 158–59, 174, 206n108
Mulvey-Roberts, Marie, 3
Murnau, Friedrich W., 58–59

The Mysteries of Udolpho (Radcliffe), 82, 112

NAFTA. *See* North American Free Trade Agreement
nahualismo, 146–48, 152–53
narrative continuity, 77–78
Náter, Ángel, 171–72
Negrótico (di Paolo and Olmedo), 183
neoclassicism, 10, 189n47
Nieto, Omar, 12
nightmares, 15, 24
The Night That Tokio Was Destroyed (*La noche que asolaron Tokio*) (Velázquez Betacourt), 184
North American Free Trade Agreement (NAFTA), 136
Northanger Abbey (Austen), 82
Nosferatu, 58–60, 67, 73–75, 178
Nostalgia of Death (*Nostalgia de la muerte*) (Villarrutia), 90–92, 98–99
Notre-Dame de Paris (*The Hunchback of Notre Dame*), 56

Obón, Ramón, 175, 182
Ocampo, Silvina, 12
Olmedo, Nadina, 183
oppression, 8, 98; force of, 10; suffering from, 22; vampires representing, 23, 42
optical illusions, 54
originality, 17, 19, 24, 173
"The Other Self" ("El otro yo"), 144
La otra orilla (Cortázar), 49–50
"The Oval Portrait," 49, 51, 68–69, 83–84

Paalen, Wolfgang, 19

palimpsests, 17–18
Palma, Clemente, 8, 21, 27, 32, 40
di Paolo, Osvaldo, 183
Paraguay, 110–17, 121, 126–29
parody, 17–18, 171, 174
Le passion de Jeanne d'Arc (*Joan of Arc*), 65–66
patriarchy, xi
Paz, Octavio, 18, 92, 133, 134–35, 188n19
Paz-Soldán, Edmundo, 73, 76
Pedro Páramo (Rulfo), 22, 81, 92–99
Pérez, Genaro, 171–72
persecution, forms of, 23
"The Philosophy of Composition," 94
Picasso, Pablo, 72
The Picture of Dorian Gray (Wilde), 4, 58, 117, 144
Piglia, Ricardo, ix
Pinto, Alfonso, 62
plagiarization, 24
Poe, Edgar Allan, ix, 1, 17, 202n6; admiration for, 15–16, 191n21; short stories by, 12–13, 42, 45–51, 58, 68–69, 82–84, 143, 145; themes of, 33
poetry, 7, 18, 32–33
Polidori, John William, 27, 112–13
Popul vuh (Maya creation story), 20, 30, 190n10
power: blood as, 168–69; to conjure doubles, 164; corrosiveness of, xi, 20; depravity of, 86; as expansive, 125; fear as, 121; hunger for, 117–18, 126; of jungle, 51; regimes in, 116; to rule animals, 121; transformation of, 128; of villains, 23
"The Premature Burial," 83

progress, reason and, 7
propaganda, 193n30
psychic automatism, 10
Puig, Manuel, 17
"El puritano," 71

Quiroga, Horacio, ix, 12, 21, 27; as drawn to film, 189n45; on film culture, 66; works by, 22, 48–53, 64, 67–72, 78

Radcliffe, Ann, 3, 10, 82, 99, 112
rationalism, 11, 24
rats, 120–21
realism, 15, 24, 65
reality: conception of, 77; Mexican social, 63; nature of, 3; questioning of, 112
reason, progress and, 7
El reino de esto mundo (The Kingdom of This World) (Carpentier), 23, 81, 85–88, 141, 149–55
resurrection, 92, 97, 106, 157–58
Reyes, Alfonso, 19, 43, 64
Reyes de la Maza, Luis, 56–57
Rice, Anne, 113
Roa Bastos, Augusto, x, 23, 88–89, 109–29, 135
Rodríguez de Francia, José Gaspar, x, 111
Romanticism, 9, 10, 33, 190n1, 1188n19; doppelgänger and, 141; modernistas drawn to, 21
Romero, Rolando, 136–37
Romero Sandoval, Roberto, 31
Roussel, Henry, 59
Rubén Darío and the Romantic Search for Unity: The Modernist Recourse to Esoteric Tradition (Jrade), 33

Rulfo, Juan, ix, 14, 22, 81, 92–99

sacrifice: human, 30, 156, 165; of personal desires, 37; tradition and, 163
sacrificial ceremonies, 23, 134, 142, 156, 164–71, 205n84
The Saint (El Santo), 178–79
Salón rojo (Reyes de la Maza), 56
Schreck, Max, 58
science fiction, 69
Scott, Walter, 112
Sedgwick, Eve, 85
seduction, 27; gastronomical, 165–69; by vampires, 105, 138; of women, 133
self-conscious Gothicism, 16, 52
self-realization, 81, 102
sensationalism, 9
sexuality, 37–41, 48, 131
sexual relations, as transgressive, 5
shape-shifting, 27, 42, 87, 146, 155
Shelley, Mary, 4, 58, 76, 99
Shklovsky, Victor, 195n68
The Shrouded Woman (*La amortajada*) (Bombal), 22, 65–66, 81, 98–107
Skal, David, 61–62
Skinner, Lee, 8, 37, 39
Skin Shows (Halberstam), 36
social change, 7–8; through art, 189n35; film as vehicle for, 195n64
"The Son of the Vampire" ("El hijo del vampiro"), 49–50, 146
La sorcière (Michelet), 159–61, 164, 169, 173, 204n59
sound, 62, 67
Spanish Conquest, 21
special effects, 62–63

specters, 70, 88
spectral couples, 23, 141
Speratti-Piñero, Emma Susana, 65
split-selves, 20, 23, 141
Splitting the Difference (Doniger), 19, 117
sterility, 11
Stevenson, Robert Louis, 4, 58, 76, 117
Stoker, Bram: dedication of, 122–23; *Dracula*, 4, 13, 21–23, 27–30, 58, 85, 111–19, 138–39, 162, 178
Stories of Love, Madness, and Death (*Cuentos de amor, de locura y de muerte*) (Quiroga), 48
The Strange Case of Dr. Jekyll and Mr. Hyde (Stevenson), 4, 58, 76, 117
The Student of Prague, 58–59, 67, 76–77
Summers, Montague, 6, 8
Sunset Boulevard (Wilder), 174
supernatural, 1–2, 112, 115, 120, 163, 188n20
El supremo dictador: Biografía de José Gaspar de Francia (Chaves), 116
Surrealism, 9, 10, 72, 91, 189n36, 189n45, 197nn30–31
Surrealists, 10–11, 18, 60, 86

Tablada, José Juan, 55
Taíno indigenous group, 153, 190n13, 202n3
Teoría general de lo fantástico: Del fantástico clásico al posmoderno (General Theory of the Fantastic: From the Classic to the Postmodern Fantastic) (Nieto), 12
"Thanatopia," 21, 34–36
Thanatos, 34
Thompson, J. Eric S., 30, 31
time travel, 12
Todorov, Tzvetan, 12
tonality, 59
del Toro, Guillermo, 175, 179–82
totalitarianism, 23, 121
Los trabajos de Persiles y Sigismunda (Cervantes), 151, 155, 203n32
tradition, 6; of magical realism, 14; sacrifice and, 163; as worn-out, 67
traditionalism, 189n47
Triple Alliance, 123–24
Tropical Gothic in Literature and Culture: The Americas (Edwards and Vasconcelos), 183
Turcios, Froylán, 8, 21, 27, 32–34, 42–48, 146
The Twilight Zone, ix
twoness, 20, 141
tyranny, 5, 81

Ugestu (Mizoguchi), 174
La última niebla (The House of Mist) (Bombal), 100–101
unconscious creation, 72
The Underdogs (*Los de abajo*) (Azuela), 53, 63–64, 197n24
underworld, 31
Unraveling the Real: The Fantastic in Spanish-American Ficciones (Duncan), 12

"La vampira," 21, 34, 38–39, 47, 145

"Vampiras" ("Female Vampires"), 21, 40, 47
La vampire (Féval), 126, 199n1
vampires, x–xii, 2, 5, 7, 9; as agent of damnation, 131; bat influence on imaginings of, 21; boundaries transgressed by, 130–31, 136; disease of, 187n6; drug lords compared to, 138; evolution of, in film, 175; in fantastic literature, 27–28; female, 36–41, 48; first use of term, 29; folklore surrounding, 30, 119, 124; immortality of, 23, 113; literary experimentation with, 50–51, 111; metaphoric, 123–28; modernistas drawn to, 33; new versions of, 185; oppression represented by, 23, 42; portrayal of, 27, 118–19; prominence of, 13; as reincarnation of former souls, 117; relationship with mirrors, 124–26; representation of, 102; as seductive, 105, 138; shift in imaginings of, 48; transformation of, 49–50; types of, 181
The Vampire's Coffin (*El ataúd del vampiro*), 175–76, 178
vampirism, 41, 48, 51
"El vampiro," 22, 34, 41–42, 48–49, 53, 67–69
El vampiro, 175–79
El vampiro (Turcios), 21, 34, 42–48, 146
Vampyr, 58, 65, 77, 85
"The Vampyre," 27, 112–13
Van Helsing, 177

Vargas, Margarita, 26
Vasconcelos, Sandra Guardini, 183
Velázquez Betacourt, Diego, 184
verisimilitude, 24
Verlaine, Paul, 32
Verónica y otros cuentos fantásticos (Darío), 33–36
Vertov, Dziga, 195n65
victimization, 41
Victorian Gothic: Literary and Cultural Manifestations in the Nineteenth Century (Wolfreys), 4
villains, 2, 20, 172; monstrous ways of, 3–4; names of, 74; as violent, powerful and immortal, 23
Villaurrutia, Xavier, 90–92, 98–99
Vincenzi, Moisés, 43
violence, 98; of authoritarianism, 123; from drug trade, 137–38, 202n70; by villains, 23
Violence and the Sacred (Girard), 143
Virgin Mary, 131–33, 177
Vitascope, 192n7
Vlad (Fuentes), 23, 89, 109, 129–39
Vlad Tepes, 122–23, 173, 201n58
Vodou priests (*houngáns*), 87, 152
Voyage of the Beagle (Darwin), 29

Wallace, Diana, 99
Walpole, Horace, 3, 5, 10, 13
Warhol, Andy, 16
Watson, J. S., Jr., 60, 84
Webber, Andrew J., 144
Webber, Melville, 84
Wells, H. G., 12
Whitman, Walt, 91
Wiene, Robert, 21, 57–59, 61, 67, 73

Wilde, Oscar, 4, 58, 117, 144
Wilder, Billy, 61, 174
"William Wilson," 143, 145
Wilson, Adolfo, 192n16
Wilson, Elizabeth, 31
women: autonomy of, 42; becoming monsters, 38–39; characterizing of, 45, 131, 201n64; domestication of, 41; freedom for, found in death, 106–7; limited position of, 81, 102–3; live burial experience of, 101–7; modernistas imaginings of, 36; as predators, 37–38, 132–33; seduction of, 133; slaughtering of, 202n70; spell of, 47. *See also* vampires, female

World War I, 57–58
wrestlers (*luchadores*), 178–79
Wuthering Heights (Brontë), ix, 5

Ximénez, Francisco, 190n10

Yo el supremo (I, the Supreme) (Roa Bastos), x, 23, 88–89, 109–29, 135

zombies, 181–85, 196n13, 196n16
Zotzil Maya, 30–31
Zotz: The Bat in Mayan Culture (*Zotz: El murciélago en la cultura maya*) (Romero Sandoval), 31